CONNECTED COMMUNITIES
Creating a new knowledge landscape

HERITAGE AS COMMUNITY RESEARCH
Legacies of co-production

Edited by
Helen Graham and Jo Vergunst

First published in Great Britain in 2019 by

Policy Press
University of Bristol
1-9 Old Park Hill
Bristol
BS2 8BB
UK
t: +44 (0)117 954 5940
pp-info@bristol.ac.uk
www.policypress.co.uk

North America office:
Policy Press
c/o The University of Chicago Press
1427 East 60th Street
Chicago, IL 60637, USA
t: +1 773 702 7700
f: +1 773-702-9756
sales@press.uchicago.edu
www.press.uchicago.edu

British Library Cataloguing in Publication Data
A catalogue record for this book is available from the British Library

Library of Congress Cataloging-in-Publication Data
A catalog record for this book has been requested

978-1-4473-4529-9 hardback
978-1-4473-4530-5 ePdf
978-1-4473-4532-9 ePub
978-1-4473-4533-6 Mobi

The right of Helen Graham and Jo Vergunst to be identified as editors of this work has been asserted by them in accordance with the Copyright, Designs and Patents Act 1988.

The statements and opinions contained within this publication are solely those of the editors and contributors and not of the University of Bristol or Policy Press. The University of Bristol and Policy Press disclaim responsibility for any injury to persons or property resulting from any material published in this publication.

Policy Press works to counter discrimination on grounds of gender, race, disability, age and sexuality.

Cover design by Clifford Hayes
Front cover image: istock
Printed and bound in Great Britain by CPI Group (UK) Ltd, Croydon, CR0 4YY
Policy Press uses environmentally responsible print partners

Contents

List of figures and table

Notes on contributors

John Ball is World Music Performer in Residence in the Department of Music, University of Sheffield.

Tony Bowring is Chairperson of Arts on the Run in Sheffield.

Karen Brookfield is Deputy Director of Strategy and Business Development at the Heritage Lottery Fund.

Danny Callaghan is Project Co-ordinator for Ceramic City Stories, Stoke-on-Trent.

Esme Cleall is Senior Lecturer in the Department of History, University of Sheffield.

Vicky Crewe works in learning and teaching development at the University of Sheffield.

Elizabeth Curtis is Lecturer in the School of Education, University of Aberdeen.

Neil Curtis is Head of Museums at the University of Aberdeen.

Oliver Davis is Lecturer in the School of History, Archaeology and Religion, University of Cardiff.

Jayne Fair is a member of Ceramic City Stories, Stoke-on-Trent.

David Forrest is Senior Lecturer in the School of English, University of Sheffield.

Helen Graham is Associate Professor in the School of Fine Art, History of Art and Cultural Studies, University of Leeds.

Fay Hield is Lecturer in the Department of Music, University of Sheffield.

Nick Higgett is Associate Professor in the School of Design at De Montfort University, Leicester.

Mark Hope is a trustee of The Barn, Aberdeenshire.

Dave Horton is Community Development Manager for Action in Caerau & Ely (ACE), Cardiff.

Robert Johnston is Senior Lecturer in the Department of Archaeology, University of Sheffield.

Kimberley Marwood is a Policy Adviser with the Integration and Communities Directorate, Ministry of Housing, Communities and Local Government.

Jodie Matthews is Senior Lecturer in the School of Music, Humanities and Media, University of Huddersfield.

Helen McCarthy is part of the Hidden Hillforts Management Team, Cardiff.

Jane Murison is Head Teacher of Keig School, Aberdeenshire.

Jeff Oliver is Senior Lecturer in the Department of Archaeology, University of Aberdeen.

Kate Pahl is Professor of Arts and Literacy at Manchester Metropolitan University.

Toby Pillatt is an Honorary Research Fellow in the Department of Archaeology, University of Sheffield.

Jan Roberts is a member of Ceramic City Stories, Stoke-on-Trent.

Phil Rowley is a member of Ceramic City Stories, Stoke-on-Trent.

Colin Shepherd is an archaeologist in Aberdeenshire.

Helen Smith is a visual artist based in Newcastle.

Gemma Thorpe is a photographer and film-maker in Sheffield.

Jo Vergunst is Senior Lecturer in the Department of Anthropology, University of Aberdeen.

Jenny Wilkinson is a PhD student in the School of Design, De Montfort University.

Dave Wyatt is Senior Lecturer in the School of History, Archaeology and Religion, University of Cardiff.

Series editors' foreword

Around the globe, communities of all shapes and sizes are increasingly seeking an active role in producing knowledge about how to understand, represent and shape their world for the better. At the same time, academic research is increasingly realising the critical importance of community knowledge in producing robust insights into contemporary change in all fields. New collaborations, networks, relationships and dialogues are being formed between academic and community partners, characterised by a radical intermingling of disciplinary traditions and by creative methodological experimentation. There is a groundswell of research practice that aims to build new knowledge, address long-standing silences and exclusions, and pluralise the forms of knowledge used to inform common-sense understandings of the world.

The aim of this book series is to act as a magnet and focus for the research that emerges from this work. Originating from the UK Arts and Humanities Research Council's Connected Communities programme (see: www.connected-communities.org), the series showcases critical discussion of the latest methods and theoretical resources for combining academic and public knowledge via high-quality, creative, engaged research. It connects the emergent practice happening around the world with the long-standing and highly diverse traditions of engaged and collaborative practice from which that practice draws.

This series seeks to engage a wide audience of academic and community researchers, policymakers, and others with an interest in how to combine academic and public expertise. The wide range of publications in the series demonstrates that this field of work is helping to reshape the knowledge landscape as a site of democratic dialogue and collaborative practice, as well as contestation and imagination. The series editors welcome approaches from academic and community researchers working in this field who have a distinctive contribution to make to these debates and practices today.

Keri Facer, Professor of Educational and Social Futures,
University of Bristol

George McKay, Professor of Media Studies,
University of East Anglia

Preface

Our aim in editing this book has been to bring out the ways in which heritage is being explored and created through community research. Both 'community' and 'research' need as much unpacking as 'heritage', of course, and the book's Introduction provides critical perspectives on these terms and others that are relevant to us. However, the point is that these shared and participatory inquiries can tell wholly different stories from those commonly associated with history, archaeology and other disciplines associated with the past, and also anthropology and social sciences concerned with the present. To anticipate our conclusion, it is the way in which time itself is open to question that seems to make the difference. Different futures might result.

The impetus for our book has come from the UK Arts and Humanities Research Council's (AHRC's) 'Research for Community Heritage' initiative, part of their Connected Communities programme. The swapping around of words for our title is a small but we hope significant move intended to raise questions for those interested in participatory and co-produced research more generally, as well as those already in the 'heritage' field. Specifically, we were recipients of a grant from the AHRC to explore the legacies and outcomes of heritage research within Connected Communities, which enabled us and our co-investigators (Elizabeth Curtis, Neil Curtis, Oliver Davis, Robert Johnston and Colin Shepherd) to host meetings and workshops, and to fund further explorations of research legacy. This book is an outcome of that process. We gratefully acknowledge the funding, and we also acknowledge and thank the many researchers, participants, communities and organisations that have been involved.

Helen Graham and Jo Vergunst
January 2019

Introduction: heritage as community research

Jo Vergunst and Helen Graham

Introduction

It seems that the past is not the same as it used to be. The promises of both history, in which the past is written from documentary evidence into a single authoritative narrative, and archaeology, in which the truth of the past can be revealed layer by layer on a site, have been redeemed by the figures of the historian and the archaeologist as experts on the past. Both have stood their own tests of time and it is not our purpose to undermine them here. Instead, this book explores how not all accounts of the past are created by those means and by those figures. We consider the ways in which the past can become something different: more akin to a journey in which the destination is uncertain than a pre-existing set of facts that is waiting to be discovered by the historian or archaeologist. The single expert figure no longer, of necessity, takes precedence in finding the way and is replaced by a looser collective made up of interested amateurs, 'communities' and 'the public', as well as professionals who may contribute their own skills and resources but by no means 'own' the research.

In this regard, the rise and proliferation of discourses around heritage are positive developments. The meanings of heritage shifted in the 1970s and 1980s from the medieval sense of inheritable property, to the now-mainstream form of historical narrative or material that resonates – somehow – into the present. Associating heritage with the present might feel counter-intuitive, and yet the ways in which heritage opens onto questions of past, present and future have proved to be both powerful and useful. In one way, heritage can be said to differ from history by way of the latter's fixation on the past compared with the former's emphasis on bringing the past into the present. Through the process of bringing the past into the present, the notion of inheritance is broadened from the individual to the communal, and from the legal to the symbolic.

Dictionary definitions of heritage are perhaps unsurprisingly behind the curve in this respect. Merriam-Webster gives us 'legacy', 'inheritance' and 'tradition' (Merriam-Webster: 'heritage'), and following a list of 'inheritance' definitions, the Oxford English Dictionary provides a further sense of heritage as follows: 'Characterized by or pertaining to the preservation or exploitation of local and national features of historical, cultural, or scenic interest, esp. as tourist attractions' (*Oxford English Dictionary*: 'heritage'). A crucial insight of the newly cohering field of critical heritage studies, by contrast, has been to characterise heritage not as fixed in specific buildings or objects, or focused narrowly on preservation and then exploitation, but more broadly as a social process of meaning making (eg Kirshenblatt Gimblett, 1995: 369; Tunbridge and Ashworth, 1996: 6; Lowenthal, 1998: 226; Harvey, 2001: 320; Smith 2006: 3).

A central theme of the book is that neither 'preservation' nor 'exploitation' – nor, indeed, simply claiming heritage as a process – adequately conveys the active nature of *inquiry* that seems so significant in much community-based heritage. In the cases presented in this book – which form our contribution to the ongoing exploration of the processes that make heritage – what enlivens relations with the past is more an ongoing process of finding out, sharing, debating and undertaking small-scale acts of stewardship. These are stories that are worked on and pieced together collectively and with meaning for current circumstances, not simply uncovered, retold and 'used' in straightforward historical or archaeological modes, or directly taken into institutional forms of governance. So, as we understand it in this book, 'heritage' is about relationships created through inquiry, between past, present and future, between people, and between people and things.

In noting the processual nature of heritage, a discursive turn has been a crucial feature of critical heritage studies. Laurajane Smith (2006) opens her influential book *The uses of heritage* with a discussion of heritage as discourse, noting how 'heritage' has become part of Romantic and nationalist ideas of the past as a source of meaning and interpretation of the present. Many other scholars have explored how discursive processes shape the past and how the past is understood in the present (eg Kirshenblatt Gimblett, 1995; Lowenthal, 1998), deconstructing what Smith terms the 'Authorised Heritage Discourse' of professional museums and official heritage sites. One response has been to critically unpack the meanings behind such renderings of the past and the politics that underlie them, revealing inequities and exclusions (Tunbridge and Ashworth, 1996). Another, as noted by Smith (2006: ch 7), and powerfully articulated by Raphael Samuel (1994) in *Theatres of memory*, which is the focus of this collection, is to fully recognise that there are other ways of producing accounts of the past. What happens when communities, or collectives of people interested in exploring their own pasts or those of the places around them, actively create their own heritage that links between past and present?

For us, one implication is that the methodological focus can be usefully shifted from a discursive analysis of heritage in the critical tradition, which tends to look back in order to diagnose and unveil power and inequality, to more appreciatively noticing, enacting and creating different kinds of knowledge through doing heritage. This is what we describe throughout this book as 'ways of knowing'. From the point of view of the communities involved with heritage through research, it is not simply about discursively arguing against a mainstream interpretation of the past, but about making their own way into an exploration of the past. While the cases here function on the 'local' level in one sense, they are considerably more than just local history. Instead, they locate what may be much broader processes in specific situations of places and people. Framing this work as 'inquiry' also draws attention to the ways in which 'ways of knowing' are also *ways of acting* in the world, ways of creating change and using the past for future-making, what we call, in the second part of the collection, 'heritage as action'.

Cross-cutting these themes, a further facet of virtually all research is that things do not go as planned, and unexpected turns, changes and outcomes will occur. Some of these are problematic in the short term but turn out to be significant in a different way later – points of learning or crossroads in which the direction of research changed. Our exploration of community heritage research feeds back into reflections on the nature of research and inquiry, including the role of the university and the possibilities of more democratic relationships of knowledge.

This, then, is the agenda for our book. *Heritage as community research: Legacies of co-production* explores the nature of contemporary heritage research in the UK involving communities. It puts forward a new view of heritage as a process of research and involvement with the past, undertaken with or by communities for whom it is relevant. Rather than just reflecting on existing discourses *about* heritage, the book's contributors present community-based research *into* heritage in which histories are explored through new modes of production: crossing disciplines, sustaining partnerships and evaluating legacies. The process of research itself, the contributors show, can be an empowering force by which communities stake a claim in the places they live.

Drawing on their experience of collaborative heritage research, contributors to the book focus on both the substance and the legacies of their work. Community-based historical narratives are combined with explorations of the outcomes, benefits or disbenefits, sustainability, and value of heritage research. All of these processes feed into its legacies, a key term for us. In this book, legacies are understood as the ways in which research or its outcomes continue into the future and have effects among people and places. Seeing synergies with our approach to heritage, we read legacy – deliberately distinct from 'impact' – as about relationships, too, between past, present and future, between people, and between people, things and the world. We see legacy as the difference that is made – the potential that is opened up – when we treat not only research and heritage, but our places, our politics and our democracies, as collaborative inquiries.

Programmes of participatory and collaborative research are now being supported by public research funding, including the UK Arts and Humanities Research Council's Connected Communities programme. This has supported a wide range of projects with the aim of working with communities in social science and humanities-based research, including work focused on heritage, from which most of the material in this book is drawn (Facer and Enright, 2016).

Conceptually, we want to bring into dialogue traditions of anthropology, critical heritage studies, and participatory and action research, as well as debates concerning community engagement in universities, museums and heritage. Working at this intersection allows us to explore the way in which concepts such as time, memory and materiality can illuminate participatory and action research. Equally, it allows learning from participatory and action research contexts to be brought to bear on the ongoing concerns of critical heritage studies and museum and heritage practice. The rest of this Introduction illuminates these themes and sets them within three main thematic threads: 'ways of knowing', 'heritage as action' and the 'unexpected in heritage research'.

Ways of knowing

Part One of the book focuses on 'ways of knowing'. These chapters explore both the distinctive processes by which collaborative and community-led heritage research takes place, and the distinctive forms of knowledge that emerge – often based in the sharing of skills, collective understanding and involvement with materials. We borrow the term 'ways of knowing' from a number of previous scholarly uses, including Mark Harris's (2007) edited collection, which explores alternatives to the Western concepts of objectivity and positivism that have become associated with research in a scientific paradigm. These include embodied and implicit forms of understanding. As Harris (2007: 4) notes, the phrase reminds us that 'any knowledge is inevitably situated in a particular place and moment; that it is inhabited by individual knowers and that it is always changing and emergent'. Moving from the individual to the collective, Helen Graham et al (2014) also use 'ways of knowing', in this case, to refer to the distinctive 'registers, values and subjectivities of collaborative research', exploring the means by which disparate perspectives can find common ground in research. A crucial starting point here – in keeping with our approach to heritage – is that approaching knowing as a process is very different to approaching knowledge as an object, which is an underpinning precept of participatory and action research (Fals-Borda, 1991; Brydon-Miller et al, 2003).

A distinction leading on from a focus on process is that our work is not about 'engagement' in heritage, if by that we mean an exercise undertaken by heritage professionals to involve communities or the public in their work. As Watson and Waterton (2010: 1) note, there has been 'a growing recognition on the part of practitioners that community engagement helps them to achieve their own objectives by marshalling public support for their otherwise arcane activities'. Such a model of engagement is predicated upon the resources to understand the past – whether substantive, methodological or logistical – being held by experts who subsequently construct an entity (the community) with which to 'engage' in their work. Through this mode of working, both 'heritage' and 'community' are fixed as different, as pre-existing each other and to be brought together via professional facilitation. In a university research context, this idea is close to those of knowledge transfer, dissemination or impact, in which the body of work pre-exists and can be conveyed relatively unproblematically to an audience upon whom it has an effect. Often, those arguing against this model of 'community engagement' emphasise instead an alternative, more process-oriented, way of working – as, indeed, we are – one where knowing is always needing to be actively reworked, ripped up, reconstituted and created by those using it in order to be meaningful. While the growing literature on community engagement in museums and heritage provides an important grounding for this book (eg Lang et al, 2006; Lynch and Alberti, 2010; Lynch, 2011; Golding and Modest, 2013; Waterton and Watson, 2013; Hawke et al, 2017), the trajectory that we take is to open up the distinctive contributions that thinking of heritage *as research* might offer.

To take an example at the intersection of heritage and anthropology, Alison Brown (2017) shows how a network centring on museum and archival collections of indigenous Blackfoot material inverts the usual model of 'engagement', which begins with academic and professional expertise, in favour of indigenous concepts of consensus and relationship-building. Museum staff in the UK followed Blackfoot protocol for handling objects, while pre-existing modes of collaboration among Blackfoot partners were respected. Staff also took part in visits to the places in North America connected with the collections. Brown (2017: 123) identifies how the very relationships of the research came to be 'co-authored' in ways not at first apparent to museum colleagues – suggesting that the standard model of community engagement can be subverted even from within the midst of collaboration.

We might usefully explore the more diverse forms by which heritage as an inquiry and an encounter take place – beyond the sharing of a resource from professional 'centre' to community 'periphery'. In many projects, it seems likely that work will proceed in a variety of ways over time. At times, heritage professionals from museums or universities may bring specialist expertise to the work, but at others, it may be communities who take the lead and set the agenda. Jo Vergunst et al's chapter (Chapter One) describing landscape heritage research in rural Aberdeenshire is an example here as various specialists have contributed skills in archaeology and exhibitions even as community members have set the overall agenda and methodology for the research. In the context of digital reconstructions of historic buildings, Nick Higgett and Jenny Wilkinson (Chapter Four) show how the expertise of university-based computer specialists is harnessed by communities to their own ends, even as the reconstructions themselves take on a wide range of roles once released to the communities.

Heritage as community research therefore involves particular ways of knowing that go beyond forms of engagement. This principle has guided much of the work in this book, and yet we can pursue the dynamics of such processes in more detail. How can we critically think through the distinctive social relations and the distinctive outcomes of heritage as a community research practice?

Co-production and enskilment

The notions of co-production and collaboration in research offer ways forward here. Keri Facer and Kate Pahl argue that collaborative research that involves universities with communities and other organisations has been valued in a variety of ways, including but going beyond the engagement model. They write:

> Such research is seen by some as a means of creating greater 'impact' on the social world and by others as a way of enhancing the quality of knowledge; by some as a form of democratic recalibration of knowledge production and others as a way of generating more robust products and services. (Facer and Pahl, 2017: 2)

Our agenda is perhaps not so broad, but this does open onto the diverse and unexpected outcomes of community heritage research, which we will return to later in this Introduction. Research in this form is a journey, usually without a clear destination, at least at the start. Facer and Pahl choose 'collaborative' as their key descriptive term, but they recognise that it is not sufficient simply to claim and demonstrate collaboration in itself. There is, we might say, a danger of fetishising collaboration in the same way as engagement, and for all these processes, we need to ask: collaboration with whom, for what purpose and with what outcome or legacy?

Collaboration comes in many forms, of course, from 'lip service' or small in-kind contributions, to joint and sustained work throughout a research process. For us, however, the co-production of research is a useful and challenging notion that adds a distinctive flavour to these debates. Research cannot be said to be co-produced by way of tokenistic participation from any partner, and if the central idea is of jointly making the research and its outcomes happen, there can be no sense of hierarchy in the various contributions that may be made. No quantitative ethical test is needed either – co-production either happens together or not at all. So, defining co-production is not a case of setting a bar at any particular level (eg more and more 'engagement' finally equals 'good' 'co-production'); rather, co-production is qualitatively different and a reckoning of the creative processes of research themselves. The cases in this book are intended not as exemplars of co-production in a simple positive sense, but rather as honest and reflexive accounts of heritage inquiries. Co-production becomes a means by which relationships can be traced and participation valued in a critical way.

Angie Hart et al (2013) formulate university and community co-production as operating through 'communities of practice' (drawing on the work of Lave and Wenger), or groups that come together in joint enterprises. In their case study of groups supporting disadvantaged children and families in the south of England, while seeking to demonstrate an equality of participation and being concerned with the ethics of the process, what seemed most crucial was the making of a functioning and meaningful community of practice to support activity.

A vital aspect of the community heritage research projects that we document in this book is, indeed, the skills that are developed among participants through what we could think of as their communities of practice. While the 'soft skills' or 'people skills' of communication, negotiation, project leadership and so on are all relevant and well documented in these chapters, it is also the range of practical research skills that are striking – even though the distinction between the two may not always be apparent. These are stories of people learning not just how to trowel in the bottom of a trench in an archaeological excavation (the common experience of amateur archaeologists joining a summer dig), but, as Vergunst et al show, learning how to develop a project in the first place, how to carry out the full range of archaeological, archival and history tasks alongside many partners. Also using an archaeological case study, Elizabeth Curtis et al (Chapter Nine) describe how schoolchildren can also be more than able to take part and take 'responsibility' in this work. Oliver Davis et al (Chapter Six) indicate how involvement in a dig creates a pathway into higher education. For Karen Brookfield et al in Stoke-on-Trent, meanwhile, knowing is enabled through distributed community networks and the kind of social support and innovations in funding models that mean participants can 'get on with it' (see Chapter Seven).

To think through this conceptually, Tim Ingold's notion of 'enskilment' as a form of inhabitation and dwelling is useful. Skilful practice is not about conforming to rules, Ingold argues, and neither is skill merely an innate capacity for a task that some happen to have. Instead, it is through a matrix of social relations that skill develops and is expressed, in conjunction with specific material forms of tools and technology. Then, more specifically, we can think of dexterity as being gained through 'the gradual attunement of movement and perception' – through bodily practice and improvisation (Ingold, 2000: 357). Novice archaeologists would certainly attest this as they learn to distinguish soil types and classify potsherds as they trowel and take part in finds processing (Holtorf, 2002), but the point also stands for those reading handwritten documents in an archive, for example, where reading and translating are highly developed skills. We could also think along these lines of the confidence that is engendered in participants as research progresses and they become more skilful in both tasks requiring manual dexterity and those involving the social relations of research (eg negotiating research questions, methods and outcomes). Community heritage as research, then, surely happens through enskilment more than it does through engagement.

Considering the ways of representing the research described here, it is tempting to imagine a continuum of participation from relatively weak 'engagement' at one end, to 'collaboration' in the middle, and to relatively strong 'co-production' at the other, along the lines of Sherry Arnstein's 'ladder of participation' (Arnstein, 1969; Facer and Pahl, 2017: 4). Attributing these labels, however, suggests a competitive ranking that does a disservice to what are commonly more democratic ethics of research with and by communities. From community perspectives, things can look different in the sense that the professional, university-based researchers who are the starting point for the ladder of participation may actually be just one partner among others. More fruitful might be to explore how different ways of working together entail different sorts of social relationships, and can also enable different forms of representation. Our chapters explore how these relations lead to different outcomes – different legacies – that are meaningful to those involved in different ways.

Dialogical approaches

To push even the idea of co-production in research a little further, it may be worth reflecting on the forms of single and multiple voicing that we present in this book. Our chapters have been created together by academics and community partners, often explicitly using dialogue as a form of writing. In so doing, they find a way of allowing multiple voices and perspectives to be present. This is a challenge to models of historical, sociological or critical interpretation that privilege the individual observer of, or about, others' practices. All the research on which this book is based has been carried out collectively in various ways, although the configuration of the research teams and participants varies.

The sole single-authored chapter, by Jodie Matthews (Chapter Three), still takes part in dialogue – or, rather, group conversations – through social media comments and debate in the field of Roma studies and the circulation of images of Roma people. Higgett and Wilkinson (Chapter Four), as a further example, go beyond just the provision of digital building reconstructions to community heritage projects in order to seek out what the responses of those communities have been to the digital work. This contribution shares the authorial voice, as do Vergunst et al (Chapter One) and Kimberley Marwood et al (Chapter Eight), but others have kept their voices apart, although very much in conversation and dialogue. Ball et al (Chapter Two) use dialogue in their chapter to explore complementary perspectives, including that of Kate Pahl as anthropologist-researcher and others as musicians-researchers. Curtis et al (Chapter Nine) also keep distinct their insights as community archaeologist, school head teacher and education academic, respectively, and the same is true in different ways for the chapters by Brookfield et al (Chapter Seven), Davis et al (Chapter Six) and Helen Smith and Mark Hope (Chapter Five).

The theme of dialogue in community heritage is, perhaps surprisingly, lacking in recent scholarship. Where notions of co-production sometimes tend to emphasise a moulding of perspectives into a single outcome (in other words, 'the' research or 'the' exhibition), we argue that co-production in a dialogic vein enables distinctions to be maintained, alternative views to be respected and a position from which diversity of outcomes may be welcomed. Robert Baron (2016) locates a tradition of dialogism within public folklore as a discipline in North America in the way that oral history and other performative aspects of culture have led folklorists to maintain a wide range of voices in their research rather than attempting to combine them into a single authoritative account. Drawing on examples from the Smithsonian Folklife Festival and other public arts events, he writes: 'Dialogically constructed modes of presentation mutually engage folklorists, community members and audiences in representations of heritage to the public' (Baron, 2016: 593).

Baron draws on the work of Mikhail Bakhtin, who provides a key starting point for thinking about dialogue and multiplicity for many other humanities scholars as well. His studies in philosophy and literature develop ideas that play out in many ways in this book, in particular, for the contributors noted earlier who have chosen to present their work through more than one voice. For Bakhtin, dialogism is the study of language as it is performed, which is always with another listener or conversation partner in mind (even one's inner self): 'language, for the individual consciousness, lies on the borderline between oneself and other. The word in language is half someone else's' (Bakhtin, 1981: 293). Bakhtin also coins the notion of heteroglossia to describe the incorporation of many subjectivities into the language of a novel, and takes this to be the fundamental and primordial mode of linguistic communication, as opposed to the monoglossic voice of the single author.

The point for our work in this book is that presenting an explicitly dialogic account of how heritage is created recognises that this basic quality of language as also a facet of sociality more generally, and the parallels between the two are striking. Anthropologists Nicholas J. Long and Henrietta L. Moore (2012: 41) approach sociality as:

> a dynamic relational matrix within which human subjects are constantly interacting in ways that are coproductive, continually plastic and malleable, and through which they come to know the world they live in and find their purpose and meaning within it.

We might argue that such subject relations happen between the past and present, and, indeed, the future, as well as just within the present.

As Robert Baron (2016: 591) also notes, there is a distinction between a dialogical approach and the generations of anthropologists who worked within a positivist framework to describe diverse cultures as static ideal-types, usually from the singular perspective of the anthropologist. While the cultural turn in anthropology began to address issues of writing and representation in the discipline (Clifford and Marcus, 1986), it was the later interest in critically rethinking notions of the field and research methods that stimulated more overt reflection on, and valuing of, collaborative and participative forms of research. Akhil Gupta and James Ferguson (1997) challenged the assumptions that fieldwork in anthropology should take place by way of the model in the sciences of 'the field' as a bounded area within which unbiased observation can take place, and since the 1990s, a new interest in collaborative research has developed in anthropology.

It is partly, therefore, with this contemporary anthropological sensibility that our contributors are reflecting from the midst of their endeavours rather than as detached observers and evaluators. Luke Lassiter has put the process of working together with participants on the outcomes of research as follows: 'Collaborative reading and writing emerges, like collaborative ethnography itself, as a *dialogue about* a particular ethnographic topic … not as a final *statement on* any particular ethnographic topic' (Lassiter, 2005: 141, emphasis in original). An important point to take from dialogical texts and reflect back into our reading of co-production is that they are never the last word, and we might say that they are 'unfinished' in the sense of leaving open further interaction and outcomes.

Metaphors and materials

The point of the chapters herein – both those that are explicitly dialogical and those that take a more traditional form – is, in part, to reflect more accurately the nature of the research process in community heritage. They have not followed the rigid plan and methodology of a laboratory experiment; rather, the work has been improvised. This might take the form of a journey through a landscape that doubles as fieldwork, which Vergunst et al (Chapter One) develop as a metaphor. A different vision might be that of the studio that Pahl et al (2017: 146) describe powerfully as a metaphorical – and sometimes actual – space for collaborative research inspired by practice in the creative arts 'that can hold difference, permeate boundaries, and be robust enough to collapse and reform'. Both the ideas of fieldwork journey and studio collectivity ground research in a socially oriented process, where shared or dialogical learning and improvisation are key.

Finding useful metaphors is always significant for this kind of research, but this is not to displace the material realities of things, sites, places and so on. Both landscapes and studios can be, after all, material as well as metaphoric entities. Thus, a further approach that underpins much of the work in this book is the attention to these material qualities of research in heritage. We might argue that the subjective relations that create sociality are not just between humans, as Long and Moore (2012) suggest, but also include entanglements with materials, things and places (Hodder, 2012).

Here, we mesh with our theme of enskilment, in that skill is frequently enacted through materials and things, which include archaeological finds, historical documents and images, and landscapes and places that bring forth the past into the present. All of these are described in different ways throughout this book. Conversely, community heritage projects are also notable for the qualities of the things that they produce, such as exhibition and interpretive materials, and 'new' places that are made available for others through heritage work – a library basement or an architectural ceramic door well in the Potteries in the case of work described by Brookfield et al (Chapter Seven). The seemingly 'intangible' outcomes of the research presented here, such as Higgett and Wilkinson's digital building reconstructions (Chapter Four), the music of Ball and colleagues (Chapter Two), and the art and film work of Smith and Hope (Chapter Five), all operate through material forms as well. In such ways, the commonly held boundaries between tangible and intangible cultural heritage become blurred (Vergunst et al, 2017). This allows us to note that 'doing' –

inquiry – is also a 'making' with the world, and its materials are active participants. The chapter by Brookfield et al (Chapter Seven) shows that learning-through-doing, specifically, how to scrape wallpaper off tiles in a basement, is a co-production of new meaning and a new material space at the same time.

There is, of course, no single 'way of knowing' that emerges from all this work, but while we emphasise the plurality of knowledges, the chapters in this book collectively stand for a recognition that no single account of the past, or at least of what we are describing here as heritage, can claim authority by virtue of a narrow claim to historical resources or expertise. Other dialogues need to be started up and listened to. Indeed, we might argue, drawing on Donna Haraway's (1988) work, that shared, positioned and partial knowing is even more powerful because of the acknowledgement of the reality of where and how the knowledge has been produced. Heritage as co-productive inquiry – a way of knowing – is therefore configured quite differently to engagement, and its ethics and politics can be judged best from within and from the capacities and legacies that the processes create.

Heritage as action

Part Two of the book focuses on heritage as action. There is a particular reason for this. Thinking of heritage as a dialogic and relational process – as we have done earlier – immediately requires more from us in terms of delineating and illuminating the nature of that process. In this book, we have been using 'research' – more specifically, 'inquiry' – as a way of opening up certain ways of thinking heritage-as-a-process. Yet, in the same way as heritage-as-a-process, thinking research-as-a-process only takes us so far and also opens up further questions.

We note an unhelpful elision at work in the turn to process. This critical move has had the effect that collaborative work is often judged primarily by its relationships, by its ethics not the quality of the outcome. As Clare Bishop (2004: 77) has put it in a participatory arts context: 'today, political, moral, and ethical judgments have come to fill the vacuum of aesthetic judgment in a way that was unthinkable forty years ago'. An allied concern has led Facer and Pahl (2017: 5) to argue for the need 'to move away from the assumption that collaborative research is to be judged only by the degree and quality of public/community engagement at all stages'. The crucial shift enabled by framing heritage and community collaboration as inquiry is to see 'knowing' not as static, but as future-making, where quality is not judged by only either its ethics (*'Have you been "good"?'*) or by peer-review ideas of quality (*'Is it good quality?'*) (which is arguably where Bishop's aesthetics lies), but by whether the 'knowledge' produced leads to action. Is the collaboration productive of meaningful potential for those involved? In response to our interest in delineating further 'process' as a critical descriptor, the theme emphasised in the second half of the book is that of 'action', with traditions of 'action research' and 'participatory action research' being mobilised in different ways through the chapters. Drawing on these traditions allows us to identify a variety of different processes at work in community heritage.

A key aspect in this – which enables the link between our themes of 'ways of knowing' and 'heritage as action' – is to see, in the words of action researcher Danny Burns (2007: 3), that research is not only produced afterwards or only through a process of reflection, but can also be understood as a process of meaning-making that is 'derived in action' – that is, seeking to know and to understand is 'part of everyday practices' (Burns, 2007: 4; see also Brydon-Miller et al, 2003). Yet, this also allows us to see that meaning-making is also world-making. Collaborative heritage is about not only making pasts, but also making futures (Harrison, 2012, 2015). Framing community heritage as *action* inquiry invites us to extend our ideas about participation and to think more fully about how heritage is a process by which people, landscapes, things and tools interact in co-producing the world, a 'participatory ontology'. On this view, world-making is always underway and can always be linked to meaning-making, just as building understanding of pasts together is also, in itself, an act of making the future.

Participatory action research as community heritage

Critical voices have often been concerned that community heritage is a manipulation, a cosy category that co-opts radical energies within professional structures (Lynch and Alberti, 2010; Waterton and Smith, 2010). Part of the move offered by yoking community heritage and action research is to more clearly articulate and contest the politics of knowledge production and world-making at play in community heritage. An early reference point for work combining action research, participatory practice and community heritage is Anthony Fyson and Colin Ward's (1973) development of 'the exploded school', published as *Streetwork*. Based on their work as educational officers for the Town and Country Planning Association, Fyson and Ward developed methods through which young people work to build knowledge about, and, through this, come to be active participants in shaping, the places in which they live. If read through the terms of participatory action research, this ethos could be summarised as: 'Understand your world, make sense of your life and develop new and creative ways of looking at things' (Heron and Reason, 2001: 1). Participatory action research traditions see radical epistemologies – what we have called 'ways of knowing' – as enabled by the 'full range of human capacities and sensibilities' being 'available as an instrument of inquiry' (Heron and Reason, 2001: 3), that is, intuition, feelings, senses, movement and physical work, as well as language. This connection with the 'full range of capacities and sensibilities' is a characteristic of the chapters included in this volume, where feelings, fun and food (Smith and Hope, Chapter Five), physical work and talk (Vergunst et al, Chapter One; Brookfield et al, Chapter Seven), conversation and laugher (Marwood et al, Chapter Eight), or litter picking and archaeological knowledge (Davis et al, Chapter Six) combine.

A theme of 'participatory action research' has been creating change, the 'A' over the 'R' in the PAR of participatory action research as Chatterton, Fuller and Routledge (2007: 218) put it. This concept of action and change has been framed in quite a variety of ways in the action research literature, from a sense of learning 'how to act to change things you may want to change and find out how to do things better' (Heron and Reason, 2001: 1), to revolutionary traditions contesting imperialist forms of 'development' and modes of capitalist economy that sustain poverty and fail to address pressing environmental concerns (eg Fals-Borda and Rahman, 1991; Gavanta, 1991; Mathie and Gavanta, 2015). Smith and Hope's chapter (Chapter Five) on a small-scale lavender oil production industry in the 1960s shows how it was a central part of the lives of those closely involved in the work and the local community in Aberdeenshire, but it also speaks to changing economies and social relationships in that community and, therefore, the role and future of the arts organisation who initiated the heritage project. The siting of heritage work in an arts organisation reinforces that shared endeavours in heritage and research are always creative process. What came to be known was not only 'what happened', but a shared sense of what the organisation might become. For Vergunst et al (Chapter One), drawing on Ingold, the activity in their heritage project offers a mode of living creatively in 'a world that is itself crescent, always in formation' (Ingold, 2012: 3). This points to the ways in which action, knowing and change are not separable, but intimately connected and socially dynamic processes. They are what key theorist of participatory action research Orlando Fals-Borda (2013 [2007]: 159) terms the 'slow rhythm of reflection and action'.

Local and responsive (not parochial)

A common theme of all the chapters is a concern with specific local circumstances. Heritage, knowledge and change are not abstract or distant categories, but ones that arise from particular social and material capacities: from musical instruments, musical traditions and improvisation (Ball et al, Chapter Two); from memories and scrapbooks (Marwood et al, Chapter Eight); from social media dialogue (Matthews, Chapter Three); and from tiles and digital photography (Brookfield et al, Chapter Seven). Taken together, we suggest that these examples show the significance of the local as a site for productive interventions in a time when the world seems complex and expansive, and where political agency seems always vested elsewhere.

Many of the chapters here indicate a sense of acting in small ways – what participatory urban planner Nabeel Hamdi (2010) calls 'small change' – as a corrective to the paralysis that many people feel in terms of their ability of influence institutional forms of decision-making. The potentials of this are clearly shown in Marwood et al's 'action heritage' as a mode of working (see Chapter Eight). They draw on radical pedagogy, which, through inquiry and personal stories being shared, shifts and creates what they call 'participatory parity'. For Marwood et al, however, action heritage is 'active not activist', in that the projects they supported did not necessarily work towards achieving wider, large-scale social change.

Yet, for others, this distinction is not clear-cut. As Matthews shows, quoting Leeds Gate (see Chapter Three), taking action through and with archives has the purpose of offering 'a challenge to stereotypes of what Gypsies were like in the past'. For Davis et al (Chapter Six), the conceptual work enabled by the contrast between the Iron Age hill fort being at the heart of political power then and the marginalisation of the political voices of those living on the Ely estate today is highly significant. Small acts of co-production reflect communities of past and bring into being a new community. Brookfield et al (Chapter Seven) evoke the energy created through distributed capacity, where 'pings' of connection are able to make things happen and help create the belief that change is possible. In the project described in Curtis et al's chapter (Chapter Nine), school students expected to take on not just jobs, but *responsibility* and leadership for the archaeological research.

There is a spirit here of politics that is about 'making change from where you are' (Bashforth et al, 2015) and seeing power and politics not as solid structures, but as open to new possibilities through small adjustments, conversations and new energies. Emma Goldman, in her explanation of anarchism, poetically captures this approach to politics that is attentive to, and emerges from, specific local circumstances: change 'is a living force in the affairs of our life, constantly creating new conditions', where 'methods must grow out of the economic needs of each place and clime' (Goldman, 2008: 29). Or, we can return to Colin Ward (1973: 23) to reinforce Goldman's point:

> Far from being a speculative vision of a future society, [anarchism] is a description of a mode of human organisation, rooted in the experience of everyday life, which operates side by side with, and in spite of, the dominant authoritarian trends of our society.

While many of these chapters may not see themselves as anarchist as such, there is a certain anarchic spirit, the ethos of Fyson and Ward's *Streetwork*, which can be traced through many of these collectives of people working together, enthusing each other and transforming the places and social conditions that they are part of through acts of collaborative inquiry.

Words and worlds: participatory ontologies

Through thinking community heritage and participatory action research together, it is possible here to link two different ideas of co-production. The first is the use of co-production in the sense we used it earlier: professionals, academics and other interested people working together to research and create heritage. Yet, there is also another significant use of co-production: co-production has been widely elaborated to argue that 'the realities of human experience emerge as the joint achievements of scientific, technical, and social enterprise: science and society, in a word, are co-produced, each underwriting the other's existence' (Jasanoff, 2004: 33).

Many disciplines, notably, anthropology, geography and science and technology studies (STS), have been concerned to develop alternative ways of conceiving the world based on how things and people, nature and culture, and the material and the semiotic are mutually productive, drawing on epistemologies that recognise the knower as intimately bound up in, and affecting, any 'object' of study. The notion of co-production, therefore, has become one way of articulating this relationality, 'the conjoined production of one nature–culture' (Latour, 1993: 107). An aspect of this approach has been to radically extend the number of 'participants' involved in any phenomenon to 'more-than-human' participation (Abram, 1996; Bastian et al, 2017), including things, plants and animals (Star and Griesemer, 1989; see also Reason, 2005). In an action research context, this insight has been framed as a 'participatory worldview' (Reason, 2005) or a 'participatory ontology'. One could see participatory action research – inquiry in the way we are using it – as a method seeking to be adequate to these philosophical insights.

In our chapters, the sense that the world is being made through 'more-than-human' participation is very present. Vergunst et al evoke the iterative relationship between activities such as digging soil, clearing sites, writing text labels and imagining the past and future, arguing that such temporal openness enables the possibility of change in relationships with landscape. 'More-than-human' participation is also present in the ways in which the chapters signal alternative enactments of key heritage practices such as 'conservation'. In the most traditional readings, heritage is identified and named as such, and is then subject to professional conservation practices, whether of collection and designation, and/or material conservation practices, such as treating the fabric of buildings or keeping the object in stable climatic conditions. Yet, taking up conservation as an action inquiry – and as participatory in the full ontological sense – opens up alternatives. Brookfield et al (Chapter Seven) show how do-it-yourself heritage approaches create sustainable contexts for material forms – in this case, architectural tiles in the potteries – through social networks.

Heritage as action, therefore, calls to mind how knowing comes to be actionable, how working from the midst of the local is by no means parochial, but rather enables a sense of agency in a complex world, and how more-than-human entanglements shape both the course and outcomes of heritage and underpin a form of research. It sees itself not just as knowing about the world, but as taking part in making the world and helping to shape its future.

The unexpected in research

Throughout our reflections on community and co-produced heritage research, we have been struck by the importance of things not going according to plan, and sometimes actually going wrong. It might be to do with the nature of the projects described in this book, which were driven as much by curiosity and even happenstance as they were by a detailed schedule or formal research proposal. It might also be to do with the different configuration of skills and experience among those carrying out the work, going well beyond the standardised research methods of professional university researchers (Brown, 2017). This is not to say that unexpected events happen more commonly in this kind of research, or are more severe in their effects. It is a truism to say that researchers in virtually any discipline need to be flexible enough to respond to the circumstances thrown up by the research. If we take ethnography to be emblematic here, Judith Okely (2012: 48) writes: 'The unplanned character of ethnography is precisely its value'. The occurrence of the unexpected in community heritage research seems to provide a distinctive liveliness that animates the whole process in a way that closely sticking to the original research proposal (even if there was one written) cannot so easily achieve. Where problems occur, they often speak to more fundamental issues about the relationship between past and present, and the authority to find and use resources that narrate the past; sometimes, if only in hindsight, they become the pivot points around which heritage – as community research – emerges.

A number of the chapters in this book develop this theme. Marwood et al's (Chapter Eight) experience of what was intended to be research on the history of a young people's hostel in Sheffield was that it only really came alive when the focus shifted from the building itself to how it was connected with the personal stories of those who used it. This felt like a failure at first as the research aim of telling the history of the building was not being met, and only later came to be recognised as productive because of the intertwining of the story of the building with those who were inhabiting it. Writing on images of Gypsy travellers circulating in the 19th and the 21st centuries, Matthews (Chapter Three) conveys the contestation and diversity of representations that continue to be shared as connections between names, places and people are made. Working with the Romani community to develop an exhibition, she writes that 'the very idea of the archive moves from being a closed-off repository to a resource for a community to preserve and share its heritage – for those within and without a Romani identity'. Opening up an archive to unexpected uses is emblematic of the course of community heritage research, in that improvisation and animation become central to the process rather than just following a predetermined route. Other chapters develop their sense of the unexpected and problematic in different ways: Curtis et al (Chapter Nine) on the 'problem' of involving school pupils in archaeological research; Ball et al (Chapter Two) on translating between co-produced music and co-written text; and Smith and Hope (Chapter Five) on the realisation that a heritage project could itself enable a new kind of conversation to emerge for a community arts organisation.

A clearer valuing of the unexpected could help to think through processes of research in this mode much more widely. It would, for example, go beyond the notion of subservience to an original plan – required more and more, we would argue, by professional research administrators as part of their 'audit culture' (Strathern, 2000) – and towards recognising the significance of the unexpected in the ways of knowing and the action that results. More broadly, it might enable scholarship on collaboration and co-production, such as that we have reviewed here, to imagine looser and more flexible forms of working together that could even be *designed* for the unexpected. An example can be found in the chapter by Brookfield et al (Chapter Seven), where a key funder, the Heritage Lottery Fund, responds to very small-scale funding needs by limiting the need for plans and a heavy layer of audit. In research on heritage specifically, we can emphasise again the sense of movement and journeying in regard to the past as a contrast to attempting to reach the 'destination' of history produced by the figure of the professional historian. The conclusion to this book returns to some of the implications of this thought, where we develop future directions for practice, policy and funders in relation to community heritage research.

References

Abram, D. (1996) *The spell of the sensuous: Perception and language in a more-than-human world*, New York, NY: Pantheon Books.

Arnstein, S. (1969) 'A ladder of citizen participation', *Journal of the American Institute of Planners* 35(4): 216–25.

Bakhtin, M. (1981) *The dialogic imagination. Four essays*, Austin, TX: University of Texas Press.

Baron, R. (2016) 'Public folklore dialogism and critical heritage studies', *International Journal of Heritage Studies* 22(8): 588–606.

Bashforth, M., Benson, M., Boon, T., Brigham, L., Brigham, R., Brookfield, K., Brown, P., Callaghan, D., Calvin, J., Courtney, R., Cremin, K., Furness, P., Graham, H., Hale, A., Hodgkiss, P., Lawson, J., Madgin, R., Manners, P., Robinson, D., Stanley, J., Swan, M., Timothy, J. and Turner, R. (2015) 'How should heritage decisions be made? Increasing participation from where you are?' Available at: http://heritagedecisions.leeds.ac.uk/publications/

Bastian, M., Jones, O., Roe, E. and Moore, N. (eds) (2017) *Participatory research in more-than-human worlds*, Routledge: London.

Bishop, C. (2004) 'Antagonism and relational aesthetics', *October* 110: 51–79.

Brown, A. (2017) 'Co-authoring relationships: Blackfoot collections, UK museums, and collaborative practice', *Collaborative Anthropologies* 9(1/2): 117–48.

Brydon-Miller, M., Greenwood, D. and Maguire, P. (2003) 'Why action research?', *Action Research* 1(1): 9–28.

Burns, D. (2007) *Systemic action research: A strategy for whole system change*, Bristol: The Policy Press.

Chatterton, P., Fuller, D. and Routledge, P. (2007) 'Relating action to activism: theoretical and methodological reflections', in S. Kindon, R. Pain and M. Kesby (eds) *Participatory action research: Approaches and methods: Connected people, participation and place*, London: Routledge, pp 216–22.

Clifford, J. and Marcus, G. (eds) (1986) *Writing culture. The politics and poetics of ethnography*, Berkeley, CA: University of California Press.

Facer, K. and Enright, B. (2016) *Creating living knowledge: The Connected Communities Programme, community–university partnerships and the participatory turn in the production of knowledge*, Bristol: Arts and Humanities Research Council.

Facer, K. and Pahl, K. (2017) 'Introduction', in K. Facer and K. Pahl (eds) *Valuing the impact of collaborative research: Theory, methods and tools*, Bristol: Policy Press, pp 1–21.

Fals-Borda, O. (1991) 'Re-making knowledge', in O. Fals-Borda and M.A. Rahman (eds) *Action and knowledge: Breaking the monopoly with participatory action research*, New York, NY: The Apex Press.

Fals-Borda, O. (2013 [2007]) 'Action research in the convergence of disciplines', *International Journal of Action Research* 9(2): 155–67.

Fals-Borda, O. and Rahman, M.A. (eds) (1991) *Action and knowledge: Breaking the monopoly with participatory action research*, New York, NY: The Apex Press.

Fyson, A. and Ward, C. (1973) *Streetwork: The exploding school*, London: Routledge and Kegan Paul.

Gaventa, J. (1991) 'Toward a knowledge democracy: viewpoints on participatory research in North America', in O. Fals-Borda and M.A. Rahman (eds) *Action and knowledge: Breaking the monopoly with participatory action research*, New York, NY: The Apex Press, pp 121–32.

Golding, V. and Modest, W. (eds) (2013) *Collaborative museums: Communities, curators, collections*, Oxford: Blackwell.

Goldman, E. (2008) *Anarchism and other essays*, Munich: Book Rix.

Graham, H., Banks, S., Bastian, M., Durose, C., Hill, K., Holland, T., McNulty, A., Moore, N., Pahl, K., Pool, S. and Siebers, J. (2014) 'Ways of knowing: exploring the different registers, values and subjectivities of collaborative research'. Available at: http://waysofknowing.leeds.ac.uk/

Gupta, A. and Ferguson, J. (1997) 'Discipline and practice: "the field" as site, method, and location in anthropology', in A. Gupta and J. Ferguson (eds) *Anthropological locations: Boundaries and grounds of a field science*, Berkeley, CA: University of California Press, pp 1–47.

Hamdi, N. (2010) *Small change: About the art of practice and the limits of planning in cities*, London: Earthscan.

Haraway, D. (1988) 'Situated knowledges: the science question in feminism and the privilege of partial perspective', *Feminist Studies* 14(3): 575–99.

Harris, M. (ed) (2007) *Ways of knowing: New approaches in the anthropology of knowledge and learning*, Oxford: Berghahn.

Harrison, R. (2012) *Heritage: Critical approaches*, London: Routledge.

Harrison, R. (2015) 'Beyond "natural" and "cultural": Towards an ontological politics of heritage in the age of the anthropocene', *Heritage and Society*, 8(1): 24–42.

Hart, A., Davies, C., Aumann, K., Wenger, E., Arandaa, K., Heaver, B. and Wolff, D. (2013) 'Mobilising knowledge in community–university partnerships: what does a community of practice approach contribute?', *Contemporary Social Science* 8(3): 278–91.

Harvey, D.C. (2001) 'Heritage pasts and heritage presents: temporality, meaning and the scope of heritage studies', *International Journal of Heritage Studies* 7(4): 319–38.

Hawke, S., Stefano, M. and Onculi, B. (eds) (2017) *Engaging heritage, engaging communities*, Woodbridge: Boydell & Brewer.

Heron, J. and Reason, P. (2001) 'The practice of co-operative inquiry: research with rather than on people', in P. Reason and H. Bradbury (eds) *Handbook of action research: Participative inquiry and practice*, London: Sage, pp 179–88. Available at: www.peterreason.eu/Papers/Handbook_Co-operative_Inquiry.pdf

Hodder, I. (2012) *Entangled: An archaeology of the relationships between humans and things*, London: Wiley.

Holtorf, C. (2002) 'Notes on the life history of a pot sherd', *Journal of Material Culture* 7(1): 49–71.

Ingold, T. (2000) *The perception of the environment*, London: Routledge.

Ingold, T. (2012) 'Introduction', in M. Janowski and T. Ingold (eds) *Imagining landscapes: Past, present and future*, Farnham: Ashgate, pp 1–18.

Jasanoff, S. (2004) 'Ordering knowledge, ordering society', in S. Jasanoff (ed) *States of knowledge: The co-production of science and the social order*, London: Routledge, pp 13–45.

Kirshenblatt Gimblett, B. (1995) 'Theorizing heritage', *Ethnomusicology*, 39(3): 367–80.

Lang, C., Reeve, J. and Woollard, V. (2006) *The responsive museum: Working with audiences in the twenty-first century*, Ashgate: Aldershot.

Lassiter, L. (2005) *The Chicago guide to collaborative ethnography*, Chicago, IL: University of Chicago Press.

Latour, B. (1993) *We have never been modern*, trs. C. Porter, Cambridge, MA: Harvard University Press.

Long, N. and Moore, H. (2012) 'Sociality revisited. Setting a new agenda', *Cambridge Anthropology* 30(1): 40–7.

Lowenthal, D. (1998) *The heritage crusade and the curse of history*, Cambridge: Cambridge University Press.

Lynch, B. (2011) 'Collaboration, contestation, and creative conflict: on the efficacy of museum/community partnership', in J. Marstine (ed) *The Routledge companion to museum ethics: Redefining ethics for the twenty-first-century museum*, London and New York, NY: Routledge, pp 146–63.

Lynch, B.T. and Alberti, S.J.M.M. (2010) 'Legacies of prejudice: racism, co-production and radical trust in the museum', *Museum Management and Curatorship* 25(1): 13–35.

Mathie, A. and Gavanta, J. (2015) *Citizen-led innovation for a new economy*, Rugby: Practical Action Publishing.

Okely, J. (2012) *Anthropological practice. Fieldwork and the ethnographic method*, Oxford: Berg.

Pahl, K., Escott, H., Graham, H., Marwood, K., Pool, S. and Ravetz, A. (2017) 'What is the role of artists in interdisciplinary collaborative projects with universities and communities?', in K. Facer and K. Pahl (eds) *Valuing the impact of collaborative research: Theory, methods and tools*, Bristol: The Policy Press, pp 131–52.

Reason, P. (2005) 'Living as part of the whole: the implications of participation', *Journal of Curriculum and Pedagogy* 2(2): 35–41.

Samuel, R. (1994) *Theatres of memory. Volume 1: Past and present in contemporary culture*, London: Verso.

Smith, L. (2006) *Uses of heritage*, London: Routledge.

Star, S.L. and Griesemer, J.R. (1989) 'Institutional ecology, "translations" and boundary objects: amateurs and professionals in Berkeley's Museum of Vertebrate Zoology, 1907–39', *Social Studies of Science* 19: 387–420.

Strathern, M. (ed) (2000) *Audit cultures. Anthropological studies in accountability, ethics and the academy*, London: Routledge.

Tunbridge, G. and Ashworth, J. (1996) *Dissonant heritage: The management of the past as a resource in conflict*, Chichester: Wiley.

Vergunst, J., Curtis, E., Davis, O., Johnston, R., Graham, H. and Shepherd, C. (2017) 'Material legacies: shaping things and places through heritage', in K. Facer and K. Pahl (eds) *Valuing the impact of collaborative research: Theory, methods and tools*, Bristol: Policy Press, pp 153–72.

Ward, C. (1973) *Anarchy in action*, London: Freedom Press.

Waterton, E. and Smith, L. (2010) 'The recognition and misrecognition of community heritage', *International Journal of Heritage Studies* 16(1/2): 4–15.

Waterton, E. and Watson, S. (eds) (2013) *Heritage and community engagement. Collaboration or contestation?*, London: Routledge.

Watson, S. and Waterton, E. (2010) 'Heritage and community engagement', *International Journal of Heritage Studies* 16(1/2): 1–3.

Part One: Ways of knowing

We are using 'ways of knowing' to link the first five chapters of this book. By this, we want to indicate that when heritage is framed as a form of community research, it is produced through plural and interacting modes of understanding and making sense of the past in the present. The phrase 'ways of knowing' offers a nod to debates in anthropology and participatory and action research, which have drawn attention to knowing as an expansive and ongoing process that might rely as much on feelings, intuition, social interaction and communication as on formal research methods. In these chapters, this more expansive – or 'extended' (Heron and Reason, 2001) – epistemology is very much in evidence.

In our first chapter, Jo Vergunst, Elizabeth Curtis, Neil Curtis, Jeff Oliver and Colin Shepherd explore how collaborative archaeological research draws on 'ecologies of skill' that 'bring together landscapes, materials, people and their social interactions'. From this, the notion of an 'archaeological imagination' is developed, in which 'more voices are heard and more people become skilled at working within their own landscapes'. The research is spatially and temporally situated in ways that open up future possibilities for environmental change.

Also concerned with how different ways of knowing – in this case, of singers, musicians and anthropologists – John Ball, Tony Bowring, Fay Hield and Kate Pahl, in Chapter Two, enact the improvisatory mode of their music-making in written form. Through a staging of a sequence reminiscent of both an improvisatory music session and an action research cycle, they explore how the process of 'do–think–say–write–do' led, over time, to drawing their differences into a shared framing for making sense of their collaboration and its implication for the transmission of musical heritage.

Chapter Three offers an emphasis on contesting popular representations, with Jodie Matthews drawing attention to the dangerous and damaging stereotypes of the Romani community in the media and on social media. Matthews explores how archives and sharing personal experience offer resources for pluralising and challenging these restricted modes of representation.

Reflecting on their involvement as academics in projects that create digital resources for community heritage groups, Nick Higgett and Jenny Wilkinson, in Chapter Four, show the significance of different expectations, time frames and perceptions to the collaborative process. In an honest exploration of these differences, they recognise that miscommunications can mean less satisfaction with a project and recommend greater conversation as projects begin to establish shared understandings.

In Chapter Five, Helen Smith and Mark Hope explore how a community arts organisation working together on the histories of lavender farming produced a series of social and metaphorical resources for working the organisation's future into being. As much to do with memory and the senses (the smell of the lavender) and the act of cutting and nurturing the lavender, the work gave the group an embodied shared reference point to the conceptual legacy of the research project.

All of these chapters are concerned with the forms of knowing that emerge when lots of different people from different perspectives actively take part. A common theme here is of an epistemology that is situated in many different collaborative activities: of archaeology, of improvisation, of social media, of making digital reconstructions and of lavender cutting. In these chapters 'knowing' contains the active participation not only of people, but also of things – whether of plants, smells, instruments, digital objects, soil, trees, charts and displays – indicating the epistemic significance of a more-than-human participation in community heritage as research, in the 'ecology of skill' evoked by Vergunst et al in the first of these chapters.

The chapters in this section also develop another dimension. Through the process of research – and from seeking to know the past and places together – new social relations and new metaphoric resources emerge. In making room for many ways of knowing and in seeking to know and to understand the past socially and in the spirit of inquiry, something akin to a prefiguration of a future-to-come is worked into being.

Reference

Heron, J. and Reason, P. (2001) 'The practice of co-operative inquiry: research with rather than on people', in P. Reason and H. Bradbury (eds) *Handbook of action research: Participative inquiry and practice*, London: Sage, pp 179–88.

ONE

Shaping heritage in the landscape among communities past and present

Jo Vergunst, Elizabeth Curtis, Neil Curtis, Jeff Oliver and Colin Shepherd

Introduction

Can community-based archaeology achieve different outcomes from more traditional academic approaches? In this chapter, we explore how ways of knowing the past can alter significantly when the landscape is encountered through collaborative means. This not only provides a contrast to how archaeology is usually practised in university and professional settings, but also enables us to study relationships with landscape that span the past, present and future. If one of the preoccupations of mainstream archaeology is the regular chronological ordering of human activity from the past towards the present, working through a collaborative methodology opens onto how time and landscape can be understood in different ways.

Research co-design and co-production undermines assumptions that the past is a stable and static entity that can be uncovered and read off layer by layer (Simonetti, 2013). By drawing inspiration from phenomenological perspectives on landscape, we explore how notions of time develop from practical and discursive involvement with landscape. These forms of activity can become mediums through which senses of the past, present and future emerge; in this way of thinking, 'time duration is measured in terms of human embodied experience of place and movement, of memory and expectation' (Bender, 2002: S103). We would add that plants, animals, seasonality and other non-human components of landscape also create senses of time. As ways of life in the landscape continue, so time itself unfolds, not simply according to a calendrical or 'clock' chronology, but also by way of the qualities of being past, present and future, and of duration and change. This holds true for the ways of practising archaeology as much as for the landscapes of the past being described. Field research on 'heritage' can serve to provoke notions of temporality beyond standard associations with the past and beyond the imposition of a sense of time onto the landscape. By these means, collaboratively exploring the past of a landscape is also an emergence of its present and future.

Our argument builds on ideas and practices of community and public archaeology. Dalglish (2013: 2) writes that community archaeology:

> is evident in the many projects which have community participation as a primary aim and in the new funding streams which support such projects ... it has become possible to see such involvement as a particular way – not the only way – of doing archaeology.

While we broadly celebrate the involvement of the public in archaeology and other heritage research, others have drawn attention to the somewhat limited successes that can result from such work. Simpson and Williams (2008: 80) note that although standard archaeological excavations are often 'the draw' for the public, there may then be 'a lack of participation in subsequent non-excavation activities'. The same might also be said for preparatory work such as surveying and test pitting, which is often hidden from public view or involvement but vital for setting the scale and scope of the research. More broadly, the task 'of really empowering the community in relation to its heritage' is much more difficult than merely providing the 'expected deliverables' of site visitor numbers, a greater level of engagement with the archaeological process and so on (Neal and Roskams, 2013: 151).

Moving practices of heritage away from the authorised heritage discourse (Smith, 2006) of professional or official interpretations that are passively received by non-experts is what is at stake here. For Abu-Khafajah et al (2015: 194), writing in the post-colonial context of Jordan, a significant liberation from such received truths is at stake: 'This liberation is essential for re-establishing the connection between lay people and heritage, reviving the role of heritage in building people's identities, and launching a future for heritage beyond tourism'. From this perspective, community or public archaeology is about substantially more than merely involving non-professionals at various, and usually isolated, points of the research process. In parallel with Abu-Khafajah et al's work, we seek an active, creative and critical form of heritage, rather than one led by an expert-driven or rigidly scientific approach whose instrumental outcome is often commodification for tourism purposes.

The material we present is not intended as a straightforward evaluation of a further case study of community archaeology, although we do describe the ways in which we have worked. Instead, it is about the broader terms of temporality and landscape in which community archaeology and related forms of heritage research *could* engage. The empowerment that scholars engaged in public or community archaeology speak of, we argue, can be usefully conceived of in terms of the ability to imagine the possible futures of heritage sites and their associated communities, and to help bring them into being. Empowerment may be complicated by different agendas, perspectives and politics; yet, at the same time, it is these very processes that give the edge – or even the vital force – to heritage research by purposefully bringing in multiple voices and practices. First, however, we need to briefly explore some key concepts in landscape, heritage and enskilment that ground the way we are thinking about heritage. We then move on to present our activities at the archaeological remains of the Bennachie Colony, together with how the future is being imagined through them.

A Scottish landscape, heritage and skills

At the hill of Bennachie, on the edge of the Grampian Mountains about 20 miles from Aberdeen in North-East Scotland, there are two main ways of getting around. Having arrived at the visitor centre or one of the car parks, one may simply follow a series of signposted paths on foot (or perhaps with a bicycle or on horseback). The paths are mostly broad and well-made, and lead to the open moorland at the top of the hill or through plantation forests of conifers that encircle it. One of these lower circuits will take you around the small collection of ruined croft houses and partly enclosed fields and pasture – now mostly a timber plantation – that comprised the 19th-century informal settlement known as the Bennachie Colony. Visitors can observe the ruins of toppled enclosure walls and the lower courses of stone buildings, along with the occasional quarry from which the stones were prised. It is, however, quite easy to miss these remains through the often thick undergrowth of broom, gorse, heather and bracken; most of the time, people pass by on their way around the forest or to the top of the hill.

The second way of getting about Bennachie is used less frequently by those who make the approximately 100,000 visits occurring each

Figure 1.1: The hill of Bennachie as background landscape

Source: Photo by Jo Vergunst

year. It involves stepping off the modern, well-laid paths and making one's way through the trees and the undergrowth. This would not be to attain a particular destination; it is more suited to simply seeing what is there or what happens along the way. There are some small paths that have been formed through common use, and areas that afford passage by virtue of not being too overgrown. It is the way of moving through the landscape that a dog-walker might experience with their dog following a scent, or that a child might entertain – to look for a stick, to hide among the bracken and heather, or just because being off the path is more interesting than being on it. It is also how those wishing to explore the history of the landscape might choose to move, at least every now and then. Where *does* the wall of that field actually end? Traipsing away from the main paths brings a distinctive set of visual and bodily relations with the landscape. In a literal sense – being less concerned with gaining the view from the top of the hill, and being on a much less even surface – the walker looks down and around, and feels the ground itself rather than just the laid path.

There are broader historical resonances to these two ways of moving that speak to the themes of heritage we are concerned with. In the Highlands and Islands of Scotland, dominant visual modes involve the gaze onto an empty landscape, perhaps with iconic mountains, rivers, forests or moors (eg the art of Edwin Landseer or, in literature, Compton Mackenzie's novel *Monarch of the glen* (1941), which was inspired by Landseer's 1851 painting of the same name depicting a red deer stag). Conspicuously, the people are absent, unless they are outfitted in tartan as a form of marketing for diaspora tourism (Gouriévidis, 2016). This vision of rural Scotland has underlain the highly concentrated pattern of landownership in which much of the Highlands, and elsewhere, has been owned by a small number of people by way of large and thinly populated estates (Wightman, 1996). Mackenzie (2013: 12) describes this way of seeing the land in Scotland as a 'colonizing optic' that presents 'narratives of a sporting estate empty of people or a place of "wildness" that must be protected from people'. Within such settings, there is an association of scenic nature with the landscape in these forms that can be traced to travellers undertaking a version of a Grand Tour in the later 18th century (following the subjugation of the Highland clans at Culloden in 1746), and became part of an emerging 'green consciousness' in the UK and beyond (Smout, 1991; Macdonald, 1998; Olwig 2002). However, locally, it also underpinned the development of large-scale recreational uses of the landscape for sporting purposes, such as grouse-shooting and deer-stalking, which themselves followed the sheep farming that was key to the removal of large parts of the rural population from the Scottish Highlands and Islands in the 19th century (Richards, 2000; Lorimer, 2002; Hunter, 2015). In short, the tropes of heritage that come through to the present are often comprised of images of a wild, unpeopled landscape, which in North-East Scotland, is combined with castles and whisky. Given the strength of such populist discourses, it is easy to forget that these places were, and are, also the homes of rural people and are also inhabited by many regular visitors. Their pasts, and how they might be brought into the present, are far less frequently considered.

To metaphorically step off this 'main path' of conventional heritage offers a chance to see and feel things differently. By this reckoning, the landscape is not simply what is contained within a view from a mountain top. Even while this kind of 'gaze' is not, these days, necessarily a powerful appropriation when undertaken by ordinary hillwalkers (Lorimer and Lund, 2008), the historical and political resonances of the landscape are also altered. Rural histories in Scotland are being told in forms both traditional and new, and rural communities have been part of the broader turn towards community heritage activity in recent years that provides alternatives to the mainstream construction of the past. This has encompassed work in community archaeology (Dalglish, 2013), the arts (Smith and Hope, this volume), crafts (Bunn, 2016), archival history (Macknight, 2011) and technology–heritage hybrids (McCaffery et al, 2015), as well as established work in oral history and ethnology (such as the continuing interest in work among Scottish Traveller communities in the 1950s and 1960s by Hamish Henderson). All of these forms of heritage activity are, in different ways, resituating the agency of communities themselves in terms of the past and present, and in terms of how they have lived with the landscape and its resources.

At the same time, the politics of the land in Scotland have taken a series of sharp turns away from traditional vested interests through the establishment of the Scottish Parliament in 1999 that had land reform on its agenda. The Land Reform (Scotland) Act 2003 instigated a community right-to-buy of land in the crofting areas of the Highlands and Islands, and recent evaluations of the policy suggest that the changing relationships and new partnerships that involve communities in the management of the land have been significant compared to the fairly small number of actual cases of community buyouts (Warren and McKee, 2011). Alongside the buyouts legislation, the Act also established a right of responsible access for walkers and other non-vehicular users to virtually the whole of Scotland's countryside. The severance of the right to control access to land from the right to own it has also changed the dynamics of rural landscape management, although, as with the community buyout rights, this has also not gone uncontested (Vergunst, 2013). The point is that the terms in which we can think about landscape are changing in Scotland and, indeed, elsewhere (Déjeant-Pons, 2006), in ways that are power-laden.

Scholars have also developed concepts in tandem that recognise forms of embodiment and politics in relation to the landscape. Where Cosgrove and Daniels (1988: 1), in an influential edited collection, used visual representation as the core for understanding landscape, arguing that 'landscape is a cultural image, a pictorial way of representing, structuring or symbolising surroundings', other reckonings of landscape have come to emphasise the collective power relations and bodily relationships engendered with and through landscapes (Bender, 2002; Olwig, 2002; Arnason et al, 2012). For Olwig, drawing on medieval European history, landscape is fundamentally created through a body politic of everyday conventions, tradition and common law, often in opposition to the gaze of the powerful. Ordinary interactions with the landscape can be as significant as those of the landowner and policymaker. Subverting the standard optic of governance, it is as much through ordinary ways of being and knowing in the landscape that 'the political' is enacted as it is through the formal processes of legislation and governance.

A further key concept for this chapter is enskilment, or, specifically, the way in which skills for engaging in heritage research, including archaeology, can be learned and shared. In 2013, we hosted a reflection and evaluation workshop for community heritage research projects in Scotland.[1] One discussion was about the skills learned in this context, and prominent among the examples given by the non-academic and academic participants alike were teamwork, negotiation, perseverance and other such capabilities. We were struck by how such 'soft skills' became an intangible outcome of heritage research. It is certainly the case that research projects involving partnerships between communities and other organisations need to draw on these kinds of skills, especially in the management roles that many of the participants in our workshop had. Yet, what also emerged was that participants and their communities had gained a wide variety of specific practical abilities to carry out the research itself: to access and use public archives; to elicit oral histories; to carry out archaeological field surveys; to excavate and analyse; and to synthesise all these into coherent narratives involving outputs such as exhibitions, publications and performances. These skills did not seem to be recognised, or valued, in the same way, and perhaps because of this, it made us want to consider their significance in more detail.

Reflecting on the specific nature of archaeological skills being carried out with communities is something that the scholarly literature on community archaeology does relatively rarely, although in Scotland, the Royal Commission on the Ancient and Historical Monuments of Scotland (RCAHMS) (now Historic Environment Scotland) has produced a practical guide (RCAHMS, 2011) that includes surveying and excavation techniques. Yet, scholarly focus often returns to the 'soft skills' such as those identified by our workshop participants. Other approaches to thinking about skills may be useful here.

Tim Ingold (2000: 353) argues that considering skills demands an ecological perspective, in the sense that skilled practice encompasses a whole field of relations in a richly structured environment, rather than simply being the property of an individual. What we might think of as 'ecologies of skills' bring together landscapes, materials, people and their social interactions. Our question is how they can produce forms of heritage that do not isolate and separate the past as a visual spectacle, as in the forms that we described earlier, but enable a much more critical consideration of temporal connection and disconnection. We make the case that through undertaking practical skills of heritage research – in this case, field archaeology and the exhibiting of the results – communities can be enabled to imagine differently, to think differently about past, present and future, and thereby to also act differently.

Our sense of 'communities' is very much inclusive of academics as well. We are, indeed, keen to explore the means and circumstances in which academics become enmeshed in the communities with which they are engaged, and we might trace the shift from engagement towards co-production that Vergunst and Graham propose in the Introduction to this volume. The hard dividing lines between academic and non-academic partners can become blurred and both 'communities' may act as a unified body – in some ways, and at some times at least – and we will go on in this chapter to discuss the limitations of this model as well. We argue that the enmeshing of interests of the 'heritage' and academic communities is a significant process in co-produced heritage processes. The coalescing of perspectives is one way in which community empowerment in and through heritage has the potential to take place.

Researching in the landscape: from survey to exhibition

In this section, we trace the progress of a collaborative heritage research project involving the University of Aberdeen and communities around Bennachie. Since 1973, the Bailies of Bennachie community group have been working to preserve the amenity of the hill and ensure public access and public interest in its history. While presence of multi-period archaeological remains has long been known about, in 2010, the Bailies began a coordinated effort to research the natural and cultural landscape of the hill through the Bennachie Landscapes Project (BLP), which was given initial shape by independent archaeologist Colin Shepherd. In 2011, the University of Aberdeen secured funding through the Arts and Humanities Research Council (AHRC) Connected Communities programme to work with the Bailies, with a specific focus on the 19th-century crofting colony that existed on its eastern slopes.[2] While the Bailies had been involved in surveying the colony in the late 2000s, further funding enabled an expanded archaeological programme, along with archival and oral historical work that was also premised on notions of co-production (Oliver et al, 2016; Armstrong et al, 2017).

Skills have been learned and shared through many different activities, including the practical, hands-on activities of archaeology in its various forms, during regular 'work party' volunteer days on the hill and a parallel programme of training and research events. A key emphasis underlying much of the archaeological work has been the use of 'low-tech' procedures and equipment because the skills required are those that can be quickly grasped through practice in the landscape.

Shovel testing

At the start of the BLP in 2011, a programme of shovel test pitting was implemented. This technique is used for determining the presence of archaeological remains not visible on the surface in order to establish the extent of cultural activities within a defined area. Shovel testing was employed during the first year of the project to help define the character of the buried archaeology and, specifically, to identify the range of artefact types and to acquire dating material that could be compared with the standing archaeology. As the method is simple and easy to learn, and may be used to test relatively large areas such as agricultural fields, it can be a very effective tool in the hands of a community group with only limited archaeological experience. To draw as much interest in the project as possible, the project commenced with a series of shovel-testing weekends. Events held on multiple weekends attracted between 30 and 40 people, including members of the Bailies of Bennachie and the wider public, from around 13 years of age upwards. Participants were divided into teams and assigned one of three gridded-out enclosed fields (typically 10m × 10m squares) adjacent to the ruined dwelling houses. Each team further divided themselves into pairs or threes and were given the task of digging 20-litre test pits and sifting the soils to look for artefacts.

Shovel testing can be tiring and repetitive over the long term, but it proved to be an extremely popular way to make discoveries about the settlement and the landscape. Test pits can often produce negative results (ie no finds), although these are important for mapping artefact distributions. Most groups identified artefacts at least some of the time and the act of discovery was much anticipated. Pieces of ceramic, metal or glass were found, wiped clean of soil and handled, shared and discussed, initially among the local shovel-testing pair and then with others. At this stage, some of the technical terms were introduced to describe the 19th-century pottery – for example, sponge ware, transfer-printed ware – while pieces of rusted metal or sherds of glass were also given an initial appraisal. Given the public's understanding of archaeologists as excavators who discover the past buried beneath their feet, test pitting may have helped to fulfil some of the expectations of first-time participants for doing archaeology (Holtorf, 2005). A school group who came to assist one weekend tested a former enclosed field with very few artefact finds, possibly because it was used for grazing rather than for arable (arable fields tend to be manured, which often contains domestic rubbish). Despite the low numbers of 'finds' compared with other areas and groups, their interest in the task remained high for the duration of their visit.

Overall, shovel test pitting was a popular activity that was able to encompass a relatively large number of people. The ease of learning the method combined with the fact that almost everyone made 'discoveries' helped to establish interest in the project from an early stage. More broadly, however, it also draws attention to the significance of finding and handling materials, which has been a theme of our reflections on co-produced heritage research (see Vergunst and Graham, this volume). While the community archaeology literature has noted the importance of fulfilling the public's expectations of archaeology as a way of securing participation (Neal and Roskams, 2013), shovel testing also enables a set of tactile relationships involving artefacts being drawn directly from the landscape. In the small conversations around potsherds, as soil was wiped away to reveal patterns of line and colour, participants began to develop their own understanding of the archaeology, as well as the practical skills to take part it in. These moments of close involvement with finds seem particularly important in community-based archaeological work, and we continue to seek ways in which they can be extended and maintained. In much archaeology, finds are all too soon packaged up and removed from local circulation into the keeping of professional finds specialists and curators according to national regimes of antiquities management (Karl, 2011).

Surveying

Subsequent phases of the project have incorporated a range of different types of methods for planning the colony site. While this included methods like dGPS (differential Global Positioning Systems) survey, kite photography and digital mapping, which are now commonly used by professional archaeologists, we placed greater emphasis on more traditional methods of archaeological survey, including a measured offset survey, the use of plane tables and detailed planning using 1m × 1m drawing grids. The real efficacy of these more low-tech methods was not only that they were accessible for our community researchers, but also that they played an important role in further developing relationships involving the standing archaeology and the participants.

Surveying the Bennachie Colony was as much about exploring and discovering remains as it was about an objective recording of what was there. The process of offset survey involves a constant moving through the landscape in order to lay out a grid and then to measure offsets from both axes. In a wooded environment (750m × 450m and covered with trees and undergrowth of varying densities, as noted earlier), this work involves clambering and crawling through undergrowth in order to define that grid and then again, many times, in order to record any features (Vergunst, 2012). Sight lines are inevitably blocked by trees and tapes get snagged on brush. However, the process brings people into direct contact with their environment, and moving through this landscape in a sometimes tortuous way also forces a close attention to environmental detail. By the time any measurements are taken, the traverse of the tape is already known implicitly.

While recording the more obvious remains, further elements are discovered. Furthermore, in order to perceive the extent of original structural lines and subsequent damage, often masking the original features, surveying becomes a decision-making process. What to record and what not to record? Where does this feature start and where does it stop? The choices become endless but measured marks have to go down on the drafting film. Individuals find themselves engaged in a dialectic with the archaeology and their decision becomes the accepted canon for an unspecified period of time. The community participant becomes the 'expert' whose decision, in this instance, is final. The dividing line between 'expert' and 'novice' blurs into a range of greys determined by a number of interdependent variables defined both by previous life experiences and experiences gained. Gradations of possibility are far more common than black-and-white assessments of right and wrong.

As the limit of inference within this historic environment is so prejudiced by undergrowth, previous site degradation and shear scale, a finer resolution than 1:50 could not be countenanced for this type of survey. Buildings were, therefore, planned at that level of definition while the larger enclosures were planned at 1:100. Plane tabling was particularly effective for recording features at a middling level of detail, in particular, at a scale of 1:200, which allowed us to represent individual crofts and their related kailyards and surrounding fields on a single piece of A3 paper. Planning using 1m × 1m drawing frames required a similar set of skills to plane tabling, but allows an even greater level of detail, at 1:20. The selection of an appropriate scale is, as in all surveying, a key aspect of not just the final outcome, but the whole field of relations involving participants, the archaeology and the landscape.

Offset surveying could be contrasted with plane tabling where points are selected from a distance and measured in. As described in the RCAHMS (2011) field manual, an idea of the site is generated by observation and points are chosen to depict that notion. With offset survey, the tape is moved routinely at intervals of one or two metres. The point at which the tape cuts the feature is, therefore, more random and the nature of the site unfolds during the process of recording rather than prior to it. In practice, however, plane tabling often took place through a conversation between the recorder standing at the plane table and the measurer moving around the archaeology, in which decisions about what significant point to map in took place according to more than one perspective. It is this capacity for generating dialogue and shared understanding, rather than individual, expert-led decision-making, that we think is important. In this case, the dialogue involves both the more distanced 'gaze' of the recorder and the mobile, tactile reckoning of the measurer, and requires a consensus to be generated between the two. Given the relative complexity of the ruined crofts, both plane tabling and offset surveying forced our participants to make very clear decisions about selecting what features would be included on the plans and what features would not be represented. This process required us to effectively untangle different kinds of material relationships – such as what was human made versus 'natural', or what features were in their original location and what features were not – in order to form a coherent picture about the site for later use.

Building survey has also involved larger-scale section drawings at 1:25 of the remaining stone walls. Looking side-on at the walls for drawing meant, at the same time, beginning to track their methods of construction. As a group, we talked at one stage about the use of small 'sneck' pinning stones that could be seen between the larger ones in the wall, which helped to create a solid wall from unevenly shaped blocks. The drawing was again undertaken in small groups, mostly of pairs (one measuring, one drawing), again generating understanding through dialogue.

Unlike shovel test pitting, with its focus on artefacts, survey and planning therefore guided attention towards features, in particular, the archaeology of buildings. The methods not only helped us to pay greater attention to materials and building techniques, but also gave us a much clearer picture of how the crofts were added to, redesigned and eventually torn down. The colony buildings have interesting and complex biographies themselves that we have come to explore in

Figure 1.2: Plane table survey

Source: Photo by Jo Vergunst.

our work (Oliver et al, 2016). Surveying and planning have taken place over several years, typically as weekend events during periods of better weather and particularly during 2013, when our funding provided for additional help. While occasionally advertised to the wider public, these activities tended to attract far fewer 'general' members of the public, and tended to rely on members of the Bailies of Bennachie and a handful of other participants who routinely formed the backbone of field working parties. The positive aspect of this more limited participation was in helping to forge a particular sense of identity within the more involved group. With this more involved group, using 'low-tech' survey and planning methods encouraged not only particular kinds of tactile and other sensory attentiveness towards the archaeology within the landscape, but also greater degrees of engagement among participants themselves. By these means, the shared process of learning about the landscape is emergent from the shared practice of recording.

Excavation

During the summer of 2013, we undertook archaeological excavations of two of the croft houses, Shepherd's Lodge and the MacDonald house at Hillside, in order to compare and contrast ways of life within the colony. The excavation was evaluative in nature. After removing rubble from the interior of both dwellings, exploratory trenches were opened both inside and outside the former structures. Excavation revealed interesting details about the different construction methods used at the two crofts. At Shepherd's Lodge, it cast doubt on a more popular folk tradition which suggests that the croft was burned to the ground during a dramatic eviction event (Oliver, 2015). At Hillside, on the other hand, the discovery of fragmented but whole pottery vessels suggests a second eviction event. While archaeological excavation has provided the project with the most fine-grained evidence about life at the scale of the household, it also encouraged a more diverse series of outcomes among those who participated. This was enabled through a number of variables, including the technical difficulties surrounding excavating, the quality of the archaeology discovered and the level of interest that it produced among the excavation teams and other members of the project.

Excavation, like some of the later survey phases described earlier, required the establishment of a more intimate group of participants. This was further reinforced by the general requirement for community researchers to participate for the full two weeks of the excavation in order to ensure a degree of continuity. The work thus provided an important setting for learning to excavate and work as a team. While the technical requirements of excavation meant that professional archaeologists played an oversight role (in particular, Oliver, Shepherd and a contracted community archaeologist, Aoife Gould), as skills and knowledge competencies were developed, team members become increasingly responsible for undertaking certain tasks, including providing site tours for frequent visitors. At one point, community members also took charge in removing rubble from the McDonald house interior. As the building debris consisted of bulky and heavy granite blocks, an efficient and safe method was required for their removal. The answer came in the form of a 'bier', a stretcher of logs tied with rope that was made by our participants.

The skills and identities of participants thus continued to develop through the field research in similar ways as occurred during the shovel testing and surveying activities. At the same time, however, much imaginative and interpretive work was also underway. On one level, the constant involvement with the interpretation and narratives of the sites through specific research techniques (survey, excavation, etc) can be thought of as imaginative work. All participants on the site have the opportunity to take part in the shaping of the temporal and spatial narrative to emerge from it. A simple example of this was in shovel test pitting around the field and garden areas of one of the colony houses. We quickly realised how deep and rich the topsoil was; in short, how much work, effort and labour had been expended

Figure 1.3: An improvised bier for moving large pieces of granite

Source: Photo by Jeff Oliver.

by those living in the croft houses to improve the soil. These were efforts that the Forestry Commission, the current main landowners at Bennachie, now benefitted from in having excellent soils to grow their conifers from. At the same time, pieces of richly decorated and colourful pottery came readily from a number of the pits we dug. Our stereotypes of poor, marginal squatters scraping a living from the land were rethought, and re-imagined, with each shovelful of soil. Now, we are thinking of the colonists not as subsisting hand to mouth, but as having their own ambitions for the future and making long-term commitments to living on the land through improving the soil, building dykes and houses (which we now survey and excavate), and raising families (whom we find recorded in archives). As it is for many farmers, the land must have been the locus for the growth and emergence of the future. The eventual failure and break-up of the colony at the hands of surrounding landowners must have been all the more painful for it.

This recognition of the future-oriented historic landscape of crofting at Bennachie contains within it the possibility of further change. This is both within the landscape itself and in community relations with structures of power and decision-making regarding the landscape. On the hill, the Bailies of Bennachie are developing management plans for the croft houses that include further historical research possibilities but also considering anew the land itself. At the Shepherd's Lodge croft, we have begun to reinstate a kailyard or croft garden, with currant bushes and other historically appropriate plants, as a way of both indicating the previous use of the land and exploring how such plants grow in the location. Another house will have a protective surrounding of native hazel trees, in a contrast with the timber production conifers that clothe much of the hillside. Shifts towards native trees and a more diverse range of benefits of forestry are slowly happening in Scotland, which, in themselves, form a new cultural imaginary of what forest landscapes could be (Collins et al, forthcoming). The Bailies themselves are able to take part in decision-making processes with the Forestry Commission and other landowners, who, in turn, are coming to recognise the significance of the narratives of the past that heritage research is producing.

Exhibiting

The BLP has also had a broader aim to communicate not just with the Forestry Commission, other landowners and archaeological specialists through publications, but also with the public. How and where this happens is a further important dynamic in research that is intended to be grounded in a community but has a less defined relationship with the wider population. If the research merely stays 'within' the community, there is a risk of cementing its boundaries rather than encouraging openness and new connections. Wider dissemination also raises questions of who is, or can be, authorised to tell the story of the research, and if the traditional role of the academic as expert interpreter can be subverted (Smith, 2006).

At the heart of the Bennachie Centre is a permanent exhibition about the hill and its heritage, which, the Centre's website claims, is 'the ideal place to learn about Bennachie' (Bennachie Centre, 2016). Such professionally designed exhibitions have become a standard of heritage interpretation, offering visitors an easy way of encountering expert knowledge. Although expensive to create, they are relatively cheap to maintain, but also inflexible and difficult to update. An integral part of research is sharing its results with others, from the telling of discoveries with friends, to academic publication, lectures, exhibitions and events. Increasingly, research funders expect the 'outputs' of research to go beyond academic dissemination, so it is far from surprising that the application for Connected Communities funding to support the BLP included a 'co-produced exhibition that will form an important strand of the dissemination of project results' (quoted from the Case for Support).

A mixed group of people from the existing BLP and the University of Aberdeen was established to develop the exhibition. Early discussions showed the tensions between the different ways in which the hill is experienced, from visiting the interpretation centre before a walk on the well-laid paths, to exploring the hill through trees and undergrowth. In the funding application, we had written that the exhibition would 'showcase archaeological and historical results of the project and provide an overview of the reflexive aspects of co-produced research'. An exhibition in the Bennachie Centre of finds from excavations and the results of archival research could therefore helpfully offer visitors an insight into the research, but could also confirm the idea of the visitor as consumer, passively viewing the work of others. The traditional, modernist model of exhibitions has seen them as being 'a linear process of information-transfer from an authoritative source to an uninformed receiver' (Hooper-Greenhill, 2000: 15), whereas more critical approaches have seen them as 'contact zones' (Clifford, 1997) in which visitors and curators are able to participate in discussions. Could the desire for co-production and reflexivity therefore be extended beyond the BLP group to include other people visiting the hill?

Rather than the different views of the purpose of the exhibition being considered as a block on its creation, they were seen as offering an opportunity for discussion about its aims and audiences that had not been predetermined by the funding application. The exhibition gradually moved from being a small agenda item in our monthly or bimonthly BLP meetings to the mainstay of debate. Long discussions (late evenings in the unheated Bennachie Centre in winter!) concluded that the exhibition would not be about the results of the project, but instead be about what is happening: 'an interim report to show where we have reached and what we are still to do', as we put it at the time. The group hoped that this would inspire other people to join in with the research over coming years. The expectation of sustainability from the funders therefore moved from the investment in long-lasting exhibition hardware to sustaining the involvement of people over the longer term.

The exhibition plans therefore ceased to be about new display cases in the Bennachie Centre, but rather became about a series of pull-up banners that could be exhibited at events and locations around North-East Scotland. Although there was initially some discussion about the banners following a broad thematic structure, it was soon agreed to focus on particular places and stories. For example, the banner on the house known as Shepherd's Lodge had the subtitle 'Evicted – House

Ablaze?' and presented the archaeological and archival evidence that addressed the local story that the house had been burnt as part of the eviction of the tenant. That focusing on the croft on Burnside highlighted the contributions to the project of the analysis of soil from test pits that showed how the colonists had enriched the soil to a deep rich loam. With the aim of encouraging other people to join in, much of the writing was in the first-person plural, with many illustrations depicting members of the BLP at work, while the contribution of individual members was highlighted by a series of short quotes accompanied by a photo of the person quoted to explain their involvement. Examples from the exhibition include:

> As we excavated the McDonalds' home it was easy to feel that we could welcome 21st century visitors – friends and relations, local people, tourists – to Hillside, showing them round the house almost as if it had been ours. If only for a moment. (BLP participant Colin Miller)

> Digging in the archive has been a great experience. My particular highlight was the discovery of papers stuck into the back of a book which listed the colonists and the conditions of lease being imposed on them in 1859, the year the Commonty was divided up by the local landowners. (BLP participant Ken Ledingham)

Care was taken so that those quoted included representatives of the overlapping groups from the University of Aberdeen and the Bailies of Bennachie.

The production of the banner drew on a range of skills, including those of a professional designer paid from the grant, with writing and editing shared among the group so that all banners were collaborative writing efforts. Main texts were edited down to a compressed but fluent 100–200 words, with short quotes and illustrations that showed people engaged in research, and examples of archival and archaeological finds. Despite individual draft contributions being criticised and rewritten by other people, that this remained a friendly and constructive process was the result of the long discussions about the aims and audiences that took place at the first meetings. In many cases, the very drafting and sharing of the texts enabled participants' imaginative ideas to be floated and discussed openly, as the previous examples show, alongside the 'hard' factual content. In their first year, the banners were displayed in the nearby town of Inverurie, in the Bennachie Centre and in the university. Subsequently, they have continued to be exhibited in libraries, community centres, cafes and events, though, at the time of writing, the banners now need updating to reflect new discoveries.

Through the process of its creation, the purpose of the exhibition therefore shifted from presenting the products of research for an undifferentiated general public, to focusing on the attempt to involve more people in the process of research. This can be compared with the contrast between visiting Bennachie by using the well-maintained gravel and wooden paths, and an invitation to join those who enthusiastically walk and clamber between the trees and over the walls of ruined houses.

Imagining past, present and future communities

The working examples of low-tech archaeological research and open-ended temporary exhibition are diverse and we do not want to convey a single narrative of co-production or temporal imaginings. Instead, the possibility for community heritage research to incorporate multiple strands and to allow shifts in identity and practice among participants is very much where its strengths lie. Here, we might recall the 'liberation' ideology of heritage research put forward by Abu-Khafajah et al (2015), in contrast to research being just the execution of a preconceived plan (see Vergunst and Graham, this volume).

We recognise that the BLP has shifted between phases of more explicit co-production and times when either university partners or those from the community took the lead in defining the questions and techniques of research. The latter often occurred, for example, in evening meetings, when all attending were invited to give their opinions and ideas, which led to particular participants developing expertise in archival history, survey work, pottery and other fields. Community members were also frequently able to act as a team, with substitutes able to step into the breach, for example, to give public talks.

Among the academics, while it is true that they often played their 'main' role (eg as excavator [Oliver], educationalist [E. Curtis], exhibition curator [N. Curtis] and oral historian [Vergunst], along with others, including soil scientists, archival historians and other archaeologists), they also experienced significant changes in their working practices and perspectives. Vergunst, for example, relearned archaeological field skills not practised since he was an undergraduate, leading him to rethink his anthropological work on landscape from this perspective. Elizabeth Curtis was inspired to develop a new course on 'making history' for her undergraduate education students, which gives them archival and other heritage research skills to take into their teaching careers. At the same time, Jeff Oliver found that letting the project take its course, including in directions that were unanticipated, was often immeasurably of more value than the more narrowly defined academic goals that we began with. All four academic co-authors of this chapter (Vergunst, E. Curtis, N. Curtis and Oliver) can reflect on how they became 'volunteers' on the project as well – enmeshed in it – by committing beyond the terms of the initial project grants, pursuing the work for its own sake and sharing in the formal and informal parts of the work, such as social events, as equals. The trick for the academics was to find the value of this kind of work in circumstances where they were also limited by restrictions placed upon them by their 'other' lives at the university, where commitments and the culture of long hours sometimes limited participation – together with the problem of having public engagement or community-based research recognised as worthy of the time spent on it.

What has emerged throughout these circumstances is a set of distinctive temporal imaginations of landscape. The point is not simply that through close-up involvement in archaeology, participants could imagine more realistically what life in the past had been like, though when directly asked, this is frequently put forward by community participants as a significant motivation for taking part in the work. Instead, it is to consider imagination in a broader sense as coupled with a person's perception, situated in a relation with the landscape rather than a form of mental activity located solely inside the head. The scope of what imagination is and can do seems to broaden through these means of research. In a discussion of the connection between imagination and perception, Ingold (2012: 3) writes that imagination needs to be thought of 'not just as a capacity to construct images, or as the power of mental representation, but more fundamentally as a way of living creatively in a world that is itself crescent, always in formation'. So, imagining the places and times of heritage research happens through participants' contact with them – on site and in the archives.

Further, those very subjects of imaginative work are never still. There is no stable moment that we can return back to or recreate; instead, participants become involved with the emergent, rather than inherent, temporalities of landscape. As Bender (2002: S103) writes: 'landscape is time materializing: landscapes, like time, never stand still'. There is no single, fixed moment of landscape that can be discovered archaeologically in the past or, indeed, ethnographically in the present. Bender's experimental and creative methods of researching a phenomenology of landscape in prehistoric sites on Bodmin Moor in South-West England open on to further connections between past and present, including her and her co-researchers' 'embodied negotiation' of landscape in the small routes, journeys and conversations taking place around it (Bender, 2002: S108), which must have had their equivalents in the prehistoric past. 'Time materialising' at Bennachie might refer to a similar process of exploring the past, present and future. The Bennachie crofters were striving for their own sense of the future, which was sometimes partly realised but, ultimately, denied to them.

It is surely in such temporal openness that the possibility of change in relationships with landscape lies. In our case, while permanent settlement on the side of the hill is no longer sought, the ability to nonetheless be there regularly, and to influence the use and management of the land, is still at stake. This is where the imagination of how the land was in the past comes to be relevant in the present and future, not simply for the mainstream heritage interest in the spectacle of Scottish history.

The low-tech skills of heritage research, then, become the grounds for imagining different kinds of futures for the landscape. This is to situate community archaeology as a practice that can go beyond the 'expected deliverables' of participation (Neal and Roskams, 2013), which, in themselves, would be unlikely to more fundamentally challenge structures of knowledge and decision-making in heritage. A hallmark of this kind of work in the future, therefore, would be not simply the participation of non-professionals in the research process, but the means by which dialogue, shared learning and different perspectives are also incorporated. As well as providing a challenge to accepted academic structures, this approach could also enable more sustainable community heritage research itself as more voices are heard and more people become skilled at working within their own landscapes.

Connecting the skills of participation in landscape research with the capacity to re-imagine temporal relations starts to invoke the possibility of positive social and environmental change. These are processes that do not necessarily need high-technology input or 'expertise' of the sort usually associated with academia. Our work at Bennachie has used low-tech engagements with the landscape that build on skills in the community. This posits a different sort of future for heritage research to that of technological modernity, and it might contribute to building a model for sustainable landscapes overall.

Notes

1   Hosted by the University of Aberdeen's Sharing All Our Stories Scotland team (AHRC AH/K007890/1).

2   AHRC grants AH/J013447/1 and AH/K007750/1.

References

Abu-Khafajah, S., Al Rabady, R., Rababeh, S. and Al-Rahman Al-Tammoni, F. (2015) 'Hands-on heritage! Establishing soft authority over heritage through architectural experiment: a case study from Jordan', *Public Archaeology* 14(3): 191–213.

Armstrong, J., Miller, C. and Oliver, J. (2017) 'Bringing archives and archaeology together: community research at the Bennachie Colony', *Scottish Archives* 21: 18–29.

Arnason, A., Ellison, N., Vergunst, J. and Whitehouse, A. (eds) (2012) *Landscapes beyond land: Routes, aesthetics, narratives*, Oxford: Berghahn Press.

Bender, B. (2002) 'Time and landscape', *Current Anthropology* 43(S4): S103–S112.

Bennachie Centre (2016) 'The Bennachie Visitor Centre'. Available at: www.bennachievisitorcentre.org.uk/centre.html

Bunn, S. (2016) 'Who designs Scottish vernacular baskets?', *Journal of Design History* 29(1): 24–42.

Clifford, J. (1997) 'Museums as contact zones', in J. Clifford, *Routes: Travel and translation in the late twentieth century*, Cambridge, MA, and London: Harvard University Press, pp 188–219.

Collins, T., Goto Collins, R. and Edwards, D. (forthcoming) 'Seeking shared and cultural values in a Caledonian forest: integrating deliberation, ecology and artistic engagement', *Ecosystem Services Journal*.

Cosgrove, D. and Daniels, G. (1988) *The iconography of landscape*, Cambridge: Cambridge University Press.

Dalglish, C. (ed) (2013) *Archaeology, the public and the recent past*, Woodbridge, Suffolk: Boydell Press.

Déjeant-Pons, M. (2006) 'The European Landscape Convention', *Landscape Research* 31(4): 363–84.

Gouriévidis, L. (2016) 'Heritage, transnational memory and the re-diasporisation of Scotland', *International Journal of Heritage Studies* 22(4): 277–90.

Holtorf, C. (2005) *From Stonehenge to Las Vegas: Archaeology as popular culture*, Oxford: Altamira.

Hooper-Greenhill, E. (2000) 'Changing values in the art museum: rethinking communication and learning', *International Journal of Heritage Studies* 6(1): 9–31.

Hunter, J. (2015) *Set adrift upon the world: The Sutherland clearances*, Edinburgh: Birlinn.

Ingold, T. (2000) *The perception of the environment*, London: Routledge.

Ingold, T. (2012) 'Introduction', in M. Janowski and T. Ingold (eds) *Imagining landscapes. Past, present and future*, Farnham: Ashgate, pp 1–18.

Karl, R. (2011) 'On the highway to hell: thoughts on the unintended consequences for portable antiquities of § 11(1) Austrian *Denkmalschutzgesetz*', *The Historic Environment* 2(2): 111–33.

Lorimer, H. (2002) 'Guns, game and the grandee: the cultural politics of deerstalking in the Scottish Highlands', *Ecumene* 7(4): 403–31.

Lorimer, H. and Lund, K. (2008) 'A collectable topography: walking, remembering and recording mountains', in T. Ingold and J. Vergunst (eds) *Ways of walking. Ethnography and practice on foot*, Farnham: Ashgate, pp 185–200.

Macdonald, F. (1998) 'Viewing Highland Scotland: ideology, representation and the "natural heritage"', *Area* 30(3): 237–44.

Mackenzie, C. (1941) *Monarch of the glen*, London: Chatto & Windus.

Mackenzie, F. (2013) *Places of possibility: Property, nature and community land ownership*, Chichester: Wiley-Blackwell.

Macknight, E. (2011) 'Archives, heritage, and communities', *Historical Reflections/Réflexions Historiques* 37(2): 105–22.

McCaffery, J., Miller, A., Vermehren, A. and Fabola, A. (2015) 'The virtual museums of Caen: a case study on modes of representation of digital historical content', proceedings of the 2015 Digital Heritage International Congress, volume 1, pp IEEE.

Neal, C. and Roskams, S. (2013) 'Authority and community: reflections on archaeological practice at Heslington East, York', *The Historic Environment* 4(2): 139–55.

Oliver, J. (2015) 'Archaeology and the Bennachie Colony: excavation of two 19th-century crofts', in C. Shepherd (ed) *Society and ecology in the history of North-East Scotland: Bennachie and the Garrioch* (vol Bennachie Landscapes 3), Inverurie: Bailies of Bennachie, pp 83–98.

Oliver, J., Armstrong, J., Milek, K., Schofield, J.E., Vergunst, J., Brochard, T., Gould, A. and Noble, G. (2016) 'The Bennachie Colony: a nineteenth-century informal community in northeast Scotland', *International Journal of Historical Archaeology* 20(2): 341–77.

Olwig, K. (2002) *Landscape, nature and the body politic*, Madison, WI: University of Wisconsin Press.

RCAHMS (Royal Commission on the Ancient and Historical Monuments of Scotland) (2011) *A practical guide to recording archaeological sites*, Edinburgh: Royal Commission on the Ancient and Historical Monuments of Scotland.

Richards, E. (2000) *The Highland clearances*, Edinburgh: Birlinn.

Simonetti, C. (2013) 'Between the vertical and the horizontal: time and space in archaeology', *History of the Human Sciences* 26(1): 90–110.

Simpson, F. and Williams, H. (2008) 'Evaluating community archaeology in the UK', *Public Archaeology* 7(2): 69–90.

Smith, L. (2006) *Uses of heritage*, London: Routledge.

Smout, T.C. (1991) 'The Highlands and the roots of green consciousness', *Proceedings of the British Academy* 76: 237–63.

Vergunst, J. (2012) 'Seeing ruins: imagined and visible landscapes in North-East Scotland', in M. Janowski and T. Ingold (eds) *Imagining landscapes. Past, present and future*, Farnham: Ashgate, pp 19–37.

Vergunst, J. (2013) 'Scottish land reform and the idea of "outdoors"', *Ethnos* 78(1): 121–46.

Warren, C. and McKee, A. (2011) 'The Scottish revolution? evaluating the impacts of post-devolution land reform', *Scottish Geographical Journal* 127(1): 17–39.

Wightman, A. (1996) *Who owns Scotland?*, Edinburgh: Canongate.

TWO

Co-writing about co-producing musical heritage: what happens when musicians and academics work together?

John Ball, Tony Bowring, Fay Hield and Kate Pahl

Introduction

> the yellow arch at Kriol Junction
> dream place of lost dancehalls
> cross-continental tracks meet and split
> crackling algorhythms
> storylines greet songlines
> koranic cries pijin beats migrated babble

A diverse group, including musicians, musical educators, academics and artists, collaborated on a project exploring approaches and creative responses to processes in the transmission of musical heritage. To realise this chapter, some of us have come together to enact a process of co-writing that forms a kind of negotiated dialogic and text-based equivalent to the co-production experiences embedded in the original Transmitting Musical Heritage project. In this sense, this piece seeks to mirror and perform the process of our project. Through the form the chapter takes, we seek to engage you with the different ways of knowing our work (Vergunst and Graham, this volume), and to draw you into the rhythms, call and response, and improvisations of our collaboration. Our way of conceptualising this piece of co-writing is strongly informed by the experiences that we have had as music-makers working primarily across oral traditions, accustomed to improvising, reacting and curating largely intangible moments.

The Transmitting Musical Heritage project involved a variety of activities and interventions, developing a range of partnerships. It continued long after the original project ended to work in schools and other contexts, and provides an enabling structure in which individuals and groups can work together on emergent projects. Three community groups (Arts on the Run, Babelsongs and Soundpost) worked in different ways to answer the question: what is transmitting musical heritage? In this chapter, we explore the process of researching how to transmit musical heritage through the process of co-writing. How this might be done was not a given from the start and we begin by exploring the question of how we work together in the co-writing process and allow for the improvisation of heritage as a form of 'knowing' and of 'action', to reference the two main themes of this edited collection. We then introduce key aspects of the projects, with a focus on the 'Music co-produced' workshop. We draw the chapter to a close by reflecting on the necessary and ambivalent relationship set up with 'the audience' in any notion of 'transmission'.

Through this process, we are bringing to the surface implicit understandings about our collaborative practice. We have tried to develop a common, unified voice and to give you the full experience of 'our music'. However, we have not always found this to be possible, so the chapter retains a quality of multi-vocality. Sometimes, in our writing, which mirrors our music-making, individual themes, instruments and voices emerge higher in the mix. Taken together, the chapter aims to provide an impression analogous to sound mixing and, at times, even reaching cacophony. In this sense, the chapter expresses the tensions of co-writing but also expresses (we hope) the shared space of practice that we have created together:

> I had a notion that co-writing would take on a similar form to my own experiences of co-musicking, that is, extended jams shaped into production through negotiation. I anticipated an animated process, involving co-conversations tailored into narrative. I recognise some similarities between the negotiating taking place over this chapter and those between co-authored music, these often relate to levels of attachment to either one's own ideas or one's own way of working. (John Ball)

Co-producing the research

Our project team involved a number of different partners, all with particularly complex sets of skills. These interrelationships embedded between the academic institution and community partners had a strong impact on the project, its processes and its destinations. It

Figure 2.1: Arts on the Run produce recorded transmissions featuring Rafiki Jazz in session at Yellow Arch Studios Sheffield, April 2013

Source: Photo © Aysegul Balkose.

involved varied approaches to practice and research, with the team and the co-producers, at times, occupying an amorphous zone where academics were academics, academics became musicians, musicians became academics and, thankfully, musicians were also ... musicians.

Several styles of research were employed on the Transmitting Musical Heritage project as prompts to surface the implicit knowledge held by the community partners, including discussion and active interventions using research methods, for example: 'Socratic dialogues', in which we engaged as a group with one question and focused on that, drawing on experiential knowledge (Armstrong and Banks, 2011); 'consensus mapping', where we used sticky notes to cluster questions and identity themes; and co-writing as a mode of inquiry, where we used shared spaces, such as flip charts, to brainstorm answers to questions. The aim was that we could all learn from different types of tacit knowledge held across each group, and so that individuals could more deeply reflect on their practice and consider the implications and consequences of their musical and administrative decisions.

The process of asking the question 'What is transmitting musical heritage?' and of getting close to a few answers came alive through the creation of a community of practice. By a 'community of practice', we mean 'groups of people informally bound together by shared experience and a passion for a joint enterprise' (Wenger and Snyder, 2000: 139–40). These were effective in creating a shared space where ideas could be developed and worked through in an informal but structured setting. Our community of practice was able to uncover tacit knowledge about playing and the process of making music together, as well as to unfold narratives about which heritage was valuable and why. This enabled a shared vocabulary of practice. Some critical points of connection were found across the project's co-productions (see end of chapter); all of them were concerned with improvisation and expression, as well as performance and audience, and in all of them, collaboration was key. Here, we draw on this process in our writing together.

Writing as production

In writing this chapter, we have had to allow for improvisation within the writing, as well as creating times and places where we have to collaborate effectively for a shared voice. Through participating together in practical exercises over time, we have done a lot of talking and a lot of sharing of ideas, and this has generated ease of understanding between us and respect for our differences:

> I think we were a bit surprised when having worked through what seemed like an exhaustive process of familiarisation and exchange, we weren't necessarily able to readily convert this into flowing text, or text suitable for the rigours of academia. I wonder if it has something to do with audience, experience and expectations of audience? We had co-written text before. This text was shared between a fairly small group who had established trust between them. (John Ball)

Our expressive and working styles are different, even disparate, but we are excited by this as we can trust in our common focus and perhaps also the musicians' impulse to find productive congruence. We should not slip into the assumption that collaboration somehow comes naturally or even magically to musicians. For many, it is a critical skill refined through years of practice of operating in diverse settings, working under the pressure to co-produce in tight frameworks and budgets. Even after many years of musical practice, it is often still problematic in the shifting sands of working environments and personal aspirations or needs:

> How does production encapsulate this vibrant and dynamic dialogue? I'd like to capture some kind of sense of the sheer dirty glamour of some of our co-production sessions, their fusions and confusions, the power of the transmissions through the net and the work of the network and the memorables of the intangibles we play with as both musicians and strategists when faced with heritages in all corners of the living rooms and in those so fragile vocal cadences as they wrap to the vibrating string and laptop code. (Tony Bowring)

The process of co-writing weaves together the various threads of the project. As academics in the project, we were used to taking the editorial role and presenting research from a single vision. As musicians, we were used to working as a group and may defer to a producer to mix the final cut. Here, we are attempting to co-edit and co-produce our ideas. In the conscious decision to not give editorial power to one individual, we found ourselves sometimes at odds with the discipline of co-writing. We are enacting the complexities of co-produced writing. This is a mimetic piece that explores an issue in the doing of it. That each of us has a voice discernible in the writing is analogous to sound mixing, where the producer blends individual contributions into a group whole; here, our voices are our own lines, and we are acting as each other's editors to create a track:

> The producer is responsible for what actually makes the cut, so plays an important filtering role. Often, the producer accommodates the breadth of ideas but helps to refine them. The producer has to hold a position of trust. Respect for the producer comes from the ability to organise and represent the breadth of ideas into something presentable. The producer has skills and expertise; these can enhance the raw materials. The producer also has to be diplomatic. The producer is an interface between the writers/performers and the audience. The space between the actual music-making and the production is always critical and can create further tensions and conflict. Production edits and therefore changes the music; that change can be sometimes exciting, deflating or disorientating. (John Ball)

'Music co-produced': the workshop

As part of our research into how musical heritage is transmitted, we created 'Music co-produced', a workshop to make explicit what happens when musicians collaborate. John Ball devised and produced a pilot workshop focused on the live co-production of music for an audience in order to create an experimental transmission of music heritage.[1] This was about co-producing music, but it taught us about co-producing writing together.

Invited musicians from various cultural traditions brought their music and its instrumentation to a conference setting. The workshop's objective was to establish a reflexive, analytical platform for looking at and talking about co-production in music via a live session where musicians engaged in creative music-making, and inviting critical interventions and reflections around the processes of co-production with an audience:

> The layers of collaboration taking place between co-producers in music settings are complex, influenced by a whole range of considerations, including patronage, aesthetics, musicianship, philosophical and political preferences, notions of heritage, tradition, and economics. For musicians, collaborative skills are a prerequisite for survival. (John Ball)

While the musicians were able to produce reasonably coherent and aesthetically pleasing music between them in a short space of time, the music was of an exploratory nature and felt limited in its scope. The session suggested that the musicians needed space and time to formulate more considered musical responses.

As with the writing, there was no shortage of ideas for consideration, but these raised a concern with how these ideas might be framed and in what contexts. Five musicians took part in the session, one vocalist and four instrumentalists. Some combinations of instruments were more familiar than others and some participants were familiar with more than one tradition. Collectively, the group dug deep to uncover some of the processes of music transmission and the unspoken shared heritages, and to unlock one of those doors to a musical space where difference can make all the difference.

In the 'Music co-produced' group, the connections were made: Nancy connected with Sarah's oral approach to collaboration based on responsive listening; Rob talked about how he structured music and how he communicates with other musicians; and Kadialy immediately connected with Rob's description of his relationship with traditional repertoire and how this forms the basis of his references for working with others. Initially, language was used to make reassuring statements on ways of working as a way of establishing an understanding of individual requirements, interests and potential connecting points; it is part of the etiquette, but also drawing lines – ones that can be crossed and ones that cannot. As musicians, language is only meant to get so far. The workshop needed both language and music side by side.

Musically, it felt important for the group and its individual members to get a sense of and to experience the collective sound in order to understand their place and to contextualise their own individual voices. There is a preliminary exploration of parameters and boundaries, while developing a sense for the collective tools present:

> For me, I initially explore a 'social area' of the vocabulary within the language of tabla, one that feels relatively safe, familiar and communicable, one through which I have historically experienced connection with others. Reflecting on his own input, Kadialy said that he consciously and deliberately played something open and inviting on the kora when asked to lead on a piece in the session. He doesn't like to apply traditional kora melodies in this context because he feels it is too suggestive and imposing. He chooses something with a drone-like quality with hints of accessible melodic phrasings. These are like a series of musical invitations. Then, when others join, he uses these emerging meeting points as prompts to explore more expansive melodic and harmonic possibilities. (John Ball)

Who are our audiences?

Writing, and music, involves audience. The audience is both necessary and ambivalent, shaping what is produced. Just as we are aware of who you, our readers, are, we were also very aware of our audience in the 'Music co-produced' workshop. We worried that being attentive to the audience shaped and limited the extent of our critical interventions:

> This is a collaborative methodology. It requires a patience with the process and some consideration. From this point onwards, successful music co-production may take time to emerge or may never do so. Though there was no specific

Figure 2.2: Arts on the Run produce live transmission featuring Rafiki Jazz onstage at National Centre for Early Music, York, September 2013

Source: Photo © Aysegul Balkose.

demand put on the musicians in terms of output, there seemed to be performance-orientated expectations arising from perceptions of the needs of the audience. Some of these were explicitly articulated by audience members. There was also a sense of good-will emanating from the audience, but it was also felt that, ultimately, they wanted proof of the success of collaboration. There is always an audience. I felt that the prevailing performer–audience dynamic impacted on aspects of critical analysis. The music presented was loosely shaped into performance and the performers possibly compromised critical interventions. (John Ball)

One of our challenges as a co-produced project was to surface expertise and recognise different skill sets while making room for a collaborative voice to develop. This raised an issue for us both in the 'Music co-produced' workshop and in developing this written piece:

Surfacing existing knowledge was a central element of this process; however, does this need surfacing through language, or can understandings be communicated musically? Knowledge is transmitted in a variety of ways: John played tabla, Sam designed a workshop, Josie transcribed music, we've delivered conference sessions talking about our work, now we're co-writing a book chapter. Some of the group are better suited to develop particular outputs … Sam does not like expressing himself in written form, Kate would be all at sea giving a fiddle concert. I'm not in the camp that wants all project-related outputs to be understandable to all audiences. Theory should not be dumbed down, in the same way that musical virtuosity should go uncompromised. Not everyone will have the skills to interpret a tabla performance, not all readers will comprehend the thickest of academic arguments, but there is scope for co-produced research to satisfy distinct audiences through a variety of outputs. (Fay Hield)

Transmitting Musical Heritage has generated a rich range of outputs, some musical, some written, some performative, some reflective. Some face academic audiences; others look towards practitioners or public audiences. These are multilayered and interact with ideas of analysis to different degrees:

Our outputs are time-based … musical, educational, activity-based, reflective and performative, but the acts of creating events, recordings and concerts have been trailed by a confetti of words in spaces. Blogs, docs, tweets, headers, footers, flyers and liner-notes have been following this project all along. Where is the music and where is the writing in these long sentences? Whose words and whose voices sing out the loudest, and in the end does it really matter as we jam together as co-producers in a hybrid zone? (Tony Bowring)

The time came. We spoke, we sang with Portuguese, Urdu, Bengali and village Mandinka disputing Yorkshire English space at the edges of the pools of sunlight through dusty windows. It can be named the zone of sonic multilingualism and nation building, through the yellow arch to the lab's control room and to its live room (we didn't know then that we would all have called it a 'global utopia' when we took it to the public stages and filled up workshops) to marry technology's twists with ancestral expertise, iconic instruments and the international dignity afforded by unyielding texts speaking declarations of human rights. The gush of transmission's emissions yielded up from tabla, dagga and berimbau's pots, from plangent steelpans drummed from slave tradery and from the wiry beauty of arabic oud or jali's kora strings, brought despair and laughter and sheer exhausted incredulity. Exit and debriefing was brusque but with promises of legacy. Energies and memories quickly migrated to hard drives, the mix and the mash of post-production, the promo-pitch's branding iron and the haggle over heritage's claims on our music. Much later, we put our feet up listened and watched Insaaniyat's reflections along with all the humans, sang along to MP3 beats in the car before festival stages wired it all up for live, declaring it Declaration Kriol as the musical layers unfolded crackling and shimmering, colour-washed for a very ancient public message, performance's ritual. (Tony Bowring)

Our co-writing group is multi-vocal and features many different skill sets and modes of working. For some in the group, writing is a daily activity, including the production of press releases, tweets and/or academic articles. For many, academic writing is intimidating and for a few, writing in any capacity is a discomforting modus operandi. Talking came more naturally, though there are still embedded tensions arising through a lack of common vocabulary and understandings, either at native-language-barrier level, or more subtly through understandings of words such as 'studio', 'workshop' and 'researcher'. However, we also recognised that this parallels our experience of music-making as we all have varying levels of proficiency in our own areas, and explored the boundaries between us to communicate musically, and linguistically, together. In all these formats, the development of safe spaces in which people were comfortable to express themselves was integral.

Do–think–say–write–do

Through our project, the musicians experimented, then came together to discuss their thoughts on the process. With significant flexibility and diversion, we tended to follow a surfacing knowledge–analysis sequence: do–think–say–write–do. We made sense of our disparate experiences as a group more fluidly and with deeper magnitude as our sense of group developed. Each element became more complex as we generated shared frameworks for understanding. As well as generating more nuanced understanding of our practice, in turn, influencing future practice, our ability to express our knowledge through writing became more sophisticated. Initial writing was blog-like, or appearing in promotional materials or tweets. As we developed trust in our own ideas, the surface became less lacquered and we were able to present more honest, nuanced and expressive accounts of our experiences and ideas. We advanced from personal speculation to shared theoretical statements, negotiated and contested to find a suitable form:

> Co-producing works for me when there has been a foundational process of co-working of ideas. This is inevitably messy and involves some kind of tension. In fact, without tension, it is probably vacuous and compliant. (John Ball)

The production of this chapter has been an involved process, a subsection of our team representing both the project and our experience of getting it into words. This is not one-sided though, and as our audience, you have been involved too. We have endeavoured to write in ways that are both true to our thoughts, within our capacity to deliver and of relevance and benefit to you. Take from us what you will. Transmitters … we are indeed. Transmission is transactional; the receivers are in control as well as the teachers – they (both intuitively and consciously) choose the aspects they wish to engage with and thus what ultimately survives. Regardless of the means of transmission, the audience is never a passive participant in the construction of heritage. Musicians can choose what they want to play, but they have to fit into the receivers' ideas too. Audiences want the version of you they understand.

Outputs into the public domain
Transmission in the city
Sheffield Babelsongs: *City of a Thousand Songs* – 2013–14 research, collection and recording of songs with roots in other countries, from singers who have migrated to the city, including the *Gypsy Blood* project with Roma musicians.

Soundpost: *Fiddle Weekend 2013* – international folk fiddle workshops, masterclasses, participatory and ensemble sessions at various venues in rural Sheffield.

Arts on the Run: *Declaration Kriol 2013* – series of intensive collective sessions, including writing, arranging, live recording and documenting new music from culturally diverse regional musicians working alongside *Rafiki Jazz*, directed by *Konimusic*.

University network days

Nexus of Expertise: a series of four intensive days spread right across the 2013–14 project period connecting together the academics, project leaders, musicians and singers from the community partners. It was choreographed to share practice, surface knowledge, find ways to develop and sustain a broad critical community of practice.

Reflection in diverting places

New Roots basement boudoir, Dungworth Village Hall, The Venue at Yellow Arch Studios: special settings in 2013–14 away from the workplace for extended and filmed talks, where oral culture, biographical scripts and creative dissonances are teased out from project musicians and artists in deep conversation with project academics.

Transmission onstage

Transmission as performance: Arts on the Run's *Declaration Kriol* featuring *Rafiki Jazz* premieres at *Sensoria 2013 Festival* Sheffield then on to York *NCEM*, the *2014 CC Heritage Jamboree Day* Sheffield, Cardiff *Connected Communities 2014 Festival* and the 2014 CC *Partners Day* at The Y Leicester.

Babelsongs present their *Liberian Choir* at the 2014 *Connected Communities Heritage Jamboree* Sheffield, a performance night in Sheffield 2014 to launch their *City of a Thousand Songs* CD, with live music from the *Gypsy Blood* CD project and more.

Soundpost's folk fiddlers *Nancy Kerr & Sam Sweeney* perform live at the *2014 Connected Communities Heritage Jamboree* Sheffield, while Fay Hield's *Full English* project performs a breakfast gig at Cardiff *Connected Communities 2015 Festival*.

Transmission workshops

Music co-produced live: a hybrid interactive performance created, discussed and developed in the moment for a Cardiff *Connected Communities 2014 Festival* audience, bringing together cross-genre musicians from project community partners.

Algo-kriol vocal workshops: *Declaration Kriol* goes digital as live-coder *Yaxu* morphs *Rafiki Jazz* and participants' vocals at *Platforma 2013 Arts & Refugees Festival & Conference* Manchester, York *St Johns University* and Sheffield *2014 CC Heritage Jamboree*.

Babelsongs workshops: Josie Wexler, Ella Sprung, Simon Dumpleton, Marek Pacan, Rose Bazzie and Claudio Salas perform workshops in Firvale and Sharrow schools, teaching the songs collected.

Soundpost fiddlers *Nancy Kerr & Sam Sweeney* present *Teaching Traditions and the English Fiddle* at Sheffield *2014 CC Heritage Jamboree*.

Online transmissions
For the broad picture, see: http://musicalheritage.group.shef.ac.uk/

For deep blogs from the Nexus of Expertise, see: http://musicalheritage.blogspot.co.uk

For transmission goes social, see: https://www.facebook.com/musicalheritage

For traces of micro-practice, see: https://twitter.com/TransMusHerit

Transmission's video documentary dramas
Frontier Media presents a special preview of the documentary *Transmitting Musical Heritage* 2013, featuring people, music and places from *Babelsongs*, *Arts on the Run* and *Soundpost*, to be followed by *Ensemble* 2015. See: https://vimeo.com/69476165

Rafiki Jazz play *Insaaniyat*, a *Frontier Media* music documentary from *Declaration Kriol* 2014. See: https://vimeo.com/83842941

Discs and downloads
MP3: *Rafiki Jazz* songs from *Declaration Kriol* released in 2014 as the MP3 album *At Kriol Junction*. Available at: https://itunes.apple.com/gb/album/at-kriol-junction/id797120516

CD extra album: *Rafiki Jazz At Kriol Junction (KoniCDE010)*: nine audio tracks and a video from *Declaration Kriol* released in 2014 by *Konimusic*.

CD album: debut disc Sheffield *Babelsongs* presents: *City of a Thousand Songs* (SBS01) 2014.

D (EP): Sheffield *Babelsongs* presents *Ciganska krv*: *Gypsy Blood* featuring *Marek Pacan & Frantisek Sandor* – the soundtrack for the film *Gypsy Blood*, 2014.

Note

1   Funded through the Arts and Humanities Research Council (AHRC) Connected
Communities Festival, Cardiff 2015.

References

Armstrong, A. and Banks, S. (2011) *Community–university participatory
research partnerships: Co-inquiry and related approaches*, Newcastle:
Beacon NE.

Wenger, E. and Snyder, W.M. (2000) 'Communities of practice: the
organizational frontier', *Harvard Business Review* 78: 139–45.

THREE

Visibly authentic: images of Romani people from 19th-century culture to the digital age

Jodie Matthews

Introduction

> The settled population, who can make very little link between the romantic images of the past and the deprived and excluded images of the present, are also denied opportunities to learn about and interpret this recent history. While at times British Gypsy history may have been a painful and controversial story, it is without question that it is still an important part of the national narrative. (Bowers, 2007: 19)

> For hundreds of years, the Traveller life was one of ancient traditions and simple tastes. Then their world collided with the 21st century. (Channel 4, 2012: voiceover)

In the course of researching Gypsy and Traveller people's access to museums, libraries and archives in Surrey, Romani journalist Jake Bowers (2007: 19) found a 'desire within [that] community to share and preserve its history'. The experience of being apparently ignored by these institutions is borne out not just in Bowers' work, but among Romani voices heard since that research was undertaken and in other areas of the UK. Some institutions have worked to counter this imbalance (see, eg, Knott, 2015), but where their histories are excluded not only are Gypsies and Travellers less likely to be able to share their cultural heritage with others on their own terms, but non-Gypsies and non-Travellers are also unable to (dis)connect the many romantic images of the past that are available in digital visual media with communities of the present.

Vilified for its sneering exoticisation of Gypsies and Travellers, but also dubiously held up as evidence for the disadvantages of Traveller culture (eg Farndale, 2011), the British Channel 4 television series *Big Fat Gypsy Weddings* is nonetheless an attempt to marry the romanticised past with the diamanté-sprinkled present – no matter how one might wish to criticise the tone and effects of that attempt. *Big Fat Gypsy Weddings* may be the most sensational and most talked-about translation of Romani heritage into contemporary culture by those outside Gypsy and Traveller communities, but it is certainly not the only one.

The politics of these translations reflect discourses of racism, commodification, culture, community and identity in the 21st century. As examples of a 'way of knowing' (see Vergunst and Graham, this volume), such popular representations could be seen as constituting a mainstream view of Gypsy and Traveller communities that has a hegemonic presence parallel to the 'authorised heritage discourse' identified by Smith (2006). A common consequence of such a discourse, Smith (2006: 71) argues, is the relegation of visitors to heritage sites – or, in this case, viewers of popular media – to the status of a 'passive audience'. The point here is that there are alternative ways of both creating and learning about Romani heritage that do not depend on these centralised, powerful forms of production that are then consumed passively. This chapter explores how heritage can be circulated and discussed through active means, including collaborative exhibitions and, in particular, social media. The conversations generated by social media resonate strongly with the theme of dialogism picked up in this volume's Introduction: what these social media users seek is not engagement or consensus in itself, but heritage that can be diverse and different. A post, a tag or a tweet can be a contribution to a conversation, and as liable to diverse interpretations as any other form of language (Bakhtin, 1981).

Gypsy and Traveller heritage into the 21st century

Leeds GATE is a company with charitable status started by Gypsy and Traveller people working to improve the quality of life for those communities. In the summer of 2016, they tweeted that the point of an archive is to be 'a challenge to stereotypes of what Gypsies were like in the past' (@GATEArchive, 5 July 2016). A year later, members of the Leeds GATE community worked with Special Collections at the University of Leeds to undertake precisely that challenge in co-curating an exhibition of the university's 'Gypsy, Traveller and Roma Collections', returning to an archive instituted by the non-

Romani Dorothy Una Ratcliffe to interpret historic paintings, photographs and sketches. In this case, focused in-person interpretation sessions and dialogue via a closed social media group (kept deliberately unidentifiable here) connected 21st-century experience of Romani identity to an archive collected by a non-Romani woman. For instance, one participant noted in relation to a painting of Hawes in the Yorkshire Dales that people still stop there en route to the famous Appleby Horse Fair. Surnames were recognised and discussed, with individuals coming forward to explain the context of images (where people were travelling, for instance, with whom and why). Wagon design was identified and appreciated, and pride in family and community was expressed. The geographical focus of these visual representations archived at Leeds University was Leeds and Yorkshire, emphasising the historical claim that the Romani community can stake in terms of living and travelling in the area.

In such dialogue, focused towards a public exhibition in 2018, the very idea of the archive moves from a closed-off repository to a resource for a community to preserve and share its heritage – for those within and without a Romani identity. These interpretations built on earlier sessions (in which I was not personally involved) organised by Special Collections staff and Leeds GATE to improve catalogue descriptions of the 'Gypsy, Traveller and Roma Collections'. The result of some of these discussions is available on the Yarn website, itself an output of an Arts and Humanities Research Council (AHRC)-funded project, 'Pararchive: Open Access Community Storytelling and the Digital Archive'. Participants in these archive sessions, again, added detail and context, but also reflected on representation. For instance, in relation to a watercolour by Fred Lawson, someone commented: 'it might have shown the scene to be more romantic/exotic than it actually was' (see 'Revisiting the Romany Collection', available at: www.yarncommunity.com/stories/389).

Similarly, in August 2016, a Gypsy- and Traveller-directed historical exhibition opened in Doncaster, specifically to address negative and homogenising stereotyping in the media (Cannon, no date; Proud Gypsy Traveller, 2016). This initiative was started and led by members of the Romani community rather than an archive or institution. Such valuable challenges from the Gypsy and Traveller community are against the problematic use and reuse of representations of, in particular, Romanies/Gypsies from the past, and an equation of particular tropes with a vintage 'gypsy style', a form of cultural appropriation. Both the Leeds and Doncaster examples combined in-person interaction with online activity and were directed towards either exhibitions or improving an archival catalogue. They are both successful in making Romani interpretations of Romani heritage visible. My own AHRC-funded workshops, from which the research for this chapter initially grew, brought together people from a number of creative and educational professions and backgrounds, and produced rich discussions about the challenges of making Romani cultural heritage accessible to non-Romani audiences – and the desirability of that accessibility. Ultimately, the outputs were academic-led (in this case, a non-Romani academic), and, by that nature, lose some of the contestation and vibrancy of lively discussion. However, in turning to the Internet, outputs such as this chapter fold many other contributors into this debate about access to visual heritage.

Drawing on those AHRC-funded workshops, archival research and Internet research, this chapter explores what we do in the digital 21st century with an archival legacy of visual images of Romani people, and how Gypsy culture is reinterpreted and appropriated online. My focus is on British representations, but national boundaries are harder to define in the context of online image sharing. From this point on, the chapter uses the adjective 'Romani' to refer to lived experience and identity (unless a source text uses a different term, which I retain), 'Gypsy' to refer to an exonym (a name applied by outsiders) for individuals and culture, including people dressed up as 'Gypsy' characters, and 'gypsy' to refer to the tag which is applied to things like 'spirit', 'skirt' or 'life' that have almost nothing to do with Romani culture and more to do with non-Romani mythologising or appropriation. In doing so, the chapter modifies Ian Hancock's (2008) suggested practice in his piece on the 'Gypsy' stereotype, though it should be noted that many people in a UK context who contributed to this research use the term 'Gypsy' positively to refer to themselves and their identity and culture. Nomenclature for these communities is contested and shifting terrain (in scholarship, policymaking and, most importantly, by people ascribing to these identities). Many of the arguments I make later about imagery are applicable to a number of Romani and Traveller groups – indeed, the representations in question often elide cultural diversity in these communities – but many assumptions and stereotypes that I interrogate have their roots in racialised perceptions of Gypsies, distinguishing them from other Travellers.

In terms of the history of the people whose representation is at stake in this chapter, it is likely that early Romani groups originated in North-Western India, moving into the Middle East and then moving westwards within the Ottoman and Byzantine empires. Sources indicate that the diaspora first moved into Europe in the medieval period. Groups within this diaspora split off from each other, spreading into Northern and Eastern Europe, others westwards and to the south. Throughout Europe, they were referred to as 'Egyptians', though this probably refers to 'Little Egypt' in what is now Greece. It is from here that the term 'Gypsy' derives. The first record of Romanies in England is usually understood as one dated 1514 (an inquest that mentions an Egyptian woman), though the English probably heard about Romani people before they saw them via accounts written in France and Germany. There is a long history of non-Romanies perceiving Romani people as different to them in their appearance and behaviour: the Elizabethan writer Thomas Dekker commented on how different the Romani people looked to the English, partly because of their 'od and phantastique' clothes (for this summary and more history, see Taylor, 2014). This visible difference from white, Western culture is at the heart of the exploration here of images of Romani people and Gypsy culture.

Frequent recourse is made in the chapter to the 19th century and turn into the 20th century, for two reasons. First, the visual culture of this period was defined by technologies of mechanical reproduction, just as ours is defined by digital reproduction. It may take just a few clicks today to reuse a digitised image, but an analogous recycling and re-contextualising process was at work in reused woodcut engravings and in early photography. Representations of Romani people had been produced in earlier periods, but the 19th century saw a proliferation of images with Romanies as their subject matter, many of which were recycled so frequently that they took on the character of 'truth' and feed into the representations produced and reproduced today. Comparing the use of images in the past with the present, the chapter considers continuities from the circulation of images in 19th-century culture to reposting in the 21st century. While a discussion of social media runs the risk of quickly looking outdated, the online period looked at (roughly, 2013 to 2016) can be seen as a point in the history of representations of Romani people and Gypsy culture, with this chapter acting both as an account and reflection on the period in which it is written, and as a marker for future analysis. While in previous centuries, the creators and collectors of images tended to see Romani people as the object of study, analyses of these historical representations must, in the digital 21st century, take account of the use and abuse of these images in their online circulation, but also the opportunities brought by online communities to express opinions, answer back, contextualise, own and disavow particular images and interpretations. There is increasing recognition that the digital offers new kinds of active engagements with visual heritage – some of which are to be celebrated while others are worrisome to those concerned with the politics of representation.

#gypsy

In the second decade of the 21st century, the primary way of gathering together images and posts on a particular theme on social media is the hashtag. In this case, it is also a way of visualising the condensation of a cultural stereotype. #gypsy is a bewildering digital space because that condensation has happened to such a degree – bringing together the occult, the Orientalist and the outdoor; the bohemian, the barefoot traveller and the chintzily domestic – that the word 'gypsy' is almost meaningless if one tries to apply to a community the images that a search on that hashtag throws up.

We are used to seeing the hashtag deployed to counter stereotypes about gender, ethnicity, class or appearance (#ilooklikeanengineer and #ilooklikeaprofessor on Twitter in 2015), and #iamroma has occasionally been used for political and identity-claiming purposes; strikingly, and relevant to the proceeding discussion, it was used as part of a campaign against the use of the term 'gypsy' in the fashion industry: 'We're a culture, not a costume' (@TheGoodBess, 7 October 2015). This kind of identity-claiming hashtag on Twitter assumes what Shenila Khoja-Moolji (2015) calls 'intimate publics' – that everyone using the hashtag shares the object of concern. However, #gypsy and even #romani or #roma do not necessarily gather in the same sort of intimate public as other hashtags because of their use by those outside the ethnic identities that those terms connote in other contexts. People use the #gypsy hashtag to make explicitly racist statements or, as I explain further later, to appeal to visual stereotypes and claim an aesthetic identity labelled 'gypsy'. They want to *look like* a 'gypsy', not *be* a Gypsy.

To use the categories introduced by James O. Young, this is a misconceived but still offensive form of 'content appropriation', one that, I argue, draws on and perpetuates the romanticisation of Romani culture prevalent in the 19th century (and that is usually a disempowering gesture, whether intended to be so or not). This becomes a moral issue when 'insiders [in a culture, here: Romani people] lack opportunities to express themselves in their own style' (Young, 2005: 141). In theory, everyone with Internet access has the opportunity to represent themselves via a hashtag (and many do so explicitly, as noted), but non-Romani fashion, interiors and book-cover designers have far more opportunities to appropriate the 'gypsy' style gathered erroneously around this hashtag than do Romani cultural producers. It is important not to oversimplify complex cultural interaction, or to ignore the profound influence that Romani culture has had on wider Europe, from music, narrative, painting and poetry, to politics, dance and dress, but here I wish to point to concerns raised in workshops and discussions that the 'gypsy' fantasy conjured by non-Romanies contributes to the disconnect identified by Bowers between a romanticised past and communities of the present. Khoja-Moolji (2015) notes that the tenuous collectivity of some hashtag campaigning only works by rearticulating long-standing conceptualisations of the object of concern, thus further reducing the opportunities for marginalised self-representation, and that is certainly the case in Instagram and Pinterest 'gypsy' tags.

Instagram was launched in 2010 as a photo-sharing service, enabling users to tag their images just as words and images are hashtagged on Twitter. Yasmin Ibrahim (2015) terms the uploading of trivial pictures from everyday life 'banal imaging'. She suggests that for the (largely young) Instagrammers, 'the everyday gets transformed into an imagery of conventions' (Ibrahim, 2015: 44). One can see how images associated with a particular hashtag on Instagram have the capacity to crystallise a stereotype such as 'gypsy' as users curate their habits into something interesting. Banal imaging aestheticises and commodifies the everyday. I suggest that a result of banal imaging is the desire to exoticise the everyday as part of its aestheticisation and commodification: 'look at me/my profile; I am worth looking at; my everyday life is exotic'. Banal imaging is, as Ibrahim (2015: 50) notes, 'an invitation to gaze at the ordinary, perfunctory and personal'. This is, to use Stephen Greenblatt's (2005) phrase, 'self-fashioning'. Rather than play this out on the Renaissance stage as Greenblatt describes, individuals define their subjectivity via social media. To commodify oneself as the decontextualised digital object of a gaze is also a drive to auto-exoticise. Users want the cultural artefacts that surround them to be not *just* banal, but exotically banal. The decontextualised nature of images on Instagram means that the specifics of that exoticisation do not matter.

Romani people have been the object of an exoticising gaze for centuries, so it is little wonder that perceived ideas about Gypsies participate in this exotic melee. Popular textual representations such as Walter Scott's (1999 [1815]) depiction of a turbaned Meg Merrilies in *Guy Mannering* (and the hundreds of stage and graphic interpretations that followed), the Eastern roots of the Romani diaspora and the people's non-whiteness in a racialised taxonomy, and suspicions of magic and witchcraft all feed into the exotic stereotype. This desire to exoticise the banal as part of its commodification is one explanation for the range of images tagged with #gypsy on Instagram. For Instagrammers, #gypsy means: dreamcatchers (more usually associated with Native American culture), independent travel, crystals, beads, embroidery, outdoor life and 'boho' style. Instagrammers tagging their non-Romani lives with #gypsy are making their everyday jewellery, interior design choices, travels, clothes and beliefs exotic. In the world of Instagram, the inauthenticity of that tag and any potential real-life connections to identity and lived experience are ignored. The irony of this inauthenticity is explored later in the chapter. Whatever the reason for the erroneous labelling of artefacts and experiences as 'gypsy', one self-identified Romani user of Twitter is quite clear about the implication: 'I dislike this new rush of #Gypsy themed/named things. This is #racism … #romani aren't your mascots' (@lakovsko, 20 July 2016).

Gypsy dress-up

This desire to wear 'Gypsy' style is not new, of course: Victorian portrait jewellery, with images of Gypsies painted onto porcelain and copied from full-scale paintings (or more likely reproduced engravings of these paintings that the jewellery artist had seen) can still be found for sale today. In 1899, an anonymous article in the *Daily Mail* (usually to be relied on in the 21st century for anti-Romani and Traveller articles; for examples, see Bissett, 2016; Glanfield, 2016; Spillett, 2016) reported that 'Gypsy ear-rings are being worn', referring to large hooped earrings. The lack of specificity in this label seen on Instagram is also traceable at the end of the 19th century: the same earrings are called 'a creole ring'. However, there is more at stake than just highlighting jewellery fashion: the earrings are also labelled 'barbaric' and 'they recall all sorts of quaint scenes in books one has read; old stories, too, of wandering gypsies and their soothsaying powers' (*Daily Mail*, 1899). Suddenly, the banal image of jewellery is explicitly linked to stereotypes of fortune-telling, 'wandering' (rather than 'purposeful travel') and barbarism.

Casual tagging on Instagram can similarly reproduce, solidify and extend stereotypes. Jessica Reidy (2013) discussed the 'politics of dressing "Gypsy"' in an article for *Quail Bell Magazine*. She concedes that, as a mixed-race American Romani in the 21st century, her own enthusiasm for dressing 'Gypsy' is 'complicated by nostalgia and privilege', effacing the cultural norms of the *Romanipen* (Romani way) for women (Reidy, 2013). The problem with the Instagram tags is that 'non-Romani people can "dress-up Gypsy" for a day with no serious repercussions, but when a Romani person dresses in traditional clothing, or even a semblance of it, the response can be brutal' (Reidy, 2013). This is similar to the ways in which members of the Gypsy Lore Society, figures such as Charles Godfrey Leland and F.H. Groome, lived like Gypsies towards the end of the 19th century, going to the extent of learning their language and travelling for a time with them, but leaving it all behind to resume their white male privilege when the feeling took them. Reidy (2013) adds that:

> Outsiders [the same outsiders failing to connect the romantic to the real in Jake Bowers' analysis] tend to think they understand us because they are inundated with Gypsy stereotype after Gypsy stereotype used to sell an image, a product, an ideology, or a way of life.

On Instagram, the posters are selling their own image but catching a ride on the exotic commodification of Romanies to do so.

Filters are used on Instagram to produce an affected nostalgia in the posted images. In the *New Yorker*, Ian Crouch (2012) suggested that the Polaroid-style, the overexposure and the light-flare effects rush and fake 'the emotion of old photographs by cutting out the wait for history entirely, and giving something just a few seconds old the texture of time'. Instagram suggests, even with its Polaroid logo, that there is something artisanal, and thus authentic, about the pre-digital – devaluing the very technology that is the condition for its existence. By 'authentic', in this sense, we usually mean genuine, original, traditional, singular, spontaneous and unfeigned. Instagram certainly appeals to the notion of the 'traditional' by valuing the 'texture of time' if not its passing, but there are a number of further contradictions to the idea of a filtered Instagram photo as authentic. First, the digital photo is a means of almost limitless and faultless reproduction; it cannot be 'original' or 'singular'. Second, the heavily edited nature of the Instagram portfolio undermines any promise of genuineness or spontaneity. The *impression* of these qualities is offered by apparently candid shots of people off-centre in a frame or the immediacy of recently prepared food, but they are part of an aesthetic of spontaneity rather than its experience. Finally, the authenticity of Instagram produced by filters is a manufactured one: it is feigned authenticity. There are two reasons that this matters so much in relation to the gypsy tag. One of these reasons – an equation of 'gypsy' with the past – is explained later in the chapter. The other is that the images tagged in this way also attempt to express an authenticity of being, itself rooted in the past or as an escape from civilisation: pizza on the beach, driving an SUV through a puddle, emulating the desire to 'drop out' like hippies of the 1960s. There are many variations on the words 'to thine own self be true' tagged in this way.

In the 19th century, the romance of an outdoor life, pre-industrial culture and carefree travel also appealed to writers and artists alike. A mid-century periodical article observed that 'gypsies' have a 'wild freedom' and 'untamed lordliness' that is 'nowhere met with in the busy city' (*Cleave's London Satirist and Gazette of Variety*, 1843). This not only appeals to the writer; it appeals to the audience of the periodicals in which it was published and republished. Towards the end of the century, the lure of the Gypsy lifestyle was so great as to warrant the publication of *Gipsy tents and how to use them: A handbook for amateur Gipsies* (Lowndes, 1890). Being a Gypsy was seen as something one could adopt or abandon like a hobby, though the term's racial connotations were never completely dissolved in this 19th-century usage. For 19th-century commentators, an affiliation with Gypsy life meant getting back to nature, away from an industrialised and artificial society. The barefoot traveller of Instagram, celebrating homespun wisdom and kooky jewellery with #gypsy inherits the representational association between Gypsies and a nostalgic investment in the authenticity of practices of the past. There is, the primitivist stereotype goes, a 'truth' to Gypsy life that modern existence has lost. As the chapter goes on to explain, this also problematically removes Gypsy culture from ideas about modernity and progress.

Pinning down the past

The past is pinned on Pinterest more directly. Rather than the use of filters to age a photograph artificially (as on Instagram), old or archival images – pictures on which the passage of time has had a material effect – are digitised and reused. The grain, sepia and creases on Instagram pictures and those on Pinterest may all be digital, but the Pinterest images examined here have a pre-history that includes a non-digital, physical existence and thus a physical explanation for the tints and lines. The analysis of image use on Pinterest is slightly different to the banal imaging of Instagram, and connects more directly to the idea of research about the past as action in the present – the heritage legacies explored in this book. Here, however, the past is drawn on in what are often instrumental ways, contributing to the construction of dominant 'gypsy' stereotypes that popular media also propagate.

Pinterest is a content-sharing platform that allows users to collect and share images according to the interests of users. For instance, a user might have a board titled 'gypsy', 'gypsy style' or 'gypsy soul'. Han et al (2014) have shown that these interests govern repins, rather than, for instance, the number of followers a user has. On Pinterest, the interest matters – and in terms of my analysis here, pre-existing interest in (and potentially stereotyped knowledge of) Gypsies/Romanies matters. Images can be uploaded or fetched from other sites (including tumblr and blogs), which means that there is a huge amount of image reuse, both across Pinterest and to Pinterest from the wider Internet. Pinboards are used like 'mood boards', particularly when the topics relate to travel, food and fashion – including tattoos. Users pin images to create a 'gypsy mood' with little attention to whether the images being pinned have any connection to Romani culture or experience, like the tags on Instagram.

Once again, the category of 'gypsy' broadens when images are pinned next to each other. For instance, one 'Gypsies' board on Pinterest is pinned with many images of traditional 'gypsy caravans', but also fairy gardens, 'Bohemian interiors' (visually defined either by eclecticism or Orientalism) and black-and-white studio portraits of people in Gypsy costume. Time and place are immaterial. Usernames have been deliberately omitted here as this chapter describes extremely widespread practice, and there is no desire to make an example of individual users. Another board shares the wagons and studio portraits but adds pictures of purple- and blue-dyed hair, crystals, 'tree goddess' candle holders, facial tattoos and quotations about finding one's 'inner shaman'. A third combines the portrait studios with archival images of Gypsy life, quotations about having a 'gypsy soul' ('a person always in need of change and/or adventure', it seems – authenticity of being, again), a Moroccan lamp and anklets. One black-and-white image, apparently of a Romani woman with a white headscarf, plaited hair, a striped jacket and full, patterned skirt reading the palm of a white woman in a hat, high-necked blouse, belted skirt and jacket in front of a tent, has been reposted on a number of websites but without any more information than that the image is 'late Victorian or early Edwardian'. A large number of the fashion pins take their inspiration from more recent history: Stevie Nicks and the early 1980s' Fleetwood Mac song 'Gypsy' (which uses the term to mean Bohemian in an artistic rather than ethnic sense).

Another very popular pin is a 1901 studio portrait of the American (non-Romani) model Evelyn Nesbit by Rudolph Eickemeyer. She is pictured with her long, dark hair hanging loose over her shoulders, a headdress with coins attached to it, a long beaded necklace, embroidered blouse and dark, velvet waistcoat. In some pins, the photographer and model are named; in many more (typically the 'Gypsy' boards), she is referred to simply as a 'Gypsy'. Many users of Pinterest therefore see these popular images as they circulate in these new contexts and associate them with the Gypsy tag, just as paintings reproduced in the Victorian *Illustrated London News* will have been the most familiar images of 'Gypsies' in Victorian culture. As workshop discussions revealed, archives that make digital versions of their photographs available find themselves working to counter the unacknowledged decontextualisation of the images they own and whose photographers' and subjects' legacies they manage. Across Pinterest, Romani lives are pinned next to 'pirate wench' blouses and patchwork skirts. Postcards, Hungarian musicians, 21st-century women in India and Moroccan interiors are all, simply, 'gypsy'.

The even looser tag of 'vintage' becomes closely associated with 'gypsy', across vintage décor, vintage pin-up girls and vintage fashion. For instance, patchwork quilts appear on 'vintage' *and* 'gypsy' boards whether they appear in a travelling wagon or not. A vintage peacock lamp appears on a 'Bohemian' board and is then repinned on a 'Gypsy Beauty' board along with 'clutter chic'. It appears again on a 'vintage eclectic' board. This image sharing brings the connotations of 'gypsy' to 'vintage' and vice versa. DeLong et al (2005: 24) see taste, aesthetics and historical curiosity as implicated in a love of vintage fashion, but also 'an ability to discriminate the authentic product'. What constitutes 'authentic' is complicated when the vintage pins are on Pinterest rather than in thrift-store articles of clothing. The 'product' is whatever helps construct the gypsy style, and the authenticity of that Gypsiness is simultaneously valued and disregarded. Stage gypsies, models and documentary images are all compounded and anonymised on Pinterest (though early photographers and painters of Gypsy subjects were not in the habit of recording their names either). In an example of anonymisation, an image from Liverpool University Special Collections of Sweetheart Heron gets repinned across Pinterest simply as 'Gypsy woman resting', losing her name and identity (University of Liverpool Special Collections and Archives, no date). She is 'authentic', but namelessly so. In an instance of inauthenticity, postcards of American operatic soprano Minnie Hauk dressed as Carmen or the Italian Lina

Cavalieri are labelled in the same way – just 'Gypsy' – as Romani women with their families in caravans.

Once more, this laissez-faire attitude to accuracy when appropriating 'gypsy style' is not new, particularly in contexts where a 'Bohemian' aesthetic is deemed desirable. 'Bohemia' is literally a former kingdom within the Austrian empire, now part of the Czech Republic. However, in 15th-century France, Romanies were thought to have come from or via this kingdom, so the word was applied to the Romani people wherever they were found. Since then, the word 'Bohemian' has evolved in French and English to mean 'Gypsy' or, in a figurative sense, an artist or literary figure cut off from mainstream society and following an irregular or free pattern of life. The *Oxford English Dictionary* credits William Makepeace Thackeray (1848) with introducing the word into English via *Vanity Fair*, but the artistic Bohemia was more famously mythologised by Henri Murger (2004) in *The Bohemians of the Latin Quarter* (*Scènes de la vie de Bohème*, first published as stories between 1845 and 1849) following the term's first use in this sense by Félix Pyat in 1834. Pyat compared the strange dress and lifestyle of young followers of the Romantic movement to that of Gypsies (Samuels, 2004: ix). Evelyn Gould (1996: 4) has suggested that the Bohemia of representations such as *Carmen* is not really a counter to dominant bourgeois social identity, but a dramatisation of it, which can be applied to the old argument that 'alternative' popular culture is, in fact, part of the dominant cultural form. What gets called 'Bohemian' recalls Gypsy eccentricity (in the literal sense of the word of being outside the centre), but from a position of centrality and privilege. Affected eccentricity in the form of Bohemianism capitalises on the historically marginalised position of Romani people.

Nostalgia permeates images tagged 'gypsy' on image-sharing sites. For instance, a blog might feature an uncredited vintage painted portrait as part of a 'Gypsy' collage – the title of this example is excluded, again, because this is a personal blog and its inclusion here is to demonstrate an aesthetic trend rather than to be a critique – but it does include the term 'Gypsy'. The blog's banner includes images of fortune-telling, palmistry and teacup reading, plus the uncredited painting actually by Angelo Asti (painter of the prototype 'pin up' used extensively in early 20th-century advertising, reproduced widely in that period and endlessly pinned up again on digital sites). This particular painting is of a 'Persian Beauty', though Asti did also paint Gypsy women. Similarly, a tweet from May 2016 (also anonymised) presents a 'beautiful snapshot from history' without any details of who the people featured are, where the picture was taken or why. This association between Gypsies and an unspecified pastness – usually a nostalgic longing – has itself a long history in the representation of Romani people. Posters of such images may do so in the spirit of friendliness and admiration, but the constant association between a 'gypsy' aesthetic and a Bohemian past has political effects, as commentators such as Katie Trumpener (1992) have noted. One issue is that – until recent projects such as Proud Gypsy Traveller – the published history of this community in Britain has largely been written by those outside it (and the current author is one of those outsiders), and is usually framed as a marginal or separate narrative to those told about the rest of the population. Bohemian eccentricity is a look, an aesthetic, which refers to that historical positioning by outsiders.

In her landmark essay, Trumpener explored the widespread literary and cultural assumption that Gypsies were a people 'without history' – without their own history, that is. They were considered, so the stereotype went, '*of* history', part of a generalised past, but not able to write their own. She explored the consequences of this misconception 'for the development and non-development of Western political discourse about Gypsy life' and traced the 'increasingly powerful Western symbolism developed around the Gypsies, and their discursive placement ... outside of the national teleologies or cumulative time of history', leading to 'a progressive dissociation and conflation of literary [and visual artistic] traditions with living people' (Trumpener, 1992: 849). In other words, white Westerners made and wrote history; Gypsies represented or evoked the past in literature and wistful images, and consequently in political life. An example from the 19th century helps to illustrate this: a poem in an 1879 edition of *Funny Folks* decries 'The Modern Gypsy'. The only Gypsy the poet wants anything to do with is the Oriental, fortune-telling, tent-dwelling 'noble "Romany Rye"/With his earrings, sash, and curls' and a far-off gaze. He wishes to banish the modern Gypsy of Kentish Town to the Orkneys or, in more recent racist parlance, 'send 'em back where they came from', which, according to the poem, is Egypt or the Ganges (*Funny Folks*, 1879). The only authentic Gypsy is one from the past, according to this rhetoric.

Trumpener saw that symbolism as increasingly powerful, and we can see in the use of the gypsy tag on image-sharing sites that its power has only increased in the digital age. Trumpener's was an early scholarly intervention on the subject of Romani ethnicity in wider work about identities; her theses regarding the stereotype of 'historylessness' were so astute as to continue to be widely quoted today, and her proposal that certain Western art forms and formations of political thought depend on the othering of the Gypsy as an archetypal pre-modern figure has been very influential (Trumpener, 1992; Van Baar, 2008). The decontextualised, dehistoricised images of Romanies, people dressed as Gypsies or tagged as 'gypsy' found online demonstrate that the symbolism she critiqued has become a 21st-century problem.

As much as the posters of these images may admire the version of Gypsy culture that they perceive, the posts amass a doubly dehistoricised heritage: their original context is not explained and they contribute to a sense of historylessness in which Gypsies become an ahistorical Other to mainstream society. They contribute to the problematic popular discourses on Gypsies and Traveller communities described at the start of this chapter. Yet, social media also provides the opportunity to respond, and, indeed, as LeedsGATE put it, to make a 'challenge to stereotypes of what Gypsies were like in the past' (@GATEArchive, 5 July 2016) that is not present in the original postings. These kinds of alternative and critically engaged groups have a clear role in what Kirschenblatt-Gimblett (1995: 370) describes as the generation of 'something new' in heritage – 'a mode of cultural production in the present that has recourse to the past', as opposed to simply lifting from the past into the present. Raising the question of what kind of knowledge is produced and communicated is integral to the sense of heritage as inquiry explored in this book.

Reclaiming heritage

A number of visual continuities between 19th- and 21st-century enthusiasms for Gypsy culture have been cited, chiefly: a 'back-to-nature' sense of authenticity of being; locating authentic Gypsy culture in the past; the blurring of artistic Bohemianism and the 'gypsy' label; and a desire among non-Romanies to 'dress Gypsy' or appropriate Romani culture without interrogating the political effects of that performance. The representation of Romani people is a powerful example of the ethical issues raised by the digital turn in the humanities and the questions of representation that research in this area must investigate. These are not, however, representational questions confined to digital media. Any form that facilitates mass circulation and re-contextualisation is in danger of repeating particular images until they appear to be the only reality. There are striking similarities in the way in which non-Romani people choose to represent, or reuse archival images of, Romani people today and the 19th-century visual heritage that they have inherited. Non-Romani cultural producers in the 19th and 21st centuries have also been seen to engage in a paradoxical effort to claim authenticity for their representations – the authenticity of the past, of 'real' gypsy spirit, and an authenticity of being. If one must conform to the authentic image to be visible, and that visibility is a condition for being part of a mainstream understanding of Romani heritage, then non-Romani image-makers and reproducers who unthinkingly use the 'gypsy' tag are complicit in effacing multiple histories and experiences.

Why does that effacement matter? There are many potential responses to this, but I want to point to two in closing this chapter. The first is specific to the Romani community, political, historical and, for some people, personal. The second takes the question to be an intellectual, methodological and ethical one about ways of doing and knowing about the past. As Bowers (2007: 19) notes in the opening quote to this chapter, 'British Gypsy history [is] an important part of the national narrative'. However, as I have detailed elsewhere, Romani 'voices are usually a ringing absence when "Britishness" in all its plural complexity is described' (Matthews, 2015: 81). In the broader sweep of European history, some attempts to silence Romani voices and repress Romani history have been murderously deliberate (Taylor, 2014). Other effacements are, like the ones detailed in this chapter, the result of making assumptions about what it is to be 'a Gypsy' and privileging sources and descriptions that conform to those expectations. In tracing the politics of representation, I aim to point out that heritage can become invisible if it does not match criteria of authenticity determined in advance by people who claim to know about but do not share that heritage. This is particularly important in relation to a community who have felt, as Bowers details, excluded from the physical spaces that researchers use to explore heritage (archives and museums), and, indeed, from many aspects of civic or institutional life (Agarin, 2014). Digital and other collaborative forums for reclaiming Romani heritage by Romani people not only fill a knowledge gap induced by a wider politics of Romani exclusion, then; they also enable *better* heritage practices – more ethical, critical and inclusive ways of knowing, perhaps – a claim that brings us to the second reason why the effacement of Romani histories and experiences should matter to heritage researchers.

In describing community history and ways of knowing about heritage, Alison Twells (2008) points out that involving people who have first-hand experience of a particular heritage, who know about it as family, community and personal history, means that 'people feel proud of their histories; they see their personal experiences validated'. This way of doing heritage offers 'a sense of belonging, a pride in place, as a factor in a civic consciousness' (Twells, 2008). Online, a professed sense of belonging and pride in real-life place can counter the nebulous, timeless, placeless 'gypsy' stereotype perpetuated by those who do not know about or choose to ignore a Romani heritage that belongs to the Romani community. Further, a 'critical discussion' about 'boundaries, exclusions, policing and regulation' is facilitated by this approach to the past and its legacies – a discussion with clear resonance for an excluded and over-policed minority in the present and recent past (Taylor, 2013). Projects such as Doncaster's Proud Gypsy Traveller exhibition and the community co-curation of exhibitions or catalogue enhancement – combining online and interpersonal communications – open this critical discussion out towards the interplay between heritage, identity and inclusion.

References

Agarin, T. (2014) 'Travelling without moving? Limits of European governance for Romani inclusion', *Ethnicities* 14(6): 737–55.

Bakhtin, M. (1981) *The dialogic imagination. Four essays*, Austin, TX: University of Texas Press.

Bissett, G. (2016) 'Toilets, baths and burnt out mattresses: incredible mountain of rubbish left behind by travellers who set up camp for just ONE MONTH on a housing estate', *MailOnline*, 22 June. Available at: www.dailymail.co.uk

Bowers, J. (2007) 'Gypsies and Travellers accessing their own past: the Surrey Project and aspects of minority representation', in M. Hayes and T.A. Acton (eds) *Travellers, Gypsies, Roma: The demonisation of difference*, Newcastle: Cambridge Scholars, pp 17–29.

Cannon, V.M.P. (no date) *Proud Gypsy Traveller: Twentieth-century Gypsy and Traveller cultural heritage in Doncaster*, Doncaster: Doncaster CVS/ Proud Gypsy Traveller.

Channel 4 (2012) *Big Fat Gypsy Weddings* (Season 2), TV programme. Available at: www.channel4.com/programmes/big-fat-gypsy-weddings

Cleave's London Satirist and Gazette of Variety (1843) 'The Gypsy-camp', 4 March, p 2 (originally published in *Monthly Magazine*).

Crouch, I. (2012) 'Instagram's instant nostalgia', *The New Yorker*, 10 April. Available at: www.newyorker.com

Daily Mail (1899) 'Gypsies set a fashion', 4 September, p 7.

DeLong, M., Heinemann, B. and Reiley, K. (2005) 'Hooked on vintage!', *Fashion Theory: The Journal of Dress, Body & Culture* 9(1): 23–42.

Farndale, N. (2011) '*My Big Fat Gypsy Wedding*: What if ignorance really is bliss?', *The Telegraph*, 5 February. Available at: www.telegraph.co.uk

Funny Folks (1879) 'The modern gypsy', 10 May, p 150. Available at: http://gdc.galegroup.com/gdc/artemis

Glanfield, E. (2016) 'Travelling in style: dozens of gipsies come from across Europe in a £400,000 fleet of fancy German cars to illegally set up camp in Derby for a two-week summer holiday', *MailOnline*, 6 July. Available at: www.dailymail.co.uk

Gould, E. (1996) *The fate of Carmen*, Baltimore, MD, and London: Johns Hopkins University Press.

Greenblatt, S. (2005) *Renaissance self-fashioning: From More to Shakespeare* (2nd edn), Chicago, IL: University of Chicago Press.

Han, J., Kwon, T., Choi, D., Chun, B.-G., Kwon, T., Kim, H. and Choi, Y. (2014) 'Collecting, organizing, and sharing pins in Pinterest: interest-driven or social-driven?', *Sigmetrics* 14: 15–27.

Hancock, I. (2008) 'The "Gypsy" stereotype and the sexualization of Romani women', in V. Glajar and D. Radulescu (eds) *'Gypsies' in European literature and culture*, New York, NY, and Houndmills, Basingstoke: Macmillan, pp 181–91.

Ibrahim, Y. (2015) 'Instagramming life: banal imaging and the poetics of the everyday', *Journal of Media Practice* 16(1): 42–54.

Khoja-Moolji, S. (2015) 'Becoming an "intimate publics": exploring the affective intensities of hashtag feminism', *Feminist Media Studies* 15(2): 347–50.

Kirshenblatt-Gimblett, B. (1995) 'Theorizing heritage', *Ethnomusicology* 39(3): 367–80.

Knott, J. (2015) 'Pitt Rivers Museum tells Gypsy and Traveller stories', *Museums Journal*. Available at: www.museumsassociation.org

Lowndes, G.R. (1890) *Gipsy tents and how to use them: A handbook for amateur Gipsies*, London: Horace Cox.

Matthews, J. (2015) 'Where are the Romanies? An absent presence in narratives of Britishness', *Identity Papers: A Journal of British & Irish Studies* 1(1): 79–90.

Murger, H. (2004) *The Bohemians of the Latin Quarter*, Philadelphia, PA: University of Pennsylvania Press.

Proud Gypsy Traveller (2016) 'The project'. Available at: www.proudgypsytraveller.co.uk/the-project/

Reidy, J. (2013) 'Romani fashion and the politics of dressing "Gypsy"', *Quail Bell Magazine*. Available at: www.quailbellmagazine.com

Samuels, M. (2004) 'Introduction', in H. Murger, *The Bohemians of the Latin Quarter*, Philadelphia, PA: University of Pennsylvania Press.

Scott, W. (1999 [1815]) *Guy Mannering*, Edinburgh: Edinburgh University Press.

Smith, L. (2006) *Uses of heritage*, London: Routledge.

Spillett, R. (2016) 'Villagers form human barricade and lie down in front of vehicles to stop Travellers setting up camp on their playing field', *MailOnline*, 21 July. Available at: www.dailymail.co.uk

Taylor, B. (2013) *A minority and the state: Travellers in Britain in the twentieth century*, Manchester: Manchester University Press.

Taylor, B. (2014) *Another darkness, another dawn: A history of Gypsies, Roma and Travellers*, London: Reaktion.

Trumpener, K. (1992) 'The time of the Gypsies: a "people without history" in the narratives of the West', *Critical Inquiry* 18(4): 843–84.

Twells, A. (2008) 'Community history', *Making History*. Available at: www.history.ac.uk/makinghistory/resources/articles/community_history.html

University of Liverpool Special Collections and Archives (no date) 'British Romani families'. Available at: www.liverpool.ac.uk/library/sca/colldescs/gypsy/families.htm

Van Baar, H. (2008) 'The way out of amnesia? Europeanisation and the recognition of the Roma's past and present', *Third Text* 22(3): 373–85.

Young, J.O. (2005) 'Profound offense and cultural appropriation', *Journal of Aesthetics and Art Criticism* 63(2): 135–46.

FOUR

Digital building heritage

Nick Higgett and Jenny Wilkinson

Introduction

In this chapter, we consider the complexities of working on jointly funded digital cultural heritage projects and explore the challenges and benefits of partnership collaborations. Co-creation and the merging of academic research with community heritage is a powerful way of delivering heritage projects, and it is argued that 'community engagement remains the only viable way of ensuring long term conservation of heritage sites' (Borona and Ndiema, 2014: 184).

In presenting our experiences of the Digital Building Heritage (DBH) project, we explore a range of issues, such as the importance of relationship building and establishing trust between stakeholder groups (Thorkildsen and Ekman, 2013), and the ways in which academic partners can support community heritage, facilitating the empowerment of the community partners (Fox and Le Dantec, 2014). We encounter the dangers of conforming to a top-down model of project leadership and management and the importance of managing the politics within the group, as well as establishing the role of the project manager in collaborative co-design and co-production (Perkin, 2010). Like Catherine Dillon et al (2014), we discuss the difficulties of meeting the varied agenda and goals of researchers and community heritage practitioners, and consider how the outcomes of projects might be measured. We also find that while initial and tangible project outputs are realised, and positive experiences of collaboration are reported, there is sometimes limited satisfaction with the overall impact of the projects.

Working through digital means gives a distinctive perspective to these themes of collaboration and research. In common with other contributors to this book, we find heritage to be emergent in the interaction between past and present, and where digital objects are concerned, this seems even more apparent. Yet, the digital is a category increasingly inseparable from other areas of life, including other parts of the heritage sector. As Fiona Cameron and Sarah Kenderdine (2010: 3) note: 'Digital technologies are implicated with historical transformations in language, society and culture, and with shifting definitions of the museum'. Digital objects – and processes – are themselves cultural and have their own 'social lives' (Appadurai, 1988), in which they circulate and are valued in different ways. Our analysis here is therefore not simply about the extent to which the 3D reconstructions are perceived as historically accurate or authentic (Galeazzi, 2018), but about the relationships that cohere around them and the links between past, present and future that they enable.

In the DBH project, researchers at De Montfort University (DMU) worked with community partners in order to bring history back to life through the use of digital technologies in 3D computer animation, 3D printing, 3D modelling and mobile geo-location. The project aimed to 'bring a new energy and shape to historic buildings (and sites) so they can, once again, play an important part in their communities' (Connected Communities, no date).[1]

Our chapter opens with an overview of the original project that ran in 2013. We discuss findings from a review of 11 heritage group collaborations from the DBH project (see Table 4.1), with particular reference to the benefits of co-production and collaborative working. We then present a reflective postscript with some final follow-up commentary based on information gathered from stakeholders three years on, a summary of lessons learned and recommendations for future projects. The main findings highlight the importance of setting clear, feasible objectives and outcomes according to the resources available, including plans for user testing, maintaining regular communication, consideration of proposed digital product usage and promotion. We also consider the way in which this type of practice-based research can lead to academic outcomes suitable for audit programmes like the UK's Research Excellence Framework.

DBH project overview

Prior to the DBH project starting, DMU held a Digital Building Heritage Open Day, inviting heritage groups to visit the university and experience the ways in which digital technology could contribute to their projects. This was an opportunity for heritage groups to consider the potential of working in collaboration with the university. A wide range of technological options were showcased, including laser technology, 3D printing, mobile phone apps, augmented reality, laser scanning and artefact reproduction (Cawthorne, 2012a).

Following this event, two further opportunities for exploring collaboration were offered in the form of smaller workshops during which participants were able to discuss and explore their aims and ambitions in more detail, with more focus on what might be technically feasible and appropriate for each group (Cawthorne, 2012b). Three months later, 11 heritage groups were successful in gaining funding from the Heritage Lottery Fund, and approached DMU for a collaborative co-production partnership. DMU was able to bid for funding from the Arts and Humanities Research Council (AHRC) and work began on all 11 projects early in 2013.

DMU took overall control of the project management of each digital product, typically having responsibility for the day-to-day logistics, providing technical specifications, monitoring progress, liaising and communicating with the various project personnel, and managing timescales. A collaborative approach was adopted, with both sides of the partnership being responsible for the initial scoping and design of the product.

Projects with a 3D digital reconstruction outcome were allocated approximately one month of time by the university staff, during which they worked in partnership with the heritage group to gather data from which they could create the digital reconstructions. Initial discussions established the aims and objectives of the heritage group to determine what was both appropriate and technically feasible to support their ambition. In most cases, the university undertook the collection of measurement data, through laser scanning or, in some cases, hand measurement. Heritage groups sourced additional data such as historical maps, architectural drawings and photographs where required. For some of the projects, additional academic expertise was sought to provide a greater understanding of the historical context and to ensure that the interpretation of the building or site was authentic and genuine. Following the initial investigative discussions, the university team explained and itemised the materials required to achieve the best results. A date was then set for this material to be delivered to the university.

The process for developing mobile applications also began with initial project scoping discussions between the heritage partner and university staff. Heritage partners were encouraged to think about the data they had available and consider how they wanted to present the information. They were asked to consider the story they wanted to tell. Both mobile projects had access to a significant amount of source data, and one of the key aspects of the design process was to create a focus and help prioritise the content. While this was a collaborative process, the heritage group was ultimately responsible for what was included in their final app, undertaking responsibility for the additional research required to supplement existing stories, collating data and sourcing such things as images, press articles and so on. Heritage groups identified the geographical coordinates for each featured item (the geo-locations of the graves or blue plaques) and provided these to the university programmers. University staff provided the technical skills, such as coding, navigation and creating the app interface.

Both applications were designed using the same platform (developed by the team), which provided a repeatable database model that could potentially be used for creating future apps of this nature for similar heritage projects. Limited time was available for user testing, although there was investment in training members of the heritage teams to update and amend the content of their applications, ensuring a sustainable future for the apps and providing the heritage partners with ongoing future control of their products.

Digital outcomes

The project produced two geo-located mobile phone applications, 11 3D digital reconstructions of buildings and other artefacts, and a 3D-printed model (see Table 4.1). These outcomes attracted media coverage in the form of newspaper articles, magazine features and radio interviews. Some products had formal launches with public events and press coverage, and some have also featured at academic conferences and symposiums. The AHRC produced a short documentary video of the overall project (Connected Communities, no date) and three of the projects were featured as case studies in a funder's evaluation (Heritage Lottery Fund, 2015).

DBH project review

In 2014, we received funding from the AHRC to evaluate the outcomes of the DBH project. Using the key aim to 'understand the values and outcomes (whether positive or negative) of Connected Communities heritage research' (Connected Communities, 2014) as the main focus, we sought to discover if, and in what ways, the digital resources produced by the DBH project had been successful.

Data were gathered through a series of semi-structured interviews with key DMU staff, including the principal investigator, the app project manager and one of the key lead developers. Participants were asked for their opinions on the impact of the digital project, its value,

Table 4.1: Heritage groups and digital outcomes

Heritage partner	Digital asset	Description
Alfred Williams Heritage Society (Wiltshire): dedicated to promoting knowledge of the late 19th- to early 20th-century poet and author Alfred Williams (Alfred Williams Heritage Society, no date)	3D digital building reconstruction video	Two minutes in length, the video provides a 3D digital reconstruction of the Swindon and Highworth Union workhouse with a fly-around the building. It is accompanied by a song that was also commissioned for the project.
Diseworth Heritage Trust (Leicestershire): works to preserve the historical, architectural and constructional heritage of Diseworth (Diseworth Heritage Centre, no date)	3D digital animated video	The 3D digital animation is four minutes long and explains the development of the St Michael and All Angels church from the 10th century through to the present day.
	3D digital building reconstruction video	The 3D digital building reconstruction is a high-resolution fly-through of the building lasting just under a minute and a half.
Friends of Court Farm (Pembrey): the largest surviving pre-Renaissance manor house in Carmarthenshire (Friends of Court Farm, no date)	3D digital building reconstruction video	Two minutes in length, the video provides a 3D digital reconstruction of the late medieval farm and the manor house, with a fly-around of the buildings.
Leicestershire Transport Heritage Trust (Leicester): researches, preserves and promotes Leicester and Leicestershire's road transport heritage	3D digital animated video	Just under two minutes, this animated video uses digital reconstructions of the Leicester Tram Depot and Car No. 31 (one of the original trams) to illustrate how the tram would have travelled from Leicester Railway Station along London Road and into the depot, including a fly-through in and around the building.
Wolverhampton Civic and Historical Society: dedicated to the history and heritage of Wolverhampton and preserving its character and image (Wolverhampton Civic and Historical Society, no date)	3D digital building reconstruction video	At around two and a half minutes, this video provides a 3D digital reconstruction of the Wolverhampton Women's Hospital with a fly-around of the building.
	Location-based mobile phone app	The mobile phone app has an interactive, location-aware, map that enables visitors to locate plaques and view relevant information in situ. The app provides content-rich data on each plaque, including photographs, and can be shared via social media.

(continued)

Table 4.1: Heritage groups and digital outcomes (continued)

Heritage partner	Digital asset	Description
Pembroke Dock Bicentennial Trust (South Wales): dedicated to the history of Pembroke Dock, which was established in 1814 (Pembroke Dock Heritage Centre, 2017)	3D digital building reconstruction video	Five minutes in length, this video presents a fly-through of the 3D reconstruction of Pembroke Historic Dockyard.
Swannington Heritage Trust (Leicestershire): to provide access to the heritage and environment of Swannington and the district (Swannington Heritage Trust, 2012)	3D digital building reconstruction video with animation	Two minutes long, this video shows an animation of a coal wagon being pulled up the incline followed by a fly-through of the engine house. The roof of the engine house is removed to reveal an animated working flywheel. The video also has a soundscape of machinery and birdsong.
The Haywood Society (Staffordshire): to secure the preservation, development and improvement of features of historic or public interest in the villages (Staffordshire Heritage, no date)	3D digital building reconstruction video	Two minutes long, this video presents a 3D reconstruction of the Tudor Bay Window from old Tixall Hall, including full rotation, close-up and top-to-bottom views.
	3D printed model of the Tixall Window	There is also a scaled 3D print of the window.
Wigston Framework Knitters Museum Limited (Leicestershire): located in what was once a Master Hosiers House with a two-storey Victorian frame shop in the garden (Leicestershire and Rutland Heritage Forum, 2015)	3D digital building reconstruction video	Two and a half minutes long, this video provides a 3D colour representation of the Wigston Framework Knitting Museum building with texture mapping and accurate authentic interpretation of the brickwork and external appearance of the building.
Friends of Welford Road Cemetery (Leicester) (Friends of Welford Road Cemetery, no date)	Location-based mobile phone app	The mobile phone app has an interactive geo-located map with details of people in the cemetery. The content of each personal story varies but typically include the plot number, the burial date, some biographical data of the person concerned and some photographs.

Note: All of the videos mentioned in Table 4.1 can be viewed on the Digital Buildings Heritage Group YouTube Channel (De Montfort University, no date). Figures 4.1 and 4.2 show examples of the outcomes.

the lessons learned from collaborative working, the research outcomes and the successes and difficulties of the process.

Site visits and semi-structured interviews were held with two heritage groups, one an example of a mobile phone app, and the other

Figure 4.1: Using the Welford Road Cemetery app (I)

Source: Photo © Nick Higgett and Jenny Wilkinson.

Figure 4.2: Using the Welford Road Cemetery app (II)

Source: Photo © Nick Higgett and Jenny Wilkinson.

a digital reconstruction and animation. Participants were asked about their experiences of collaborative working and their relationship with the university partners, the impact and use of their digital product, the most beneficial aspect of the project, and how they would advise similar groups who might consider undertaking a project of this nature.

All heritage groups were invited to complete an online survey, the key purpose of which was to ascertain how the groups were using the products, what their initial objectives were in taking part in the project, whether or not the digital product had helped them achieve these objectives, and how beneficial their involvement in the project had been to the organisation.

In what ways has digital heritage brought value to the stakeholders?

Digital heritage products provided significant value to the heritage partners and their projects. The 3D-printed model of the Tixall window and video reconstruction was one example of a product that was being used to show visitors a new interpretation of something that was no longer visible, bringing context and meaning to a building in a way that complements and enhances the surviving remnants of the Old Hall.

The digital reconstruction of things that no longer exist and cannot be seen, such as Court Farm or Pembroke Dock, have helped the heritage sites to further develop their own research by providing them with a richer visualisation of their buildings and enabling them to better understand their heritage. Accurate visualisations have helped to confirm previous historical research and inform new ways of viewing and interpreting these sites.

The mobile phone applications have improved the audience experience, enabling visitors to access rich and relevant content. Both products have enhanced the interpretation of the artefacts and provided new ways of telling the stories about the people and the places involved. The geo-location features have enabled visitors to navigate the site in ways that were not previously possible.

Digital products have also supported the heritage partners in providing richer interpretation for their visitors: a visitor to Welford Road Cemetery could now use the app to find a grave, discover the story of how the individual died and perhaps see a photograph or read a press article about their life. Digital reconstructions and animations have made it possible to show how buildings, such as Diseworth Parish Church and the Framework Knitters Museum, have changed over time, using engaging and accessible media.

What was the value of being involved in the DBH project?

Involvement in these projects also helped heritage groups to learn more about the potential for developing and using digital resources to interpret and promote their heritage. The projects broadened horizons and raised the ambition of heritage groups, making them feel more positive and excited to develop further digital assets. In talking to the heritage groups, we discovered a tangible sense of pride and a feeling of being 'taken seriously'. Participation in these projects had raised not only their confidence, but also their profile, making them feel more confident, particularly in relation to future bids and dealings with funding bodies and other key organisations. Academics and researchers enjoyed and professionally benefitted from the challenge of developing new skills, practising existing ones, working at the 'cutting edge' of technology and discovering new ways of solving problems in order to deliver the highest-quality digital product that was technically and economically feasible.

The projects also provided DMU staff and students with unique opportunities to work on 'live' projects in a way that was not typically part of their academic environment. The process of developing client-based relationships and the experience of working on this type of collaborative enterprise were reported as both novel and invaluable opportunities. The projects provided a distinctive learning environment and research resource for MA and PhD students, offering the experience of working with real case studies providing actual, first-hand, exposure to all the pressures and processes that occur within real, rather than theoretical, experiences. DMU has a particular ethos for developing strong links with its local community and it was felt that the project provided an ideal platform for creating and building such relationships.

Both the university and the heritage sites had used the projects to raise their profiles through press coverage, web presence, social media, conferences and symposiums. The DBH project blog was active and current, with regular posts on all projects. There were numerous examples of the project staff showcasing the co-created digital resources at regional and national events/conferences, and, similarly, a good range of examples where projects had been featured in the media.

In some cases, heritage sites not only benefitted from the digital product itself, but were also able to employ their research and the resulting content to create other resources, such as brochures and booklets. One example of this was the Friends of Welford Road Cemetery, who not only produced a range of printed, themed cemetery trail leaflets, but also gathered sufficient material to potentially enable them to write book:

> "We simply could not have achieved what we did without
> the collaboration of the university. The value is priceless

and we believe the full benefits are yet to be revealed and valued.... It has achieved an output that no other media could have done; it has brought a visual aspect that people can relate to immediately, even though we have covered just a small part of what could be done." (Sian Dureau, Pembroke Dock, 2014)

How did the process of collaborative research contribute to the creation of the digital heritage resource and what can be learned from this process?

It would have been impossible to create these digital heritage assets without a collaborative process. Each project partner contributed specific and unique skills, experience and expertise, all of which were essential to the final outcome. The heritage partners understood and could source the content and the material. They alone knew the context of their heritage and how they wanted to promote the aims and ambitions of their organisations. Technical expertise from DMU came in the form of skilled and expert personnel and equipment. The combination of these experiences, skill sets and resources was necessary for the final product, and neither partner could have achieved the same result alone.

There was evidence for both reliance on and respect for the skills, knowledge and abilities contributed to the project by each of the partners. The collaborative approach supported an environment in which historical knowledge and technical expertise could be exchanged with shared anticipation. There was an understanding that this would facilitate the creation of innovative solutions for presenting and interpreting heritage. Although similar products could have been created using commercial design companies, the reality was that small heritage groups, such as those represented in this project, would have been unable to afford this option. Additionally, a commercial company would be unlikely to have access to the same variety of skills, expertise, technology and machinery available from the university, and, indeed, the opportunity for multidisciplinary work within the university was valuable in itself.

One of the challenges of the collaborative approach was the inevitable sharing and accommodation of different working practices, some of which had worked well, and some of which were less effective. The development of a 'work-package' process to gather data provided an effective project management tool, encouraging heritage partners to develop new skills in electronic communications and file transfer, and also, on occasion, in professional time and project management, and is an example of sharing good working practice.

However, in some cases, it was felt that the university took the role of 'leading' the project and that they had, what seemed to be, a 'final say' in some of the design decisions. Some heritage partners expressed a feeling that they had 'not quite got what they had asked for'. Further examination of these instances showed that, in most cases, the university was making these decisions based on technical and resource restrictions, and not through their own preferences, though this may not have been communicated to the heritage partner. One example of this was the mobile phone applications. Initially, it was hoped that these would be available on both Android and iPhone platforms but the limitations of both time and money meant that this was not possible and so both applications were created and launched as iPhone apps only. The problem was not perhaps with the decisions that were made, but with the communication of these decisions and the consequence that this had on the relationship between the two groups. Establishing 'necessary trust and mutual commitment among partners' (Thorkildsen and Ekman, 2013: 157) is an essential part of any cultural heritage collaborative design process.

One aspect of the collaboration that worked well was the focus that the project provided. The discipline of sourcing material for a digital product required significant thought around the purpose of the product and what it was meant to achieve. Working together, the heritage groups and the university team were faced with questions such as: what do we include and what do we leave out? Heritage groups were encouraged to develop their research skills, categorise content, prioritise their material and focus on the story that they wanted to tell. They had to think about the ways in which they wanted their material to be presented. For example, with the Wigston Framework Knitters Museum, it was agreed that the rendered version of the building, showing the brickwork, would be limited to the final stage of the building as this would be the most historically accurate representation. Not all of these collaborations were comfortable and, in some situations, the process of creating the digital representation raised questions about some of the existing historical evidence and the way in which it had been interpreted by the heritage group, resulting in difficult conversations about accuracy and authenticity. In most cases, this was resolved by further research and examination of the evidence, ultimately providing a better and more accurate understanding of the building or artefact; however, in a minority of examples, these discussions remained inconclusive.

What aspects of the project worked well and what got in the way?

The management of the project was evidently successful in developing, creating and delivering tangible digital heritage products for each of the heritage groups. Evidence from the review supports this and also provides a number of useful lessons for future projects.

Examining the project sequentially, from inception to legacy, provides a useful overview of the leadership and management of the process. At the outset, there were good processes for capturing the needs of the heritage partners and demonstrating the technical abilities of the university, via the open day and subsequent workshops. However, the unexpectedly high volume of successful heritage groups wishing to work with DMU resulted in projects not being afforded sufficient time for initial scoping activities. Much of the early work, including the open day, was speculative as it was not known which groups would be funded to work with DMU. Time pressures remained an issue throughout the project and we heard frequent comments that there was inadequate time available to fully complete products.

The issue of insufficient resources, particularly in terms of academic time, was mentioned a number of times as a significant difficulty, and scheduling around the requirements of the academic calendar was particularly significant. Unfortunately, delays in project progress resulted in projects slipping into the autumn teaching period, when academics were less available, creating additional pressure for the academics concerned and resulting in some projects being rushed to completion or not having all the features originally discussed.

Although these projects were ostensibly collaborative, there was, in most cases, a feeling that the relationship was between a client (heritage group) and a provider (DMU). On the whole, this relationship worked well and there is good evidence that the partners communicated and worked together effectively; however, we also found that the 'client' expectations of the project might not always have been in line with those of the 'provider'. In some cases, the heritage groups had a limited understanding, and an unrealistic expectation, of what would be technically possible within the available time and resources. They relied on the DMU team to provide guidance and leadership on this, and, in most cases, this was successful. However, it was clear that some groups may have been given enthusiastic and ambitious visions as to what was possible and the type of digital product that they would receive, for example, providing both iPhone and Android versions of apps. Managing the expectations of stakeholders should be part of project scoping, and, again, this mismatch in expectations could be due, in part, to insufficient attention being paid to this at the outset of each project.

Another aspect of this was the enthusiasm with which both academic and heritage partners approached the projects. It is clear that there was a good deal of excitement at the start of these projects and a certain amount of discussion around possibilities and what could potentially be achieved. It is possible that the heritage partners interpreted this as what would actually happen, rather than what could potentially happen. As the project progressed, and the realities of time and technicalities became clearer, the outcomes of the project were adjusted, leaving some heritage partners with an impression that they had not quite got what they were expecting. Another mismatch in understanding was around working methods and the allocation of resources. We found that some of the heritage partners thought that partnership with DMU meant that they had a dedicated relationship with the team over the period of their project. In reality, of course, the university teams were working on various projects simultaneously, and while the heritage partners understood this in principle, it is evident that some felt that they should have had more contact time.

One observation from the review was the subtle impact that what we might describe as cultural differences between academics and heritage groups might have had. Academic staff typically work in an environment that values and promotes experimentation and creativity, and is potentially quite fluid. They are usually comfortable in circumstances in which they may not necessarily know what is possible, but are willing to try something out to see if it works. This is the underpinning nature of creativity and innovation. Positive conversations, perhaps seen as exploratory by academics, may have been regarded by the heritage partners as being more concrete. If this was the case, then heritage partners may well have been disappointed when the final product did not match all that was discussed.

Another observation from the review was the occasional disparity in values between the academics and heritage groups, for example, when what one group regarded as important was not necessarily seen as such by the other. An example of this was a discussion regarding one of the 3D reconstructions in which the heritage group expressed disappointment that their building was not 'coloured in' but left as a white object, while the university team regarded this as more stylish and in line with professional museum display. This is less an argument about accuracy or the integrity of the reconstruction, and more about stylistic differences. The heritage group wanted something that they felt looked more attractive and were disappointed with the white detail, whereas the university team viewed this as clear and professional. Working practices and the ways in which heritage groups operate also impacted on the project in other, more tangible, ways. For example, the governance and management of these groups and the fact that many heritage groups are run by volunteers influenced the availability of heritage staff and decision-making practices. Some projects were delayed because certain decisions had to be taken by a governing board that only met once a month.

One issue that arose with some, though not all, of the projects was that the heritage group was not always certain that the project had finished. The ongoing nature of the development of their products and the fact that they were waiting for some minor tweaks and changes meant that they were not formally aware that the project had been completed, although they did know that the product had been uploaded to YouTube or launched on the App Store. A common feature with creative projects of this nature can be that it is difficult to know when they are complete as there is often a continuous and constant process of revision and refinement. In our case, there was no formal conclusion such as a 'sign off' meeting or equivalent process. Consequently, some groups reported that they were not certain as to the status of their project. Finally, there was an interesting 'post-project' observation by heritage partners that through the additional research they had done for their projects, many of these projects had generated a substantial amount of content that, while not used directly for this project, remains an invaluable resource for future projects, digital or otherwise.

How successful and effective was the digital resource in meeting the original aims of the project?

The limited time available for the each project also meant that there were few opportunities for user testing or evaluation. We found no evidence that any of the heritage sites had undertaken formal testing of their products, although there was informal anecdotal evidence via emails and other visitor comments that audiences had enjoyed the products and found them interesting and informative. There was no evidence that these products had attracted new visitors to these heritage sites, but, again, this had not been formally investigated, so if there were new visitors, this was unrecorded.

The lack of any formal evaluation means that finding tangible evidence to demonstrate the effectiveness of these products was difficult and limited to such data as YouTube video views or App Store download statistics. While this provided some indication of usage, they were not immensely positive and may well be misleading in terms of assessing the impact of these products. The YouTube statistics indicated that the most viewed video had over 1,490 views and the least around 40. However, this is not a complete picture as we did not know how the heritage site had chosen to use this product and it would certainly be very wrong to assume that the number of views is a measure of one product being more successful than another. We looked at the web presence of the heritage groups to ascertain if and how they were promoting the product. Results were varied: most did not mention it, a couple featured it on the front page and others made reference to the fact that the product was in development, whereas it was, in fact, completed and available.

Three heritage groups promoted their products with high-profile launch events, all of which had received local press coverage. At least one of the products had been part of a six-month exhibition and there was evidence that others had been shown to group members and public audiences at events such as open days. This would indicate that these products had been successful in helping the heritage groups raise their profile and promote their heritage to their local communities.

Discussions with the heritage groups suggested that they either did not know how much their product was being used or were not yet in a position to use it. This might suggest that the creation of the product was not part of their overall strategic planning, but was perhaps more opportunistic, something that they did because they had the chance to, rather than something that they had considered to be of operational value. In one case, the product had been developed with the view to attracting schools to the website. This had not happened and, when asked, we discovered that there had been no supplementary activity to engage schools, which suggests that the product on its own was not sufficient to attract this new audience and that additional promotional activity would be required to make this happen.

Follow-up case studies

Three years following the completion of the project, we contacted the heritage groups to find out how they were getting on with their digital outcomes. In terms of the apps, one was still available but the other had been removed from the App Store after two years. This was because the group found it difficult to update and they also wanted something more accessible. Instead, they focused their efforts on their web presence. However, they felt that the project raised the group's awareness in the media and had made the group, most of whom are pensioners, much more aware of the impact of information technology (IT). This had resulted in an increasing use of social media and lots of 'new stuff' on the website, such as 360-degree views and flyovers. Therefore, the app produced did provide a long-term legacy through the experience of developing it, which had 'switched the group on to digital opportunities', as they said to us. The other app is available through the group's project website and is also used in training and workshops on heritage and disability. Although this group felt that the project was a success, on reflection, they felt that any future work needed a clearer and more precise written agreement on deliverables as they felt that the outcomes did not fully meet their expectations. More positively, they felt that the digital technology utilised had 'added interest and dimension for audience' and in terms of legacy had enabled them 'to build a portfolio of heritage work as an organisation with ambition and wider interest'.

In summary, the evaluation review found the following:

- All projects were successful in producing a digital product that could be used by the heritage group.
- All projects were completed within agreed timescales and within budget, though in at least one case, the heritage group felt that it did not meet their expectations.
- Approximately half of the digital products were used by the heritage groups within a public setting to promote their ambitions and operations.
- The digital products were used to increase and develop the profiles of both partners through press coverage, social media and academic symposiums and conferences.
- The collaborative aspect of the projects increased the knowledge and skill sets of both partners.
- The digital products provided new ways of interpreting the assets of the heritage groups.
- Co-production of the digital projects stretched and developed both partners in terms of research and working in new and different ways.

What follows are recommendations that we would make for future projects of this nature.

Strategic planning and project management

Clear objectives should be set so that you know what you want to achieve. Key to the success of any project is defining and understanding the main objective of the project. In many cases, the stated aim of these projects was to achieve increased audience engagement, and those who succeeded in this understood the nature of their target audience, designing products that suited this need, and promoted them appropriately, for example, exhibiting the Pembroke Dock reconstruction video in the town library. Future project teams should be encouraged to think about when and how people will use their product and consider the needs of the visitor in their design process.

Project scoping – understand the feasibility of your project

The size and scope of a project should be clarified and communicated at the outset of a project with all partners in agreement as to what is feasible and what is viable. Considerable pressure and frustration was created for the project partners where the scope of the projects was more than could be achieved with the available resources. Scoping worked well with those projects that were clear about the resources they had and what they wanted to achieve. It worked less well where the outcomes were not clearly defined at the outset and were subject to regular review and alteration.

Plan for product testing and involve users

Effective testing of digital products requires a number of different approaches, ensuring that the product actually works, that users can and will use it, and that the product achieves the aim for which it is intended. These activities should form part of the project plan and should be incorporated at the initiation of the project. The volume of projects supported by the DBH project and the time for completion restricted the opportunity for developing and implementing any testing strategy. For some projects, this was less of an issue, for example, the video reconstructions work; however, without further evaluation, there is no evidence that they have met their aim. The limited amount of testing and time available for the mobile apps meant that the products were working but, at the time of the review, still had bugs and issues requiring resolution before they could be considered fully functioning. The potential impact of this is that users might become frustrated with the product if they perceive that it does not do what they think it should and may cease to use it. Product testing should be included in the project plan, even if this limits the amount of content available. It would be better to have less content that works well than more content that is considered unusable.

Product and project evaluation

Consideration should be given as to how and when evaluation of the products and the project as a whole should be conducted. There was good evidence that the project had been successful in creating the products, working collaboratively and developing good engagement between the stakeholders. However, there is less evidence as to the effectiveness of these products in attracting new audiences or engaging people in new ways with the heritage, which was a clearly stated objective of most of the heritage groups. Further research is required to assess more accurately the impact that the products have had on audience engagement; however, information on this would be very difficult to ascertain as there was no evidence of initial benchmarking and therefore no tangible baseline to demonstrate increased usage or engagement. The process for evaluating both the project and the products should be part of the initial project plan and data should be collected at the outset and throughout the project.

Collaboration and building relationships

Developing strong relationships with and between all project partners will not only make this type of project easier to manage, but also potentially lead to better outcomes as expectations and requirements are better understood. Those working on projects of this nature should be mindful of the subtle cultural differences that might exist between partners and ensure that all communication is suitably delivered and understood. Regular and appropriate communication, occurring at key points in the project, will help facilitate good relationships and, in turn, contribute to positive project outcomes. It must be remembered that effective communication does not happen by accident, but should be a planned and well-managed activity. This requires an investment of time from all involved, particularly, those leading or managing the project. The establishment of a communication strategy as part of the project initiation will help all parties understand their contribution and responsibilities in this area.

Conclusions

Although each project resulted in a tangible product, it was, from the university's point of view, disappointing to see how few were being used to their full potential. Heritage groups should be helped to consider how they will use and promote their digital product, and should consider the whole lifespan of the product and not just its creation. Care is also needed regarding user and audience expectations, and more advice should be provided to the heritage groups regarding the inclusion of users in the design process. This would increase understanding of how people are likely to engage with the product and help the design team make informed decisions as to the needs and requirements of the users and how these can be accommodated within the product.

What is interesting here is that the digital objects take on something of a life of their own, and have their own agency within the collaborative relationship. To connect with another broader theme of this book, collaboration can neither be taken for granted nor entirely planned for; rather, it is contingent upon the motivations and resources of those involved. As Perkin (2010: 109–10) notes in the context of museums, inherent power imbalances may exist between community and heritage professionals that need to be overcome to achieve the success, impact and sustainability of a project. The cases described here show that the resources of time and expertise are not evenly distributed and yet can shift within the collaborative frame. Here, we see that as the groups began to learn about their heritage sites for the narrower purposes of this project, they often began to develop research that took them in new directions. This is, in fact, characteristic of heritage as a 'way of knowing', which commonly has not an easily identifiable end, but rather a series of further openings (see Vergunst and Graham, this volume).

This open-endedness also speaks to the nature of the digital objects themselves. In a discussion of 3D artefact and landscape reconstructions, Galeazzi notes the continuing subjectivity within the technological processes of digital reproduction that mitigates against any sense of absolute authenticity in the final product:

> The true value of 3-D replicas of archaeological sites and monuments resides not in the creation of an objective and perfect copy of the original but in the ability that such a copy can give to researchers to analyze and interpret – and

to students and the general public to understand – cultural heritage. (Galeazzi, 2018: 272)

From the perspective of this volume, it is the means by which such digital objects lead into research and involvement with heritage, rather than provide an 'answer' to a problem, that is most notable.

Practical considerations remain important in this kind of work. From the university's perspective, the number of projects supported in the time available created significant pressures, resulting in some products being rushed and delivered with less functionality than was originally planned and agreed. Lessons for future projects are about scoping but also about being realistic about what can be achieved with the resources available. For the academics, meanwhile, the pressures to produce research that can be measured and assessed using traditionally recognised systems such as peer review and the Research Excellence Framework are immense, and the fact that projects of this nature do not easily result in such output needs to be addressed. It should also be recognised that these projects are very positive in other valuable areas, including creative output, impact and public engagement.

Note

[1] We acknowledge funding from the Connected Communities programme of the UK Arts and Humanities Research Council. Heritage groups were funded by the UK Heritage Lottery Fund.

References

Alfred Williams Heritage Society (no date) 'In the shadow of the workhouse'. Available at: www.alfredwilliams.org.uk/workhouse. html

Appadurai, A. (1988) *The social life of things: Commodities in cultural perspective*, Cambridge: Cambridge University Press.

Borona, G. and Ndiema, E. (2014) 'Merging research, conservation and community engagement: perspectives from TARA's rock art community projects in Kenya', *Journal of Cultural Heritage Management and Sustainable Development* 4(2): 184–95.

Cameron, F. and Kenderdine, S. (2010) *Theorizing digital cultural heritage*, Harvard, MA: Massachusetts Institute of Technology Press.

Cawthorne, D. (2012a) 'Mind mapping and soul searching at the first AHRC Digital Building Heritage Workshop', Digital Building Heritage. Available at: https://digitalbuildingheritage.our.dmu. ac.uk/2012/11/16/soul-searching-at-the-first-ahrc-digital-building-heritage-workshop/

Cawthorne, D. (2012b) 'Sun shines on Digital Building Heritage Conference/Open Day', Digital Building Heritage. Available at: https://digitalbuildingheritage.our.dmu.ac.uk/2012/05/28/sun-shines-on-digital-building-heritage-coneference-open-day/

Connected Communities (no date) 'Using 3D Print Technology to Bring Lost Buildings Back to Life', Video. Available at: https://connected-communities.org/index.php/project_resources/using-3d-print-technology-to-bring-lost-buildings-back-to-life-video/

Connected Communities (2014) 'Call for funding proposals: New legacies of heritage research'. Available at: https://connected-communities.org/index.php/news/call-for-funding-proposals-new-legacies-of-heritage-research/

De Montfort University (no date) 'DBHeritageatDMU'. Available at: www.youtube.com/user/DBHeritageatDMU

Dillon, C., Bell, N., Fouseki, K., Laurenson, P., Thompson, A. and Strlic, M. (2014) 'Mind the gap: rigour and relevance in collaborative heritage science research', *Heritage Science* 2: 11.

Diseworth Heritage Centre (no date) 'The Trust'. Available at: www.diseworthcentre.org/trust

Fox, S. and Le Dantec, C.A. (2014) 'Community historians: scaffolding community engagement through culture and heritage', DIS 2014, 21–25 June, Vancouver, BC, Canada.

Friends of Court Farm (no date) 'Welcome to the Friends website'. Available at: http://focf.info./

Friends of Welford Road Cemetery (2012) 'Friends of Welford Road Cemetery'. Available at: www.fowrcl.org.uk/

Galeazzi, F. (2018) '3-D virtual replicas and simulations of the past. 'Real' or 'fake' representations?', *Current Anthropology* 59(3): 268–86.

Heritage Lottery Fund (2015) 'All our stories evaluation'. Available at: www.hlf.org.uk/all-our-stories-evaluation

Leicestershire and Rutland Heritage Forum (2015) 'Wigston Framework Knitters Museum'. Available at: www.lrhf.co.uk/properties/wigston-framework-knitters-museum/

Pembroke Dock Heritage Centre (2017) 'A brief history of Pembroke Dock'. Available at: www.sunderlandtrust.com/about-us/brief-history/

Perkin, C. (2010) 'Beyond the rhetoric: negotiating the politics and realising the potential of community-driven heritage engagement', *International Journal of Heritage Studies* 16(1/2): 107–22.

Staffordshire Heritage (no date) 'The Haywood Society'. Available at: http://staffordshireheritage.weebly.com/the-haywood-society.html

Swannington Heritage Trust (2012) 'Swannington Now & Then'. Available at: www.swannington-heritage.co.uk/index.html

Thorkildsen, A. and Ekman, M. (2013) 'The complexity of becoming: collaborative planning and cultural heritage', *Journal of Cultural Heritage Management and Sustainable Development* 3(2): 148–62.

Wolverhampton Civic and Historical Society (no date) 'Wolverhampton Civic and Historical Society'. Available at: www.cityofwolverhampton.com/

FIVE

Legacy and lavender: community heritage and the arts

Helen Smith and Mark Hope

Introduction

This chapter explores how new perspectives on organisational practices are revealed when participants in an arts practice research project decide to focus on a local heritage subject. The Lavender Project, as this arts project became known, is a case study in an Arts and Humanities Research Council (AHRC) Connected Communities collaborative doctoral award (CDA) between Robert Gordon University (RGU) and community partner Woodend Barn (The Barn), a rural arts centre in the North East of Scotland. The CDA came about because of a long-standing relationship between Fiona Hope and Mark Hope, co-founders and trustees of the Barn, and Anne Douglas, co-founder of On the Edge Research, a network of people and organisations concerned with the relationship of contemporary art to rural cultures (see: https://ontheedgeresearch.org/). When the AHRC's Connected Communities programme was initiated, the idea of a CDA hosted by the Barn seemed a logical extension of the work of both the Barn and On the Edge in exploring the role and practice of the artist in society. The CDA invited the successful applicant, visual artist Helen Smith, to consider how, through art, the Barn might address their organisational challenges and future sustainability.

Reflecting the dialogical and plural approaches to knowing discussed in the Introduction to this volume, in this chapter, participants with different roles across their organisation reflect critically together upon difficult and complex topics, including the future direction of their arts centre. The dialogues are characterised by humour and metaphor, referencing the heritage subject and their experience of this research process. These reflections shed light on how collaborative participatory arts research, when combined with a local heritage subject identified by the participants, can open new spaces for criticality between communities, generating durable, negotiated change.

Talking about legacy

Helen Smith and Mark Hope begin with a conversation about legacy, a significant concept because it prompted reflection on the value of collaborative research for all participants. This kind of research is not simply about finding answers to a problem, but about developing a process for inquiry and dialogue, and so its legacies can be hard – but important – to identify. The ideas and language emerging from this initial conversation were used to inform the approaches taken to discussing legacy with other participants:

> MARK: Where does legacy start given that the whole of life is a continuous flow of possibilities and we have no way of knowing which possibilities are going to unfold? Possibilities that do unfold are presumably dictated, in part at least, by all previous conditions and actions, so all past conditions and events are potentially significant.
>
> HELEN: The idea of legacy, then, seems to involve a movement from somewhere in the past to somewhere in the future. It feels to me that writing this involves looking in both directions while we try to make sense of the landmarks that have influenced our direction of travel and we feel are continuing to shape the future.
>
> MARK: I like the idea of legacy involving a movement from past to future and hence the need to look both backwards and forwards. Our conversation has reminded me of why I am nervous about legacy as an idea: in my mind, the idea of legacy implies a singular effect, which has a singular cause at a specific point in time. In reality, every effect has multiple causes and one's perception of cause and effect is only relevant at the specific time at which it is formed.
>
> When we talk about 'creating a legacy', we verbalise a specific intention to create conditions where future events exhibit something(s) that would not otherwise have occurred. If we create something physical, be it a work of art or a building, it is easy to see what has been created, although we might still argue about its origins as well as its legacy. However, what about the realm of ideas, feelings and emotions?
>
> HELEN: Ideas might generate actions or values that create change in society. Their legacy is tangible. Feelings

and emotions seem less tangible. It is more difficult to imagine how we might talk about where they start and how they unfold.

MARK: I think our actions are informed by our feelings and emotions as well as our ideas but I agree that it is hard to pin them down. In any case, when we ask 'What legacy was created?', we would ideally need to separate out specific outcomes that would not otherwise have occurred. Our lack of knowledge about what might naturally have taken place is by no means the only difficulty. Additional challenges relate to the time frame that we consider and the type of change that we are looking for.

HELEN: I have noticed that we are switching between the terms 'change' and 'legacy' when we speak. This is possibly because our project and much other practice-led research in the Connected Communities programme seeks to know how research generates change. We seem to be linking the legacy of research with events that can be noted or quantified as distinct changes to what went before. Maybe we need to expand this to include the terms 'impact', 'insight' and 'influence' in order to acknowledge different types of change and ways of speaking about the legacy of research?

MARK: Superficial (eg physical or organisational) changes can be visible very quickly if they relate to things that we regularly observe or measure. By contrast, changes to personal attitudes and values may be much harder to observe and may take years to become visible. We might presume that changes to personal attitudes and values are more important than physical changes but the two are generally interlinked. For example, we might observe a number of changes that we can directly attribute to a project – for example, at a relatively superficial level, we might decide to measure audience feedback and display annual statistics in some way. This might be a useful legacy provided the new practice is continued. For that to happen, we probably need an adjustment to the personal attitudes and values within the organisation, for example, staff observe that recording audience feedback is useful in various respects, so they not only continue to gather data, but also seek to refine the data gathered and their analysis in ways that serve the organisation (eg by informing programming or improving marketing). One might generalise this example by asserting that for legacies to be enduring, they need to change the culture of an organisation, or, given that culture is always in a state of flux, build upon certain aspects of the culture that are beneficial for the organisation in the sense of furthering aspirations and goals. Whatever legacy is observed, it may reasonably be asked: 'How durable is the legacy?'.

HELEN: We have also mentioned that individuals who are open to the potential of arts practice research and what it might offer their organisation or community are significant to the context in which legacy occurs. For example, the specific history and traditions of artists' practices, such as Allan Kaprow (2003) and Suzanne Lacy (2010), influencing this research are underpinned by the pragmatist view that art offers a unique space to see the world in new ways, thus allowing new visions to emerge as a consequence of collaborative art practices (Dewey, 1987 [1934]; Schön, 1996). As participants of arts research processes, maybe any changes that occur within them are important to our conversation. However, as you say, how is this made visible? If we think of the potential legacy of a research experience like the Lavender Project in relation to the individuals who participated, the effects of that experience could occur in any other aspect of their future. For example, I now live and work in North Shields in the north-east of England. One legacy of the Lavender Project could, therefore, be said to be taking place in new contexts in another region of the UK and in a time frame that is far beyond the scope and time frame of a doctoral research project such as this.

Our argument, therefore, is that tracing the legacy of arts practice research is a complicated concept involving an intangible interconnectedness between events. We agree that any durable legacy benefits from an openness, or at least a sceptical interest, by participants that the arts create conditions in which individuals are able to experience new ways to operate and perceive the world. Given this as a starting point – an often invisible aspect of the research process – the factors which demonstrate that this process has either influenced, generated new insights or had a tangible impact are generally subjective and difficult to show. It is, therefore, the process of art as collaboration, its management and its analysis through conversations that has the potential to shift views or change minds. Exploring heritage through the arts opens on to many of the questions identified in the Introduction to this volume. If heritage research is about a 'process of meaning-making' that involves the past and the present (Vergunst and Graham, this volume, p 14), the possibility of art to reflect on experience and perception is certainly relevant. An arts-led inquiry might lead to new and interesting directions for heritage.

Participatory action research and arts practice research

The Lavender Project research was informed by two traditions: participatory action research (Facer and Enright, 2016; Facer and Pahl, 2017) and arts practice research. In participatory action research, the research 'problem' is identified collaboratively between the researcher and a community partner, often with, as discussed earlier, a hope that the research will enable positive change. In arts practice research, 'practice is a key method of inquiry and where a practice is submitted as substantial evidence' (Nelson, 2013: 9). Yet, as Douglas (2016: 1) has indicated, practice-led research also has this active connection to creating change: 'Practice-led research through the arts ... is frequently framed by interplay between the histories and traditions of practice and current social and cultural change'. Working with these two traditions, Helen's PhD thesis, 'Artist as navigator: understanding how the social qualities of art influence organizational change' (Smith, 2015), is concerned with understanding how the experience of art as a social process can influence the ways in which different communities within an organisation navigate their way through the turbulence brought about by specific internal and external influences.

Reflecting the action research approaches described in the Introduction to this book, a community of people actively involved in different aspects of the arts centre was invited to imagine a sustainable future for their organisation. In common with strands of participatory action research, where insight is derived through everyday action and a cycle of action and reflection, the work was developed not as separate 'research' events, but within the everyday life of the organisation over a period of three years. This occurred as a collaborative, public and reflective process of artistic interventions. A strong commitment to knowing that was much more than cognitive was at work, with senses, bodies, movement and relationships all values in the research process.

Introducing the Barn

At the outset of the Lavender Project, the Barn was in a state of flux following the appointment of the first full-time paid director – the Barn had previously been run by a combination of paid staff, the Barn's Board and a large number of other active volunteers, some of whom had previously had a substantial role in developing the Barn and directing and/or delivering aspects of the programme. Hence, the Barn's organisational structure was more cellular than hierarchical, with as much bottom-up as top-down management. In its most recent business plan, the organisation describes itself in the following way:

> The Barn is Aberdeenshire's leading multi-arts centre, based in Banchory on Royal Deeside. An inspirational and welcoming space, the Barn offers a diverse and ambitious cultural programme for all ages – encompassing theatre, music, dance, comedy, talks and visual art – which attracts 20,000 visitors a year. A collaborative team of staff, artists and 60 volunteers work together to devise and deliver an annual programme of around 150 performances and 200 creative workshops, ensuring that rural audiences can enjoy access to high-quality work from the best national, and local, artists and performers.
>
> For over 20 years the Barn has championed environmental and ecological awareness, including the creation of a wild garden and 110 community allotments, positively influencing the lifelong learning and well-being of local residents and visitors. Creative projects frequently explore the connections between art, the environment and sustainability.
>
> The Barn plays a key role in supporting artists, at all career stages, to create and develop new work through a series of ongoing residencies, commissions and research projects within the local community. (Woodend Arts Limited, 2017)

The Barn's origin as a volunteer-run organisation was still reflected in an affiliate structure – a network of semi-autonomous groups with different interests and ways of working. This resulted in a relatively unstructured management system. This way of working was challenged by the substantially increased programme that had been presented over the previous few years, facilitated by substantial Scottish Arts Council (later Creative Scotland) funding.

It was clear that the organisation needed to adapt to its new size and scope. All agreed that change was necessary but exactly what sort of change was open for debate. In particular, there were differing views about the appropriate role of volunteers in an expanding, 'more professional' organisation. Should the Barn director and staff team direct all Barn operations and events? Could leadership and/or direction of parts of the programme be negotiated or shared, and, if so, how?

The Lavender Project

The Lavender Project emerged as a significant intervention following other events in which Helen became immersed within the organisational and creative life of the Barn. For example, she was invited to chair an annual 'Development Day' and to produce an exhibition, 'Fold', for the visual arts programme. This led to an interest in creating the conditions for different communities to come together to identify their own research strands. A key point here is that the participants who came together to research and deliver the Lavender Project had very different roles and experiences of the organisation. They included staff members, volunteers and trustees. The following extracts from Helen's thesis recall the conditions under which the Ingasetter Lavender Company became their subject:

> In December 2012 an invitation is made to a group of 12 people to come to a New Year's dinner at the Hope's home to discuss a sustainability event and exhibition. The aim of the dinner was to find a subject containing rich and interesting stories through which we could discuss what we might mean by sustainability and in particular the specific organizational and wider sustainability of The Barn.
>
> The conversation led off from Genevieve's conviction in art's ability to explore the issues of ecology in interesting and imaginative ways without being didactic. An open, collaborative and exploratory approach to ecology became a benchmark for how we might think about working sustainably: To build and strengthen ourselves, and our community through the process.
>
> Our conversations about artists and ecology triggered further conversations about nature and environment in the Banchory area. Topics such as the specific location of alder, habitats for red squirrels, however, the Banchory lavender

plant and issues around seed collection and storage drew out detailed knowledge. It was interesting to experience how a topic that reveals very specific and interesting facts builds energy in the room.

I remember travelling home from Banchory to Aberdeen after the New Years dinner. I typed in 'Lavender Industry North East Scotland' and was amazed and excited to find a link to The National Library of Scotland (Gordon, 1965) [see Figure 5.1]. After hearing people talk about the beauty of the Lavender fields it seemed incredible to find myself watching women working in those very fields. The stories became a new kind of reality in a profound way that I wasn't prepared for. Maybe this is how an archaeologist feels when they discover an artefact they have only ever read about or

Figure 5.1: Visitors to the Lavender Project watching 'A Deeside Industry' (Gordon, 1965)

Source: Photo © Helen Smith.

heard stories of? It is over three years since this happened. If I sit and focus on the moment I am trying to explain, I can still feel the affect of seeing the women cutting the lavender with their scythes and watching the man in the distilling room extract the oil into the condenser. (Smith, 2015)

The sharing of this film is an event or intervention into the life of this community organisation. This is the pebble dropped into the water. The ripples, or legacy, of this act became the Lavender Project, a participatory and public piece of research into the Ingasetter Lavender Company. It became a people's exhibition of artefacts, memorabilia and recorded interviews. Participants collaborated to research and edit a series of 12 informational posters (see Figure 5.2), a programme of public events, including reflective discussions, a public launch

Figure 5.2: One of twelve information panels telling the story of lavender on Deeside

Source: Photo © Helen Smith.

event, and a marketing campaign. All of this activity had purpose and direction: to explore the sustainability of the Barn from an ecological and organisational perspective.

Through contacts with the local community, participants invited people who were known to have worked in the factory to an event where the film was screened. One person, Enid, was one of the young women cutting lavender in the film. She became the manager of the company and donated stories, contacts and photographs to the project. A link to the film was included in a press release written and distributed by a participant to local, regional and national press about the forthcoming exhibition.

When Scottish Television (STV) decided to film a news item about the research, they gained permissions to include extracts of the 1965 film in their news item:

> The exhibition attracted publicity in all of the local and regional newspapers. 600 people visited the exhibition and this was recorded in the minutes of a gallery meeting in November 2013. Lavender Project – Visitor numbers were given by Helen Smith. The numbers were 396 in the gallery book, 150 at the opening event and around 50 during other Barn events. The event was also seen in newspapers and on TV. (Extract from Gallery committee minutes, 14 November 2013 – Ref. HSR/No)

> The Lavender group delivered five public events during the period of the show. This included an afternoon tea-party in the gallery for the women who had worked at Ingasetter. They shared more details and reflections on their working life together with Brown, Duncan, Chambury and Fiona Hope. While chatting they were filmed by an STV journalist for an early evening news report that was watched by 400,000 people. (Smith, 2015: 123)

Reflective conversation between participants: what is the legacy of the Lavender Project for the Barn?

Almost two years after researching the Ingasetter Lavender Company, the core group of participants came back together to reflect on their feelings about the legacy of the Lavender Project. Mark and Helen developed a set of questions to guide the conversation that Mark chaired. Helen chose not to be present because participants were being asked to consider possible consequences of their engagement in the research during a period following the Lavender Project when Helen had not been present. Helen felt that if she was present, they would feel the need to explain events to her rather than use the time to be reflective about their shared experiences and knowledge of the development of the organisation. Instead, Helen transcribed the conversation from the film footage and passed this on to Mark, who has selected the following extracts. Helen then offers some analysis following each extract of conversation, seeking to draw out the themes. The views regarding ideas of legacy are threaded through this analysis in relation to the concepts of impact, insight and influence as a means of bringing our argument to a conclusion. The participants were Fiona, Genevieve, Hilary, Mark and Tony. All were involved in the Lavender Project and remain involved in the Barn.

Connecting our communities through creativity and friendship

> MARK: "'Connecting our communities through creativity and friendship' [reading Barn mission from new publicity material]."
>
> GENEVIEVE: "OK. I mean, that is so relevant to what we are discussing this afternoon."
>
> MARK: "Exactly ... I was going to ask you to consider the extent to which ... the experience of Lavender informed, or influenced, what's been going on. So, through that period we have had all this unpleasantness. We have had the Development Day listening to everybody and all the gripes, complaints and problems. We've also had the writing of the new business plan. I think, for me, actually this didn't come out of Lavender, but it's one of the things that has influenced the whole process ... whether you are staff-led and -directed, or staff-facilitated and volunteer-led, or collaboratively led. That was a major break point. The different philosophies if you like, and we have landed on this: 'The Barn's mission is to work collaboratively though the arts connecting our communities through creativity and friendship'."
>
> GENEVIEVE: "But that's exactly what Lavender did."
>
> MARK: "And I think you could say, to oversimplify Lavender, we did it in practice."
>
> FIONA AND GENEVIEVE: "Yeah."

MARK: "We actually walked that walk, rather than telling people things, which has some value, we actually did it."

GENEVIEVE: "Well, I can't help feeling that the experience of Lavender, good and bad, informed that or fed in subconsciously. For me, art has always been working at the edge of consciousness, pushing that boundary, sustaining creative art or ecological art or both.... That's where I came in really, talking about edges and boundaries ... and if you're not doing that, you're simply treading water."

TONY: "My thinking hasn't been influenced by Lavender as to what I want from the Barn. Lavender is an illustration of obtaining that. It's not something that has changed my thoughts. It has always, if you remember how long I have been going on about community, community, community. So, if I'm asked is that influenced by Lavender ..."

MARK: "You'd say no?"

TONY: "I'd say no."

MARK: "But, actually, it has focused everybody's minds, not least in all the other volunteers, that what we had was worth fighting for rather than just bye-bye, it was a nice idea and its time has gone. We have actually reinvigorated why we do it, and the importance of it, and Lavender has just been an example for demonstrating that."

GENEVIEVE: "Well, I'm not a director, so I have no idea of the timeline of influence, so it may just be that Lavender demonstrates those principles rather than influenced the wording, but it did do that, for me, it would be a huge shame if it did that, tick box, move on. I think it's got to be built on."

A recent leaflet produced since the completion of the Lavender Project with a new mission statement triggers this debate about the influence that engaging in the Lavender Project has had on the underpinning ethos of the organisation. Genevieve, who is not a trustee and has not been involved in writing it, sees a direct link to her experience of the Lavender Project, saying "this is exactly what we did". She describes the collaborative process of the arts in terms of "pushing boundaries" and "not treading water". In her eyes, this appears to be a tangible legacy of the research for the organisation. In contrast to this, Tony, who is a trustee and was highly involved in writing the leaflet, sees no direct links with his experience of the research. In fact, he reinforces the idea that he has not changed his opinion about the value of community to the organisation. The important issue here is that there is agreement that the ethos does express the values of the organisation. What is less important for the organisation is complete agreement about the influence of the arts practice research upon their newly articulated ethos. For the research, this demonstrates that consensus between participants on such matters is unpredictable. In terms of understanding its legacy, this indicates how the openness of individuals to the principles of art and its particular qualities are significant for knowing if, for example, this mission statement would have been written prior to their engagement in the Lavender Project.

The process: leadership, collaboration, volunteers

> MARK: "I'm just teasing out whether you can see the benefit, or whether you felt, from your perspective, there were some benefits in this looser way [of working] in terms of there being more creativity from the group. It being a bit more egalitarian, which, therefore, is a bit chaotic in some ways. Did you see benefits in that at all, or not really?"
>
> TONY: "A few. It was the first significant project I have done without project people around me."
>
> HILARY: "It wasn't just the voluntary sector, it was the fact that you were working with artists rather than engineers."
>
> GENEVIEVE: "But it did develop and it only developed because we didn't have a clear idea of what we were trying to achieve. We didn't actually know what was going to come out of it. The energy came from the idea … every action created, if you like, a reaction, but something else as well. So, there was no way it could be project-managed in the way that you would the oil industry."
>
> HILARY: And, actually, that was the crux of the whole project really, wasn't it. Because looking at it as a future model for the future sustainability and creativity of the Barn, then that's how we operate. That's how we encourage creativity."

The Lavender Project purposefully brought together a group of people with different experiences of this organisation. As might be expected, they also have different professional and life experiences. For example, the specific difference between how artists and engineers might operate is highlighted. Legacy, therefore, is spoken about in relation to these different perspectives. This develops the argument that the prior life and professional experience of individual participants is significant to the potential legacy of any practice-led research. What this also introduces is the idea that there are multiple legacies to research. There is a richness for the organisation and the findings in this, which is a positive reason for inviting or selecting a diversity of participants. For example, talking about their different life experiences in relation to styles of project management feeds into observations about the creative process involving making something new. The 'unknown' as a place to be travelling towards, particularly in relation to others with different approaches to oneself, is described as being chaotic. This is seen as a model for how the Barn operates and is linked to an ethos of encouraging creativity. The legacy of the Lavender Project involves opening up a reflective and critical space for the organisation to consider how it might operate in the future, and it has done so through an exploration of the lavender industry in the past. This is, again, an example of how the unexpected in heritage research, as well as arts, can be so productive (see Vergunst and Graham, this volume).

Experiencing increased community interest in the creative programme

> HILARY: "The outcomes of drawing different people into the Barn and the people who met up with each other, and who we met through it, was really precious, and that's something we need to sustain. I always love an education day. That was great. That was just a lovely thing to do – to bring a school in to engage with the Barn.... For me, it was about the people coming in at the end really and making connections."
>
> TONY: "I think that connection with the community was certainly for me the big thing."
>
> HILARY: "Communities, I'm not sure if I'm going to be able to articulate this thought very well, but people who are coming in to take part in these projects don't all need to understand it at a very intellectual level. That's one of the things really. People can be frightened of the Barn because it's seen to be too erudite."
>
> FIONA: "Yes, 'I'm not an artist so I can't walk through the door'."

MARK: "We had over 600 people who came to the gallery, many of whom had not been to the Barn before."

HILARY: "It did bring in people who wouldn't normally come to the Barn and those are the people we want to reach."

MARK: "So, there are those two things. Connecting to the community, which I think we all agree is fundamental to the Barn's survival …"

GENEVIEVE: "And those are things that I really love to do. I'm not so interested in the programme – films and theatre and so on. I'm much more interested in the day that we had with Strachan School. I thought it was fantastic."

TONY: "I think it's vital. I think without doing what you are enthusiastic about, the Barn is nothing."

The Lavender Project engaged both new and more diverse people in its organisation. An arts project that took a locally significant heritage subject as its focus appears to have been successful in contributing to this outcome. The legacy of this is that the group actually experienced how their organisation worked with heritage in order to involve its local community and many others. It gave them a taste of how this feels as a benchmark for the future. Quantitative data, such as visitor numbers, are a highly tangible legacy and are remembered in relation to qualitative feelings and emotions expressed by participants. Understanding the interconnectedness between types of legacy as facts and feelings is a characteristic of practice-led research and is significant because the experience of both will influence future decisions and actions in a deeper, potentially more durable, way.

New networks of people where I live

FIONA: "One of the highlights for me was interviewing Enid because I didn't know of Enid's existence. She's an older member of the community and it just opened this door into all these other people in Banchory who I didn't know of. It was so joyful for me and she was so grateful to us for opening up this door into her world, where she was so important in the community. And for me, it just reminded me all over again just how important it is to connect with older people."

FIONA: "There's such a warmth towards those lavender fields and the memory evokes the smell. 'I used to walk to school', people have said to me, 'and I could smell the lavender field. It just makes everybody so happy'."

HILARY: "In the exhibition, when I was stewarding, I'm just remembering people coming in and saying: 'it's the smell that takes me back to my childhood and walking to school'."

Arts practice research involving public events has the opportunity to attract visitors to exhibitions or other cultural activities. This creates the possibility for a different way of influencing communities as audiences or participants, as well as via traditional and social media. This is a web of different types of legacy that has the research process and its subject at its centre.

Lavender cuttings as a metaphor for the future

MARK: "The openness to new ideas, from wherever they come."

TONY: "And I think that was remarkable.... The project, for all the reasons you have said, worked very well. The follow-up ..."

MARK: "Remains to be done?"

TONY: "Still remains to be done. You know, it's now a year later."

GENEVIEVE: "It's in process. A lot of people devoted an awful lot of time to the project and they basically had to catch up with their lives meanwhile and PhDs and other things, but it is ticking over and there is nothing wrong with these things actually gelling."

MARK: "And gestating?"

GENEVIEVE: "Yeah."

HILARY: "I've been nurturing my lavender. I have one."

GENEVIEVE: "I need some instructions from you because I need to take some cuttings from mine. But don't tell me this is the wrong time because it's the only time."

FIONA: "I should take cuttings and I haven't either."

HILARY: "I got two cuttings from Lizzie and I killed one of them but the other one is looking quite good at the moment."

FIONA: "Well done."

MARK: "Can we return to the future thing because I think
    that is important."
HILARY: "My lavender is the future."
MARK: "Absolutely."
HILARY: "Taking cuttings is the future."
GENEVIEVE: "In many ways, you could say taking cuttings
    is what we are talking about."

Frustration at the lack of 'follow-up' within the organisation implies an expectation of some sort of legacy from the research that has not been fulfilled. Managing different expectations of legacy is worth considering in collaborative research in the arts, heritage or other fields. Participants suggest that taking time following an intense period of collaborative research has its own value by letting the ideas and effects of the experience gestate or gel. This indicates that legacy can require a period for reflection and leads to participants playfully developing their own metaphor for change and growth for the future of their organisation.

Conclusion: legacy and lavender

To conclude, we return to our question: what is the legacy of the Lavender Project for the Barn? As our conversation progressed, it became apparent that we were using different concepts to express legacy. Initially, we spoke about 'change' and this became important in how we are thinking about the legacy of this research. Types of legacy that participants mentioned included conditions for change, physical objects (art and buildings), ideas leading to actions, changing values, emotions or feelings, and arts research practice. It seems that some forms of legacy exist in relation to each other. For example, in an organisational context, structural and attitudinal legacies of research can combine to create a deeper cultural change. However, we also had difficulties in speaking about legacy and identifying legacy, which included:

- uncertainty in knowing what might have unfolded anyway;
- time frames in which we are considering the legacy;
- types of change we are interested in; and
- different types of legacy becoming visible over different time frames, for example, physical types of legacy may be more visible and take less time to appear, which is in contrast to legacy involving changes to attitudes or values.

We have found that the social, cultural, economic, political and personal contexts leading up to events are significant to their potential legacy. Therefore, it feels necessary to identify a time frame around any event being discussed. The durability of legacy might be a test of its effectiveness over time. To understand the legacy of an artwork, it appears that the conditions that make the artwork possible are as important as the influence of the artwork after it has taken place. For example, the long-term relationship that the Barn has had with its research partners before and after the Lavender Project appears to be an important factor in the influence of this research. Prior to 2010, Board meetings of Woodend Arts Limited (the charity that runs the Barn) never discussed art or arts practice in relation to the way in which the charity was managed; the two things were seen as entirely separate. This is no longer the case; the involvement of various members of the organisation in delivering an arts project and the presence over several years of an artist researching the way the organisation works undermines any assumption that artists have little to contribute to management. Individuals and their relationships are therefore important to legacy. For the Lavender Project, this includes those who saw the potential of an event or an idea, those who retain long-term relationships with a community or organisation, and those who transfer the legacy of research to new contexts.

It has felt necessary to frame our reflections in this way. Isolating the moment of the research project would have diminished the possibilities of understanding its legacy. Participants spoke about this in terms of 'follow-up' or allowing the effects of participatory research to gestate or gel.

We have defined artworks as events that intervene or disrupt the everyday life of the organisation. If understanding the legacy of a particular event is one aim of a research project, then it seems necessary to make an intervention of some sort that would otherwise not have occurred. Sharing the film A Deeside Industry with participants became a significant intervention into the life of the organisation, by which heritage became relevant to arts practice. The search to find the workers portrayed in the film and to understand the history of the industry and why it ceased became the motivating energy underpinning the project. The search for cuttings of the particular type of Lavender propagated at Ingasetter remains an ongoing legacy of the project.

Looking back at the same time as looking forwards seems to be a characteristic of thinking about the legacy of research. How we remember is influenced by our experience, and our memories of the past are constantly evolving as our life experiences continue. In the same way, how we imagine the future is subjective and continually changing. We each do this from our individual positions and the differences emerge in conversation with each other. Asking participants to consider the legacy of an arts practice research project has involved them in simultaneously thinking about the past and its effect on the future. The different approaches taken by artists and engineers to project management and collaboration have created two different approaches to how the project is remembered and how any legacy it may have for the organisation is expressed and acted upon. For example, one legacy of the project is described as 'lavender cuttings that need nurturing'. At the same time, it is spoken of as 'a demonstration of a set of principles to be promulgated'. Both acknowledge that the experience has been personally rewarding and important for the future of the organisation. Yet, the shift between organic metaphor and 'management-speak' also shows how heritage is contested and its meanings are socially produced between the past and present (Waterton and Watson, 2013).

Thinking about legacy in this example, and in heritage and arts research more generally, is complex. People involved in the project inevitably have very different perspectives when they reflect upon their experience, and this mitigates against a single dominant narrative of heritage or art as a form of collaborative inquiry. For some, in this case, lavender cuttings are the most important legacy; for others, it is more about ways of working. Tensions that exist may be creative and productive, as well as negative; it all depends upon how those tensions are managed. The experience of the research has the potential to influence this: through the process of collaboration from start to finish of the Lavender Project, members of the organisation had to work through various disagreements at every stage. The fact that there was no predetermined outcome for the project meant that all ideas needed to be heard and sifted, and then (collective) conclusions acted upon. The aim of writing this article in conversational forms is intended to enact a dialogical mode of acting in collaborative research (see Vergunst and Graham, this volume).

In addition, one could regard the evolution of the art and ecology strand of work at the Barn as a legacy of lavender. The Lavender Project was not an isolated event; it built on prior events, but it added vital energy and enthusiasm to that existing strand of work and it engaged a wider network of people in its delivery. Perhaps we should regard this as a legacy in itself. Evolution of practice leads to enhanced skills and better experiences. The practice will initially be located in a particular space or spaces, but if people are touched by the work, the legacy will be felt wherever those people go.

References

Dewey, J. (1987 [1934]) *Art as experience*, New York, NY: Penguin Group.

Douglas, A. (2016) 'Context is half the work: developing doctoral research through arts practice in culture', in C. Cartiere and M. Zebracki (eds) *The everyday practice of public art: Art, space and social inclusion*, Abingdon: Routledge, ch 8. Available at: https://openair.rgu.ac.uk/handle/10059/2060

Facer, K. and Enright, B. (2016) *Creating living knowledge: The Connected Communities Programme, community university relationships and the participatory turn in the production of knowledge*, Bristol: University of Bristol/AHRC Connected Communities.

Facer, K. and Pahl, K. (2017) *Valuing interdisciplinary collaborative research: Beyond impact*, Bristol: Policy Press.

Gordon, K. (dir) (1965) 'A Deeside Industry'. Clansman Films, National Library of Scotland. Available at: http://movingimage.nls.uk/film/2641

Kaprow, A. (2003) *Essays on the blurring of art and life* (ed J. Kelly), California, CA: University of California Press.

Lacy, S. (2010) *Leaving art: Writings on performance, politics, and publics, 1974–2007*, Durham, NC: Duke University Press.

Nelson, R. (2013) *Practice as research in the arts: Principles, protocols, pedagogies, resistances*, Basingstoke: Palgrave MacMillan.

Schön, D.A. (1996) 'Generative metaphor: a perspective on problem-setting in social policy', in A. Ortony (ed) *Metaphor and thought*, New York, NY: The Press Syndicate of the University of Cambridge.

Smith, H. (2015) 'Artist as navigator: understanding how the social qualities of art influence organizational change. A methodology for art as a social practice', PhD thesis, Robert Gordon University, Aberdeen.

Waterton, E. and Watson, S. (eds) (2013) *Heritage and community engagement: Collaboration or contestation?*, London: Routledge.

Woodend Arts Limited (2017) *Woodend Arts Limited Business Plan: Sustaining creativity, engaging ideas, 2017–21*. Unpublished report.

Part Two: Heritage as action

'Heritage as action' groups together our final four chapters. Each chapter is explicitly concerned with action itself as a form of research practice that enables both understanding of the past and change in the present. Thinking of research in this way draws on a well-established tradition of action and of participatory research, where cycles of action and reflection enable knowledge. Underpinning action research is the epistemic commitment that we are always in the middle of things and there is no objective or unentangled place for research. Instead, you need to start from 'where you are' and to 'dig where you stand' (Lindqvist, 1979).

In Chapter Six, Oliver Davis, Dave Horton, Helen McCarthy and Dave Wyatt explore, through different perspectives, the role that shared archaeology and heritage work play in the Caerau and Ely Rediscovering Heritage Project (CAER). Through enabling people to contribute in different ways, and to different intensities, it has sought to hold the production of archaeological knowledge and social and political change in dynamic relationship.

In Chapter Seven, Karen Brookfield, Danny Callaghan and Helen Graham, with members of the Ceramic City Stories team (Jayne Fair, Jan Roberts and Phil Rowley), elaborate the idea of 'DIY heritage' based on their work in the Potteries. They do so through exploring a specific event and how it worked to create moments of connection – what the group call the 'Stoke Ping'. The authors draw on wider DIY traditions 'to describe an ethos of horizontal community action, of mutual aid and of making alternatives now'. The chapter argues that DIY approaches challenge models of exponential growth that often exist in funding, policy and activism, and instead favour the magic of small moments and connections. Yet, they also show – through a recent innovative Heritage Lottery Fund initiative – how funding can be deployed to enable rather that constrain DIY horizontal, small-scale and action-led approaches.

In Chapter Eight, Kimberley Marwood, Esme Cleall, Vicky Crewe, David Forrest, Toby Pillatt, Gemma Thorpe and Robert Johnston develop a concept of 'action heritage' to show how 'the practices and processes of researching are transformative in themselves'. Through telling a variety of stories about their community heritage programme, they suggest that working together to produce understanding of the past has 'social and cultural impact around themes of cohesion, participation, social justice, community voice and identity'.

In our final chapter, Elizabeth Curtis, Jane Murison and Colin Shepherd show how involving schoolchildren in active inquiry and sharing in responsibility for research can challenge the 'content-driven model of learning' in school. Through the different perspectives of a researcher, a head teacher and a community archaeologist, they outline a lived curriculum, where they learned together not only *about* archaeology as a practice and the history of their landscape, but also *through* archaeology to understand their curriculum and their community.

Taken together, the chapters make a powerful argument for research as an active and lived inquiry, wrestling back a commitment to change from the metaphor of 'research impact'. Instead, they offer a richer sense that how we work together – underpinned by an emphasis on means over ends – is what creates and opens up future possibilities.

Reference

Lindqvist, S. (1979) 'Dig where you stand', *Oral History* 1 (Autumn): 26–30.

SIX

The Caerau and Ely Rediscovering Heritage Project: legacies of co-produced research

*Oliver Davis, Dave Horton, Helen McCarthy
and Dave Wyatt*

Introduction

The Caerau and Ely Rediscovering Heritage Project (CAER) was established in 2011 and is a collaboration between Cardiff University, Action in Caerau and Ely (ACE) (a local community development agency), local schools, residents and community groups. From the beginning, the guiding principle has been to actively involve community members, groups and heritage professionals in the co-production of archaeological and historical research. The project is focused on the Cardiff suburbs of Caerau and Ely. These are two of the most socially and economically challenged areas in Wales, but are also home to several regionally and nationally important heritage sites, including a large multivallate Iron Age hillfort. Until the instigation of CAER, these sites had received little attention and potential opportunities for using heritage to enhance social and economic well-being were entirely unrealised. Over the last seven years, the project team have employed a range of co-productive strategies to harness this potential through the *process* of researching heritage. In many respects, CAER has been effective precisely because it is about 'Heritage as Action', as it is framed in the Introduction to this book. The knowledge, energy and creativity of local people have been expressed through their engagement both with their local heritage and each other. It is the action of doing things together that has led to local communities having a stake both in the archaeology and the future of the area. As the project has developed over such a length of time, there have been many successes, but also many challenges. Using CAER as a case study, this chapter reflects on the potentials and problems of long-term co-production with communities, providing a range of perspectives from the key project partners involved.

Caerau and Ely: housing and heritage

Caerau and Ely are adjacent electoral wards on the western fringe of the city of Cardiff, although they possess a strong sense of shared identity and are often referred to together as 'Ely'. The housing estates that constitute each ward are home to a combined population of around 26,000 people. At the beginning of the 20th century, the area was essentially rural. However, after the First World War, with growing demands for housing to provide 'Homes fit for Heroes', in 1922, the area was taken inside the Cardiff City boundary and a programme of house building was initiated founded on 'Garden Suburb' principles. Ely was initially regarded as a rural idyll, an aspirational place to live for those who had previously been condemned to live in the slums of Cardiff docks. A second phase of house building was undertaken after the Second World War, and by the 1960s, the majority of residents were employed with the large industrial manufacturing companies that had premises in the area. Unfortunately, due to falling demand, these major industrial employers closed down in the late 1970s and early 1980s. Many local people lost their jobs and there was no replacement employment in the area.

To a large extent, the area has never recovered from this and faces considerable social and economic challenges, particularly high unemployment. Approximately 40% of the population receive income-related benefits (compared with 19.3% across Cardiff), unemployment is around 15% (compared with 4.4% across Cardiff) and 14% of households with dependent children do not have an adult in employment (compared with 5.2% across Cardiff). The Wales Index of Multiple Deprivation identifies 11 neighbourhood areas within Caerau and Ely as being in the top 10% most deprived neighbourhoods in Wales. The employment statistics correlate with poor educational attainment, although this has been improving in recent years. Only 49% of 16 year olds have qualifications equivalent to five GCSEs at grade A★ to C (compared with 65.3% across Cardiff) and only 7% of school leavers go on to higher education (compared with 32% across Cardiff). There is significant evidence to suggest that experiences of poverty impact significantly on the health of residents: babies born in Caerau and Ely have lower birthweights than others across the city and male and female life expectancies are also lower than the Cardiff average.

The challenges faced by these communities are complex and exacerbated by a local sense of marginalisation and stigmatisation within contemporary Cardiff. Economic and political power has become concentrated in the city centre and Cardiff Bay, where the devolved National Assembly for Wales and Welsh government sit. Nonetheless, many Caerau and Ely residents have a strong sense of connection with the area built upon extended family ties and strong friendships developed over generations. Such networks help to create a strong sense of community spirit among residents and are reinforced through a long history of community development and activism. Despite this, broader public perceptions of the area within the city tend to be negative, often focusing on the community's deficits and a small number of high-profile stories, most noticeably, a disturbance in 1991 that was reported in the national press and came to be known as 'the Ely riots' (Campbell, 1993).

Such negative views overlook a rich history that has the potential to challenge many of these perceptions. Indeed, Caerau and Ely possess some of the most important heritage sites not only in Cardiff, but in all of Wales. On the southern fringe of the housing estates and framed to the south by the line of the A4232 Cardiff bypass is Caerau Hillfort (see Figure 6.1). The hillfort is distinctly triangular in shape and is around eight hectares in size, making it one of the largest hillforts in South Wales and comparable to better-known English examples such as Danebury (Cunliffe, 2003) and South Cadbury (Barrett et al, 2000). The hillfort is a Scheduled Ancient Monument, which means that while urban development has extended to the foot of the hill, it has not encroached upon it. The interior of the monument is privately owned and actively maintained by a tenant farmer as pasture for horses and cattle. This creates a vibrant contrast between the urban context of the housing estates and the steep wooded fringe and open grassland of the hillfort. Before the instigation of CAER, the hillfort had received little archaeological attention apart from a topographic survey by the Royal Commission on the Ancient and Historical Monuments of Wales (RCAHMW). However, recent geophysical surveys and excavations co-produced with local people and the CAER team have shown that it was densely occupied in the Iron Age, and it was clearly an important centre in prehistory, hosting a powerful community that likely controlled access to the rich agricultural resources of the Cardiff area. Such a situation provides a stark contrast to the modern realities of this part of the city.

One particularly important discovery is that the hillfort overlies the remains of a Neolithic causewayed enclosure. Such sites are an

Figure 6.1: Aerial photo showing the distinctive triangular Caerau Hillfort (with excavation in progress) surrounded by the housing estates of Caerau and Ely

Source: © Crown copyright: RCAHMW (reproduced with permission).

extremely rare type of monument and represent the earliest known examples of the enclosure of open space. Around 70 such enclosures are known from England, but only two others have been confirmed in Wales (Davis and Sharples, 2017). Excavations have also uncovered the remains of Roman-period occupation within the hillfort and there are indications that the entire site may have been refortified in the early medieval period.

The north-east corner of the hillfort has been subject to considerable remodelling in later periods. A medieval ringwork, probably of early Norman date, is set adjacent to the ruins of St Mary's Church. The church is first documented in the 13th century as a chapel of Llandaff, though it became a parish church after the Reformation. The building has been restored several times, and remained the parish church into the 1970s, when it was deconsecrated. The church is now a ruin and has become a place for young people to engage in activities away from prying eyes – unfortunately, including graffiti and vandalism of the building – although it is regularly maintained by a passionate local group known as the Friends of St Mary's. The church has an important role in helping to define place and identity. Its position at the top of a hill provides a highly visible landmark for local people in the housing estates below, many of whom remember it functioning as the parish church. As such, there are deep emotional connections with this place and, for some, the church's state of disrepair is analogous to how they see their community (see Figure 6.2).

About a mile to the east of the hillfort, in the centre of the large open space of Trelai Park, are the remains of a large and well-preserved Roman villa, one of only a handful in Wales. The villa has been investigated three times, most latterly and significantly by the famous 20th-century archaeologist Sir Mortimer Wheeler in the 1920s (Wheeler, 1920, 1921). Wheeler identified an important complex of buildings dating to the 2nd to 4th centuries AD, but, today, the villa's remains are entirely grassed over and there is no interpretation on site. Encircling the villa was Cardiff racecourse, established in 1855. Crowds of up to 40,000 drawn from across South Wales and the west of England attended races here, including the annual Welsh Grand National, until the outbreak of the Second World War. The site of the racecourse was used for a variety of purposes outside of flat and steeplechase racing, including as an airfield in the early 20th century, but no visible remains exist today.

On the northern side of Ely, a number of Bronze Age metalwork hoards have been discovered following the course of the river, suggesting that this area may have been an important ritual landscape

Figure 6.2: St Mary's Church sits in the north-eastern corner of the hillfort

Source: Photo © Oliver Davis.

.at this time. The remains of a deserted medieval village also survive on the very north-western fringe of the housing estates (Davis, 2016).

Without doubt, Caerau and Ely possess important heritage assets that describe an area that has, at various times, been at the heart of power and political decision-making in the region, and, at others, been somewhat peripheral. The issue, however, is that the value of these heritage sites to enhance social and economic well-being or help reinforce pride-in-place has, for the most part, not been acknowledged (cf Cadw, 2013). None had received recent archaeological attention for instance and the significance of the various sites was little known. The lack of work and interpretation signage at Caerau Hillfort was particularly perplexing given that it is Cardiff's largest and oldest Scheduled Ancient Monument. The recognition of the contradiction between the significance of this heritage to the story of Ely, Cardiff and Wales and the insignificance of its role in those established narratives was the basis for the development of CAER.

Development of CAER

CAER was born from a series of initial informal meetings between academics from Cardiff University, ACE, heritage professionals, local school representatives, community groups and residents. This broad church of collaborators provided a mix of skills and strengths, from academic research and community development, to the understanding of local needs and networks. Dr Oliver Davis, an archaeologist with research interests in Iron Age hillforts, had visited Caerau Hillfort several times and understood its potential for a research project. Knowledge of the Iron Age in South-East Wales, and of hillforts in particular, was very poorly understood and there was a clear research need to explore a hillfort in the region (Davis, 2017). The CAER team realised early on that co-produced archaeological investigations at Caerau Hillfort could provide answers to key research questions, but also help to address local social and economic challenges by developing educational and new life opportunities for participants.

From the outset, the project's framework was co-designed by the CAER team and reflected the diverse range of interests and motivations for involvement. The six key project objectives decided upon were to:

- foster a positive 'sense of place' for Caerau and Ely grounded in the area's rich heritage;
- create educational and new life opportunities;
- promote skills development;

- challenge stigmatised perceptions of the Caerau and Ely district;
- raise local, regional and national interest in archaeology; and
- break down barriers to higher education.

These objectives were not focused upon the results of archaeological or historical research. Rather, they concentrated on how such research might be employed to transform negative stereotypes that coalesce around these communities and to attempt to address some of the challenges that they face socially and economically. Such instrumentalisation of archaeology has seen increasing critique in recent years by those who see such action as subjugating archaeological research objectives to political, economic or social needs. Yannis Hamilakis (2004), for instance, has bemoaned how archaeology as a discipline is constantly asked to justify its 'relevance' to the real world and demonstrate that it can benefit the individual financially and socially. Such tension between scholarly ideals and contemporary political and social struggles is reflective of how archaeology is increasingly seen as having a dual purpose – with loyalties to both professional archaeologists and to non-archaeologists who nonetheless value the past and its power to address contemporary concerns. From the beginning, the academics involved in CAER were well aware of its position as 'social-purpose archaeology' but approached this neither uncritically nor with the intention of employing the 'archaeologist-as-social-worker'. Indeed, the core CAER team were deliberately drawn from a range of backgrounds that included archaeology, community development, art, history, teaching, social science and heritage. The project was consciously framed as 'archaeology integrated with broader political and social agendas'. Working with the communities and professionals of Caerau and Ely in equal and reciprocal ways to explore the area's rich heritage was therefore as a process through which understanding might be enriched by tapping into local knowledge and passion, but, more importantly, through which contemporary social and economic challenges might be addressed.

From the outset, the key project principle was to value the contribution of all participants and partners, and create a mutually beneficial and reciprocal relationship. While the academic members of the team were aware of a range of recent literature exploring such ways of working with communities (eg Hale, 2012; Hart et al, 2012), CAER's approach to co-production was, in fact, largely modified and adapted from the successful strategies employed by ACE in relation to community development. These placed local people at the heart of archaeological and historical research and included activities such as geophysics, excavations, artefact analyses, exhibitions, art installations, films, heritage trails, performances, accredited courses and experimental archaeology.

Since 2011, through securing a series of successful funding grants, CAER has grown steadily and somewhat organically to become one of ACE's key community initiatives. Over that time, the project has involved more than 2,500 active participants in co-produced research and engaged with almost 15,000 visitors at various events and excavations. The project has built strong partnerships with 15 institutional partners (eg Cardiff Council, the National Museum Wales and the Cardiff Story Museum) and seven local schools, involving over 1,500 pupils in co-produced activities including archaeological research, art installations and film-making. The project has also instigated initiatives for young people facing exclusion from school and delivered six free accredited adult learner courses to 79 local adults (including unemployed and retired people), two of whom have now been accepted onto an archaeology degree at Cardiff University. Up to 2016, most funding was secured through the Arts and Humanities Research Council (AHRC), in particular, the Connected Communities funding stream. This has understandably facilitated mainly research-led activities. However, in 2017, the CAER team secured development-phase funding for a large Heritage Lottery Fund (HLF) grant. This involves developing proposals for transformational heritage infrastructure at Caerau Hillfort, including a heritage and education centre, interpretation media, heritage trails, and a learning suite at the local new-build secondary school.

Such metrics can provide useful benchmarking tools but say little about the specific social outcomes of the project. CAER has always emphasised the potential transformative effects of participation in heritage research and it is therefore the qualitative data regarding the social effects on project partners and participants that we find most meaningful, and provide the focus for the remainder of this chapter.

Reflecting on CAER

In assessing the impact of CAER over the years, our evaluative approach evolved somewhat organically from a 'separate' to an 'integrated' strategy, where an evaluation plan was developed co-productively with project participants (see Ancarno et al, 2015). Evaluation has come to be seen as a reflection on action rather than a feedback-gathering exercise. A range of evaluative strategies have been employed, but the most successful and authentic are those that are participatory. That is to say, community members and partners are actively involved in the evaluation, either helping to design the evaluation plan or conducting peer-to-peer interviews to record impacts and experiences. An analysis of evaluation data concerning local residents' experiences has already been published (Ancarno et al, 2015: 122–7). This indicated that involvement in the project had been largely beneficial for both themselves and for the communities of Caerau and Ely, although concerns over the continuity of involvement and project sustainability were raised. The focus in the remainder of this chapter will be on the experiences of participating academics and community partners through a series of testimonial reflections. The participants were encouraged to be truthful and to contribute a critical analysis of their involvement.

A view from the university: Oliver Davis

I am very much an archaeologist with a particular interest in Iron Age hillforts. I have lived in Cardiff since 1998 and had visited Caerau Hillfort several times before CAER began. I was amazed at its complexity and scale and the potential it had for research (the interior was largely pasture and seemed suitable for geophysics and excavation), but this seemed contradicted by its almost complete avoidance by other academics. I harboured a desire to start a project, but given the various site management issues, this seemed impossible without the support of the local community. After completing my PhD in 2010, I obtained a post with a local archaeological company, with whom I gained some experience in 'community archaeology'. While writing my thesis, I had thought little about the impact of my research beyond academia, but my involvement in some community archaeology projects showed me the power that heritage had to engage with people and gave me confidence that a project at Caerau might be possible. I began attending meetings in Caerau and Ely with local community groups and talking to people about the idea of starting a project exploring the hillfort. There was lots of interest and I even led a tour of the site for local residents, but there seemed little hope of gaining sufficient funding to get the ideas off the ground. Early in 2011, an academic post came up at Cardiff University for a community archaeologist. This seemed like an ideal opportunity for me to combine my interest in public engagement with my desire to obtain an academic position. I was shortlisted for interview and, as part of that process, I was required to pitch an idea for a community project, so I presented my idea of exploring Caerau Hillfort. I did not get the job, but I was subsequently approached by academics from the university (Dave Wyatt and Niall Sharples) who thought that the idea was a good one and felt that the development of a project at Caerau could dovetail well with the university's impact agenda.

CAER itself developed from many of the networks that I had established over the previous year. We held several meetings between the university, the local secondary school, interested local residents, ACE and others. Managing these relationships meant building trust. In particular, although the university could provide resources, expertise and formal links to further education opportunities, there was some initial reluctance, particularly from local residents, to committing to working with such an institution. Reflecting concerns expressed in the academic literature on both community research and heritage (Waterton and Watson, 2011), this seemed to be largely based around the fear that the university was simply parachuting itself in for a short period of time to conduct research *on*, rather than *with*, these communities. To me, the fears seemed entirely justifiable and we needed to demonstrate a genuine commitment to working with these communities in the long term. This is why co-production has been so valuable. Involving all partners in the co-design and co-creation of project activities has meant that, from the beginning, we responded to local needs and produced outcomes that mutually benefitted the community and university without overly prioritising one or the other.

Initially, funding was limited to small grants from the university and other partners, but it was enough to allow us to undertake small interventions. Such activities, like geophysical surveys and art projects, produced genuine new research, but also helped to raise the profile of the heritage of the area and to engage local people. The issue was that these activities were irregularly timed so that it sometimes felt as if the project was only progressing slowly. In reality, this was inevitable due to funding constraints. I myself was actually working for the RCAHMW at the time and so any time I gave, which was considerable, was outside my normal working hours. However, the slow pace of these initial activities was actually a crucial strength (although we did not plan it that way) since it allowed for the steady development of trust and friendships with key partners like ACE and Cardiff Council. The relationship with ACE has been particularly important. As a community development organisation, they could initially help support the development of the project but needed convincing about the ongoing benefits of a heritage project to a community that was facing much more pressing needs. The linking up of heritage research with volunteering, educational opportunities and well-being was instrumental in this. This early work also helped to create a much-needed counter-discourse to the negative framing of the area. This was reinforced through the filming of a *Time Team* programme at the site in 2012. While the archaeological results of that programme were limited, it caught the attention of the local community and presented Ely in a positive light to an audience of several million on television.

A significant step forward for CAER was the award of a substantial grant from the AHRC's Connected Communities funding stream in 2013. This allowed me to be employed on the project almost full-time for a year and to be based both at the university and also embedded into the community with ACE, where I worked for half of the week. I helped facilitate the organic and rapid development of the project as networks were established, and cemented the relationship between the university and ACE. It also allowed us to undertake a substantial excavation at the hillfort for four weeks. This was extremely well attended, with many local people visiting and actively involved in the excavation.

It was always going to be difficult to maintain this momentum beyond the funding year. I had obtained a lectureship at the university so my time was now much more in demand, but we had created networks and trust that were in danger of collapse if we could not maintain project continuity. Small funding grants from the HLF and university allowed us to maintain some presence in the community and we managed to scrape together just enough money to undertake another excavation in 2014. Further successful awards of Connected Communities funding (eg Heritage Legacies and On Shared Ground) allowed us to reflect on project impacts but undertake only small-scale engagement activities. We desperately needed new funding sources to maintain project activities on the ground, but also to facilitate even small infrastructural developments such as the installation of interpretation furniture at the hillfort. There were other challenges, too, particularly as we became drawn into community politics. As a collaborative project involving many different partners, it became increasingly difficult to disentangle the university from those partner organisations. In reality, this is a strength that provides access to significant resources and networks, but it is sometimes problematic when dealing with a small number of residents or groups who have long-standing antipathy towards those partners. For instance, over time, the university became no longer seen as an independent 'player' within these communities since it has become inexorably linked to project partners. As such, we can no longer sit on the fence when tensions between community members, groups and partners surface, but must face up to and engage with such tensions, which can be uncomfortable and time-consuming.

In 2015, we began the development of an HLF 'Heritage Grant' application. This seemed like the obvious choice for funding since, whereas AHRC grants were based around research, an HLF grant would allow capital investment. Naturally, the application was co-produced with partners and local community groups from the outset, which took it in so many different and unexpected ways, but also meant that it took a long time to develop. We were successful at first stage and awarded development funding from the HLF in December 2016, with a development year starting in June 2017. However, this process highlighted a tension between the complexity of applying for large-scale funding and the maintenance of ongoing project activities. There are clearly capacity-related constraints for academics – large grant applications require considerable inputs of time – but from the community and partner perspective, there is a need for project continuity. We have attempted to bridge this divide by continuing to run small-scale activities 'on the ground', often drawing on the capacity of partners that seven years of collaboration helps to facilitate.

From my perspective at the university, I often ask myself two questions: 'Do we manage to co-produce high-quality research?'; and 'Do we actually make a social difference through the project?'. In response to the first question, I believe that the answer is 'yes', although the focus of that research is often unexpected and the results surprising (eg the 'Hart of Ely' project has recently shifted our focus to modern and ancient relationships with crafts and craft skills; see University of Cardiff, no date) – but, after all, that is the whole point of co-production, as noted by Vergunst and Graham in the Introduction to this volume. The second question is more difficult to evaluate. We can certainly point towards considerable quantitative data pertaining to the numbers of people engaged, but this tells us little about the quality and impacts of those engagements. More pertinent are personal testimonies, particularly those obtained from peer-to-peer interviews. Some of these are deeply moving, reflecting how involvement has increased confidence, benefitted health and well-being, or even improved behaviour in school (eg the evaluation by Ancarno et al [2015] provided insights into the therapeutic nature of co-produced research). Co-production is difficult; it requires a large input of time and resources, but it can have significant impact on people's lives. I would encourage all my colleagues within the academy to aspire to co-production methods and the benefits that it can bring to one's research and the way one sees the world.

A view from ACE: Dave Horton

I have lived and worked in Ely and Caerau for over 11 years. At the beginning, I was employed as a community development worker by Cardiff Council under the Welsh government's Communities First programme. In 2010, we began planning with local people to create an organisation that would sustain community development activity beyond any single government programme, could employ local people and manage local facilities, and would provide some autonomy and 'voice' for local people in dealing with decision-makers and those in power. ACE was founded in May 2011 and has since grown a membership of over 1,000 people and a series of projects that aim to tackle disadvantage. For the last few years, I have been employed as the development manager, independent from the Communities First programme and responsible for overseeing the development of the organisation according to a local vision.

ACE has developed a particular set of values and a closely related approach influenced by theories of co-production and asset-based community development. This means that we value the expertise, experience and skills that local people themselves bring to the table, and that we seek to approach our work positively and with a sense of opportunity, identifying local assets and strengths rather than focusing solely on the problems that people traditionally associate with our community. This approach has seen us engage hundreds of people in community action (some of whom have formed their own community groups) and has enabled us to identify and develop buildings and land that were previously neglected and going to waste.

One of our hopes in founding ACE was that an effective community organisation might attract new opportunities by 'opening the door' to partner organisations who can contribute to community life. The CAER heritage project is our best example of this yet. We found ourselves with significant networks among community members and had identified interest in local heritage as a key opportunity for engagement and learning. However, we had none of the knowledge or skills necessary to develop this work further and to capitalise on the opportunities afforded. CAER has provided an opportunity for partner organisations to play to their strengths, with ACE building on years of community engagement to facilitate participation and Cardiff

University bringing historical knowledge, research and archaeological skills. In this sense, it is a model for effective partnership. An important factor here is the value that key university staff have placed on ACE's role in developing networks and facilitating participation. This takes long-term, skilled work from qualified and experienced community development workers. Our experience has too often been that large, well-resourced, public sector agencies expect to reap the benefits of this work for free. Cardiff University's CAER team staff understood early on the dangers of this presumption, and the potential implications for the sustainability of organisations like ACE, and have been proactive in seeking to cover the organisation's community development costs associated with the project.

There are neighbourhoods within our community where virtually nobody progresses into higher education. This is one of the starkest available indicators of disadvantage and inequality. For most local people, access to a university education is not even considered a possibility. In this context, we value very greatly the long-term presence of university staff within Ely and Caerau through CAER. The relationships formed between local people and committed university staff help to place higher education on the radar for people. Where this is most effective, it creates a form of bridging social capital (social capital located in relationships between people of different groups and social classes) (see Putnam, 1999). The potential implications for learning and social mobility are well documented. One of my favourite stories from CAER involves a six-year-old lad from Ely digging up our first 6,000-year-old Neolithic flint tool and taking it straight to Professor Niall Sharples to identify together. These kinds of interactions and relationships can embed themselves firmly in the mind and can be transformational in terms of people's perceptions of what is possible for themselves and their community. They require time, though, which, in this case, means a long-term presence for the university within the community. Our experience is that project delivery staff from the university understand and are committed to this approach but that senior academic staff are sometimes harder to convince and are focused on the traditional university sites (usually in the city centre).

Identifying assets in a community such as Ely and Caerau is not necessarily simple. Economic resources of the traditional kind are lacking. Physical resources such as public buildings and land are limited and are often neglected and of poor quality. Asset-based community development in this context requires organisations like ACE to be creative and open-minded in identifying potential assets and to base this work on valuing the social assets that clearly exist in the form of strong social networks, volunteerism and good will. CAER has enabled us to identify local heritage sites, local historical knowledge and memory as important assets that can provide a basis for creative participatory regeneration. Initially, these assets were engaged with the aim of facilitating learning and volunteering opportunities. Evaluation demonstrated the personal impact that these activities had on individual participant mental health and skills development. Our next stage – the CAER 'Hidden Hillfort Project' (funded by the HLF) – has enabled us to begin exploring the wider regeneration potential afforded by our local heritage assets, including the development of tourism and social enterprise. In the longer term, there is every potential for the project to make a positive economic impact on our community. It has many of the ingredients of a powerful, transformational community regeneration project: genuine community participation and co-production; the identification and development of key community assets; skilled partners who are playing to their strengths; gradually increasing access to resources; and a growing set of diverse skills held among a wide group of volunteers and staff. We look forward to telling the new story that will emerge and dealing with the challenges that will inevitably arise together.

A view from the community: Helen McCarthy

My involvement with CAER began in 2013, when I enrolled on one of CAER's archaeology courses (delivered through Cardiff University's Live Local Learn Local scheme). Although I had left full-time education at 16, I had always been an 'armchair archaeologist', forever reading books and watching documentaries, but all from the comfort of my own home. Now, I had the chance to take part in a project that was actually happening close to my home. I felt that I could not continue to make excuses, and the time had come for me to get my hands dirty, literally. Any apprehension I had about being in a classroom again quickly evaporated, and I was immediately made very welcome.

The next logical step for me was to visit the Iron Age hillfort site during excavations. I was given a tour and introduced to a trench supervisor. As an amateur, I cannot explain the excitement that I felt at actually being on a 'live dig'. My supervisor took time to explain all the processes, all of which I did myself. I was made to feel part of a team, and at no point was I made to feel inadequate or uncomfortable.

Since 2013, I have been involved in many more accredited courses and activities, and I now count the team and other volunteers as friends. As a group of people with different educational abilities and skills, we have developed a feeling of friendship and community, all because we share a common interest in history and our local heritage. This bond has caused us to take ownership of our own locality. As a 'CAER team', we have litter-picked, repaired the hillfort ramparts and created local heritage trails – such varied activities reflect the diverse nature of community heritage projects. Ultimately, we all share a communal desire to make our estate a better place to live.

In 2017, we were catapulted into a realm that could only once have been imagined when we were awarded a development grant from the HLF to undertake the 'Hidden Hillfort Project'. It enabled us to take on the lease of an old disused Gospel Hall that sits below the hillfort ramparts with the intention of turning it into a local heritage centre. Community members have taken part in architect workshops and been given a full voice. If all this year's hard work is successful, a further grant will enable us to actually renovate the Gospel Hall and have further excavations in the area.

In March 2017, I was honoured to be asked to serve as community representative on the Hidden Hillfort Management Team. I have also represented CAER in a 'Co-creating Communities' presentation in Bristol and a community archaeology workshop in Lincoln. I have also enrolled at Cardiff University, taking part in their Pathway to a Degree and Exploring the Past courses. I have the project to thank for all of this as I would not have had the confidence to do any of it prior to that adult education class five years ago.

As the winner of two major community archaeology awards (Times Higher Education Awards 2017: Outstanding Contribution to Local Community; National Coordinating Centre for Public Engagement Engage Competition 2014 Award: Overall Winner), we now occupy a national stage, and 2018 will see us go from strength to strength. I am very proud that I am a part of a wonderful project and very much look forward to what the future holds for us.

Conclusion

Co-production is not something that just happens. It takes time and commitment to develop and requires the building of trust, and often friendships, between partners and participants. While the reflections in this chapter provide different perspectives on co-production and participation with CAER, the common theme is that the most important aspect has been the development of such relationships. In CAER's case, these have been nurtured from initial small-scale pilot activities and events designed to establish working relationships and networks, to eventually large-scale projects with ambitious aims that cross-cut multiple communities and partner organisations. Continuity of key staff involvement from the many partner organisations has facilitated the long-term maintenance of collaborative and co-productive working practices and has been the crucial element in the project's success. It has allowed some relationships, particularly between Cardiff University and ACE, to flourish as partners and participants bring their various strengths to the table. For instance, in many respects, the working practices of the university academics have been shaped by the co-productive principles at the heart of ACE, while the university has contributed research skills and access to new educational and social networks. Inevitably, over such a length of time, a few relationships have soured, particularly as partners and participants get drawn into community politics. Yet, this does not detract from the guiding principles of the project in which we remain open to new possibilities and the new twists that new participants can bring. At its heart, CAER values the open, honest and reciprocal relationships between partners and participants which mean people that can contribute at a whole range of levels (Durose et al, 2012a, 2012b; Hart et al, 2012). From 'long-termers' to 'toe-dippers', everybody has a role, a contribution and a stake in the project according to their skills and needs. Without this co-productive approach, it is unlikely that a project exploring the archaeology of this place would have been possible.

At the very beginning of the project, we realised that the heritage of Ely and Caerau highlighted a great contradiction: the presence of a large and complex hillfort suggested that Ely was an important political and power centre in prehistory, yet such power dynamics had been inverted in modern times. This is a potent narrative that emphasises the temporality of power relationships and social inequality, and, in some ways, has helped shape our interpretation of the archaeological evidence. After all, the construction of a hillfort would have required the cooperation of a large number of people, drawn from disparate groups, but whose participation in such activities helped to bind them together into a new community. Such prehistoric 'communities of practice' (Hart et al, 2012) provide an intriguing parallel with those formed through the process of co-produced archaeological research.

References

Ancarno, C., Davis, O.P. and Wyatt, D. (2015) 'Forging communities: the CAER Heritage Project and the dynamics of co-production', in D. O'Brien and P. Matthews (eds) *After urban regeneration: Communities, policy and place*, Bristol: The Policy Press, pp 113–30.

Barrett, J.C., Freeman, P.W.M. and Woodward, A. (2000) 'Cadbury Castle, Somerset: the later prehistoric and Romano-British archaeology', English Heritage Archaeological Report 20.

Cadw (2013) 'Historic environment strategy for Wales: headline action plan'. Available at: https://gov.wales/topics/culture-tourism-sport/historic-environment/cadw/historicenvironstrat/?lang=en (accessed 16 August 2018).

Campbell, B. (1993) *Goliath: Britain's dangerous places*, London: Methuen.

Cunliffe, B. (2003) *Danebury Hillfort*, Stroud: Tempus.

Davis, O.P. (2016) *Excavations at the deserted medieval village of Michaelston-super-Ely, 2016: An interim report*, Cardiff: Cardiff Studies in Archaeology 37.

Davis, O.P. (2017) 'Filling the gaps: the Iron Age in Cardiff and the Vale of Glamorgan', *Proceedings of the Prehistoric Society* 79: 1–32.

Davis, O.P. and Sharples, N. (2017) 'Early Neolithic enclosures in Wales: a review of the evidence in light of recent discoveries at Caerau, Cardiff', *Antiquaries Journal* 97: 1–26.

Durose, C., Beebeejaun, Y., Rees, J. and Richardson, L. (2012a) *Illuminating the evolution of community participation*, Swindon: AHRC Connected Communities.

Durose, C., Beebeejaun, Y., Rees, J. and Richardson, L. (2012b) *Towards co-production in research with communities*, Swindon: AHRC Connected Communities.

Hale, A. (2012) *Linking communities to historic environments: A research review summary*, Swindon: AHRC Connected Communities.

Hamilakis, Y. (2004) 'Archaeology and the politics of pedagogy', *World Archaeology* 36(2): 287–309.

Hart, A., Ntung, A., Millican, J., Davies, C., Wenger, E., Rosing, H. and Pearce, J. (2012) *Community–university partnerships through communities of practice*, Swindon: AHRC Connected Communities.

Putnam, R. (1999) *Bowling alone: The collapse and revival of American community*, New York, NY: Touchstone Books.

University of Cardiff (no date) 'Hart of Ely'. Available at: www.cardiff.ac.uk/city-region-exchange/our-work/funded-projects-2017-18/hart-of-ely

Waterton, E. and Watson, S. (2011) *Heritage and community engagement: Collaboration or contestation?*, London: Routledge.

Wheeler, R.E.M. (1920) 'A Roman fortified house near Cardiff', *Journal of Roman Studies* 11: 76–85.

Wheeler, R.E.M. (1921) 'Roman buildings and earthworks on the Cardiff racecourse', *Transactions of the Cardiff Naturalists' Society* 55: 19–45.

SEVEN

Do-it-yourself heritage: heritage as a process (designing for the Stoke 'Ping')

*Karen Brookfield, Danny Callaghan and Helen Graham,
with members of the Ceramic City Stories team
(Jayne Fair, Jan Roberts and Phil Rowley)*

Introduction

The stage was set: a hidden gem and 'secret' space; a pool of tiles, different colours and shapes. Across the room was a cascade of ceramic fragments. Further away from the entrance was a bookcase full of books and pamphlets. Buckets and scrapers were positioned around the walls. Tea and cakes stood ready to be served on beautifully patterned, eclectically mismatched services. The day was 27 June 2015 and the occasion was a Do-It-Yourself Heritage Day at Minton Free Library on London Road in Stoke-on-Trent.

We want to take you into the anatomy of this event to introduce the idea of do-it-yourself (DIY) heritage, that is, heritage as it is produced through people's actions, conversations and relationships. Danny Callaghan, Jan Roberts, Jayne Fair and Phil Rowley organised and ran these events under the banner of Ceramic City Stories (other volunteers present included, Simon Ball, Phil Rawle, Jane Wells, Kristian Foster and Steve Shaw). Danny Callaghan was involved with Karen Brookfield (Heritage Lottery Fund [HLF]) and Helen Graham (University of Leeds) in a project 'How should heritage decisions be made?'. Karen and Helen came to take part in the Do-It-Yourself Heritage Day having visited Danny in Stoke as part of the research project in order to explore and articulate DIY heritage approaches. This chapter is a product both of the 'How should heritage decisions be made?' research (Bashforth et al, 2015, 2017) and two follow-up conversations in 2016 and 2017. In these conversations, the Ceramic City Stories group reflected with Karen and Helen on the ways in which the group has used the approaches deployed at the Do-It-

Yourself Heritage Day events at the Minton Library to grow and to develop ways to collaborate.

Underpinning this article – drawing on current debates in critical heritage studies (Smith, 2006) and community-led research (Burns, 2007; Facer and Enright, 2016) – is an exploration of both 'heritage' and 'knowledge' as emerging through social processes. Recognising heritage as a process has been a crucial critical intervention; it has challenged the idea of heritage as a value fixed in an object or building through preservation and managed by expert-led organisations on behalf of a public. Yet, once you start to think of heritage as a process, it does open up other questions, especially when you are thinking about the themes of this book: community participation in heritage and community participation in research. Not least, if we say that heritage is a process and knowledge is a process, then what kinds of processes are they? How might knowledge processes and heritage processes be connected in a way that opens up who is involved? What different kinds of processes in research and heritage can be actively designed to enable a plurality of both different ways of knowing and different heritage governance models to emerge?

In this chapter, we develop the idea of DIY heritage as a specific kind of process, one that relies on the chemistry of conversations and fruitful moments of connection. One of us, Jan Roberts, describes this as 'the Stoke Ping', evoking the alchemical moments of local life where something shifts: new ideas emerge, new understandings cohere, horizons expand or a sense of possibility or hope is felt. This makes the Ping sound mysterious, as if it will either just happen or not happen, and there might be something to this. However, the core argument of this chapter is that it is possible to design events and projects in order to make the Ping more likely, and that is exactly what Ceramic City Stories has sought to do.

Heritage as a process ... but what kind of process?

As already noted, since the emergence of heritage studies, a crucial critical intervention has been to conceptualise heritage as a process. The concept of 'heritage-as-process' has been used to argue for a longer and more geographically expansive framework and to recognise that 'Every society has had a relationship with its past, even those which have chosen to ignore it' and the process of heritage is 'what people tell each other about their past; about what they forget, remember, memorialise and/or fake' (Harvey, 2001: 320). The concept of heritage-as-process has most frequently been drawn on to emphasise that heritage is

Figure 7.1: Tiles following some playful engagement

Source: Photo © Danny Callaghan.

produced by people now in an ongoing present; that heritage is an act, a doing. As such, thinking heritage-as-process can be seen as part of a much wider turn to 'verbing' in critical humanities and social science, such as Doreen Massey's (1991) influential conceptualisation of place as a process. In this vein, David Lowenthal (1998: 226) has argued that 'heritage, far from being fatally predetermined or Godgiven, is in large measure our own marvellously malleable creation'. Barbara

Kirshenblatt-Gimblett (1995: 369) has described heritage as a 'mode of cultural production in the present which has recourse to the past'. Gregory Tunbridge and John Ashworth (1996: 6) have argued that heritage is produced through the way in which 'the present selects an inheritance from an imagined past for current use and decides what should be passed on to an imagined future'. Laurajane Smith (2006: 3) has extended the debate to argue that:

> all heritage is intangible. What makes these things valuable and meaningful – what makes them 'heritage', or what makes the collection of rocks in a field 'Stonehenge' – are the present-day cultural processes and activities that are undertaken at and around them, and of which they become a part.

Clearly, thinking about heritage as a verb has enabled a move away from any idea of heritage as defined by fixity and stasis, and towards a conceptualisation of heritage as produced through social interactions, debates, discussions and decisions. Yet, it is also the case in the quotes used earlier that quite a lot of varying and quite different types of 'processes' are being described. For example, we have: the process by which Historic England list a building or the United Nations Educational, Scientific, and Cultural Organization (UNESCO) decide to add a site to their World Heritage list; the processes by which museums decide to accession something into their collections; the process of aboriginal women speaking about places that matter to them; a parade of mining banners; and a performance for a tourist crowd. They are all processes, but the questions that clearly arise from the critical space opened by thinking heritage-as-process are: 'How might the political dynamics of these processes be articulated?'; and, our shared concern here, 'How might we proactively craft heritage processes that are more democratic and open?'.

To draw back to the themes of this book, lurking within all heritage processes are ideas of knowledge or knowing and therefore of research. Many heritage processes rely on some notion of expertise linked to formal governance forms (the museum, the list, the schedule). In other words, knowledge, the ability to define heritage and authority in its management have often been connected. However, in contrast, what we are going to explore in this chapter are the ways in which Ceramic City Stories enact heritage as an *action-led* and *distributed* process. Crucially, the effect of actively designing spaces for *action-led* and *distributed* processes to happen is that different ideas of knowledge and governance (care, management, decision-making) also arise.

DIY Heritage Day, Minton Library: distributing knowing and the ability to do it yourself

The Minton Free Public Library and Shakespeare Institute was designed by architect Charles Lynam and built in the late 1870s on land donated by Colin Minton Campbell. The building housed a library, a museum and, in the sub-basement, a public canteen. These functions were designed to complement a school of art (still standing next door) and a public baths, originally located immediately behind both buildings. The library originally overlooked the location of the extensive Minton China Works, though this has since been demolished and a supermarket built in its place. In the 1960s, the city council took over the library and ran the town's municipal library in the building until it was relocated in 2009. For a few years, the building was used as offices by the UNISON trade union, but it then stood empty until the local authority sold it at auction in November 2014. The DIY Heritage day was enabled by a local businessman who had recently bought the library and was interested in its history and preservation.

Having heard of the work of Ceramic City Stories, the new owner of Minton Library invited Danny Callaghan to view the building and assess the condition of tiles and architectural ceramics. On the first of these visits, an exciting rediscovery was made in the sub-basement: hundreds of Minton wall tiles had been hidden for half a century behind wallpaper, paint and library fixtures. During the visit, the owner and Danny found that all four walls were clad in hundreds of tiles with decorative block print made in the 1870s. The visible tiles suggested a wide range of literary themes depicted, including Old and New Testament, Shakespeare's plays, Aesop's Fables, Tennyson's Idylls of the Kings and nursery rhymes. After further research, it was found that artwork had been undertaken by John Moyr Smith, C.O. Murray and Thomas Allen, three leading Minton artists. After further discussions with the building owner, Danny and Ceramic City Stories were invited to undertake remedial conservation work and deliver an initial public engagement programme. This led to the DIY Heritage event on 27 June 2015.

Back to the event: networks and nodes

> "Danny and I first met in a random café. I call it
> the Stoke 'Ping'! 'You've been doing something, so
> have I. Well, I never!' It happened a lot in Minton
> Library, 'Oh, haven't seen you for 20 years'." (Jan)

We opened this article by setting the scene. Now let us enter the event as it was in full swing.

In the far corner of the room, three women are working together to scrape the wallpaper off the wall to reveal another line of tiles. It is hard work. One, Helen, suddenly realises that it is a Shakespeare play tile that she is uncovering. Another, Karen, adopts a tile and even though the paste is very sticky, is determined to reveal it fully. Near the entrance, Danny lifts up a boy to have a scrape as he talks to the boy's mother. As new people come in, they look and point; some remember when they had seen the tiles in the past when it was a canteen.

Not far away, a family play with the tiles that Simon Ball, a master-tiler, has brought. They make shapes with the tiles, match colours and line the tiles up like dominos. At the same time, Simon talks to their grandfather, who had worked in The Potteries (this ceramic-producing group of towns in the English Midlands) all of his life. They also discuss how to look after similar tiles in the hallway of their family home.

Over in the tea space, a group chat. People say that they had walked past here a lot but never been in before. There is a quiet hum of conversation. Lots of people either worked in the ceramic industry or had family who had done so (including at Minton's over the road). Shared stories included different ceramic companies in other parts of the city, specific specialist jobs undertaken and turning pottery over to 'read' backstamps (makers' marks).

Then, as more and more people arrive, something starts to happen. The women who are scraping begin to share the techniques that they are developing as they go along (scrape up and down, then side to side). New people come up and ask how to get started and techniques only just learnt are passed on and then adapted and improved quickly.

People who have only just arrived ask others what this is, they say that they have just popped in after shopping at the supermarket; they are curious. Helen and Karen – who are not part of the Ceramic City Stories team and only know what they have learned that day – tell them what they know. When they do not know something, they introduce that person to Phil, Simon, Jan or Jayne. Conversations continue between individuals:

Figure 7.2: The event in action

Source: Photo © Danny Callaghan.

"I worked down the road at Spode."

"Oh, I worked there in the 1960s, when were you there?"

"I was there a bit later in the late [19]70s – I was a sponger and fettler."

"My Great Grandma was a painter at Minton's."

"My family has supplied specialist brushes to the pottery industry since the 1800s, including Minton.... I'd put money on my Great Granddad supplied the brushes that your Grandma used in the studio!"

Over the day, around 200 people come in. Some stay for 10 minutes, have a quick look around and go. Some get stuck in, either to the tile scraping or to the conversation, and stay for hours.

Reflections: what made the event work?

Almost a year after the June 2015 DIY heritage event – and after the Ceramic City Stories group had run 11 follow-up events – the group all got back together to reflect on the event. What folllows is an edited version of our conversation. We all thought that something special happened that day, so we began by asking each other the question 'What made the event work?':

> JAN: "I think it was important that we weren't in anybody's face. We left them alone. Some people wanted to sit down and chat for two hours, but if you want to come in and then go, that was fine too."
>
> PHIL: "I was surprised that some people wanted to stay for an hour or longer."
>
> DANNY: "That was the chatting. It was the mutual learning that was going on."
>
> JAN: "And if they didn't want to talk, they could just scrape and clean the tiles. You didn't have to have a role. And the roles you did have could change over the event."
>
> JAYNE: "I think this feeling would also have happened in other venues. It wasn't only having the tiles to scrape that made it work. It was as much to do with ethos as the surrounding."
>
> JAN: "We definitely weren't precious about it. We were saying: 'This is what it is. You're welcome to stay. If not, no problem'."
>
> KAREN: "I liked that the event was for adults as much as children. A lot of things you see advertised are predicated on having children with you. But at the Minton Library event, there was room for adult conversation as well as family activities. The other element that really worked was the theme. I went to a similar event in London and it was just lots of different stalls. There was no common thread. Even though there were lots of small activities in different parts of the room, your event in the library had more connection."
>
> JAN: "There was cross-fertilisation between the activities."
>
> PHIL: "We were taking people around from place to place within the room."

KAREN: "As you moved around, there was always something to hold on to in terms of how these things fit together, rather than just 'It's an open day'."

JAN: "There was a shopping list of opportunities. If what I was offering wasn't quite right, I could pass people onto someone else in one of the other areas of the room."

HELEN: "That was what I thought was very impressive about the event. I'd learn something from one of you and then I'd talk to someone else and I would pass on what I'd just learnt. If someone wanted to know something more, then I just grabbed one of you. Sometimes, a criticism of these types of events is that without structure, people who have genuine expertise and knowledge are not valued. But with this distributed way of working, you were the nodes in the network. People who did know a lot, like all of you, probably talked to a greater number of different people, whereas I probably had more intense conversations with fewer people at the margins. Yet, there was a sense of shared purpose and a sense that we were accomplishing something together."

JAN: "This whole event design was possible because, in many ways, we're not the experts. I was not trained in a certain way of doing or thinking. Because of this, the [people coming in] recognise kindred souls. It's not about 'I'm an arts graduate of this or that'; it's about sharing, learning and swapping."

PHIL: "Other events in the city tend to be more structured. It's like they are saying 'We're doing this and that's all we're doing'."

JAYNE: "There is a certain scale; some local events are big extravaganza. That's fine. But ours is different. It is more fluid because it is at a more flexible scale."

JAN: "It was their space, their library. It was not a constructed space, a heritage space. Not new and posh. It doesn't matter if you drop your cake crumbs. You are in a comfortable space for them to make the connections for you."

As the conversation developed, the group started to reflect on the issue of how to think about and conceptualise the legacy of the event:

DANNY: "My only concern was that there were a lot of near misses. It was really difficult. It was manic on that first day. It is hard to work out how to take it to that next level? We didn't record much. I think that's the next step. But we knew there was an issue there. It always feels a bit like 'Taking a photograph, takes your soul'. Instead, we focused on creating a comfortable safe space, without judgement. People just listening to and sharing stories and just giving space for those conversations to happen between people. It was really difficult not to be in people's faces. If you are, then people get self-conscious and think 'I'm not sure I really want to do this'. The things people were sharing were so valuable and so personal; it was like this mistrust, if that is valuable to you, how are you going to use it. It's the legacy of an exploitative culture. But there is something there about recording and we need to find a better way of doing it."

JAN: "The other thing is more joined-up thinking. There is lots of ping-ponging going on but does it need to be joined up?"

DANNY: "Maybe. But there was an authenticity to the event. It wasn't rarefied. There were the 'usual suspects' who are important and always make an effort to get to things, but there were a lot of people who just came from the streets close to the library, which was particularly exciting. Regardless of trying to solve some of the bigger city things from a strategic point of view, an ongoing conversation happened and relationships were forged that continue to this day. It feels like there is something alive and something very healthy that took root during that 'residency'. There are different individuals and groups doing stuff around The Potteries. But, yes, there is also always a sense of everyone not quite pulling together. I'm just not sure how much it matters."

The group discussion raised the idea that maybe the challenge was to *keep the process going* without this logic of capturing, recording and pinning down. It also raised the idea that these alchemical Pings can maybe never really be fully joined up – or maybe that the only way of joining them up was through making lots and lots of small and informal spaces for people to come to document things themselves and to find for themselves the Pings and their own networks.

DIY heritage: the principles underpinning a distributed and action-led process

Danny has been developing some of these DIY approaches for a long time. The term 'DIY' obviously has its history in the do-it-yourself movement of painting, decorating and fixing, rather than paying someone else to do the work for you. Yet, the term has been picked up and used in all sorts of creative and political contexts (eg McKay, 1998), and chimes with approaches associated with action research (for the connections between the traditions, see Burns, 2007: 50–2). In each case, there is an ethos of doing – so action itself – as well as an emphasis on taking initiative and taking responsibility rather than waiting for someone else to lead. In this sense, 'DIY' has become used politically to describe an ethos of horizontal community action, of mutual aid and of making alternatives now (Ward, 1973; Honeywell, 2011). Thinking heritage as DIY therefore seeks to value self-generating action as a way of creating extra-institutional forms to support meaning, value and conservation (Graham, 2017).

Danny's exploration of what DIY approaches mean to him – in dialogue with Helen and Karen – formed a crucial part of the work done as part of the 'How should heritage decisions be made?' project. The moment when Helen really came to understand the approach came on a trip around Stoke. Danny was explaining about a mosaic tile design set into a door well with the name 'A Allerton' inlaid. It was important to the previous shop owners, a family called the Snapes. Danny reflected on why a DIY ethos became necessary:

> "Even in terms of the local lists and certainly in terms of the conservation team, no, you are not going to get anywhere near it…. [A door well] is the last thing the conservation officers would be able to get into their field of vision when there are Grade 1 and Grade 2 buildings that they are struggling to protect. But, at the same time, it is a unique piece of ceramic.
>
> The best thing you can do is: step 1 – preserve it virtually, take a photo, then capture the stories. So, first, we've got this family – the Snapes – talking to each other. They've agreed for it to be in the public domain. It's on the Tile Trail on Historypin. Then you've got a dialogue happening locally. [As part of the Tile Trail,] we had a walkthrough and a little tour: 'Ah Snapes, I remember Snapes'…. Then I said [to the family], 'Have you talked directly to the

builders? Tell you what, if I'm that way, I'll find out about the development'. So I went and spoke to the builders.... I explained about the doorstep – told them the story about Snapes: 'Do you know the histories of mosaic production? They are all made in local bottle kilns'. They are local builders: 'Wow, makes you proud'. They've not been told to dig it up. I said: 'It's on our Potteries Tile trail'. 'Oh I'll tell my boss. Be a shame to dig it up'. You give it an alternative value. One of the guys connected with us is a master-tiler. I suggest 'Maybe we could do a restoration class'. You create a public event." (Danny)

This thinking became the DIY Heritage Manifesto.

The really crucial shift that Danny is making here is to link developing a shared sense of the significance of the door well with care for it, the micro-governance of the builders not ripping it up and people visiting it on the Potteries Tile Trail. Often, understanding the significance of heritage is seen as coming *before* formal governance mechanisms such as listing, collecting or displaying. Yet, here, they are enacted as hyper-local, informal and mutually dependent processes.

In the DIY approaches developed by Danny and by Jan, Jayne and Phil through Ceramic City Stories, heritage, research, understanding, recognition and governance are, therefore, interwoven. In the example of the A Allerton door well, there is an ongoing fuelling of interest and care. The Stoke Ping is one of finding new connections with people with shared interests but it is a Ping that – as with the door well – actively produces and sustains heritage socially and materially. This can be seen as a mutually constitutive process of creating heritage through also creating space for *its community*, the community that can then sustain it, and itself grow. This could be framed as an iterative material-social approach to conservation, nourishing the sense of material care (revealing the tiles, not ripping up the A Allerton door well) through *social* care (that people's interest is nourished and able to flourish and grow). In this way, the A Alleton door well is materially sustained as the networks both of tiles and people extends and grows.

How has DIY heritage and the 'Stoke Ping' developed since?

This thinking of heritage as networked is of particular significance in The Potteries as the area is made up of six towns and no defined 'city centre' (although consecutive regeneration plans have sought to

Figure 7.3: The DIY Heritage Manifesto

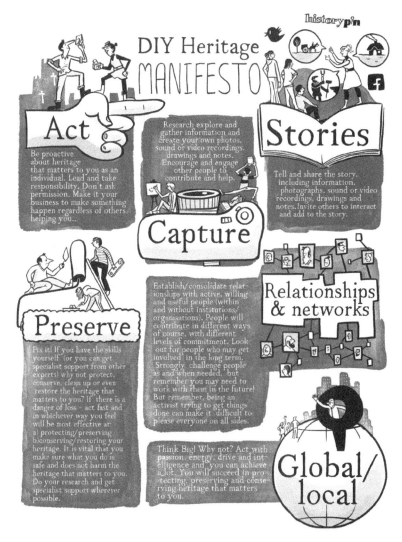

Source: Image by Fiona Blair. © Helen Graham on behalf of the 'How should heritage decisions be made?' research team.

develop Hanley, one of the towns, as the recognised city centre, albeit with only limited success). Bisected by two large A–roads and difficult to navigate, especially using public transport, people tend to visit Stoke (due to the railway station) and Hanley (for shopping) but less so the other towns. In the context of The Potteries, while the principles are more general, there is therefore something specifically necessary and resonant about taking these DIY approaches. The Stoke Ping is partly about enabling people to find the individual connections with those living in different towns and urban villages, rather than relying on a centripetal model where the aim is to 'rationalise' strategic resources (museum, library, retail and cultural offers) and, in principle, bring everyone together.

Since then, the Minton Library Residency the Ceramic City Stories group – through their work with the Fun Palaces Ambassadors programme – have extended their 'pop-up' approach. We all met up again another year on and reflected on how their approaches had developed further. We specifically explored persistent questions for both community research and community heritage: how might DIY approaches intersect with formal decision-making structures (like the local authority and the planning system) and with institutions (such as archives and museums)? What kinds of models of funding enable action-led and distributed approaches? How might DIY approaches underpin more open and participatory ways of thinking about the governance of heritage?

Formal structures

Part of being DIY is, of course, that you do do-it-*yourself*. One challenge has been how to ensure that people can do the things they want without getting tied up in formal organisation questions around undertaking formal risk assessments or ethical reviews (an issue also noted in Gilchrist, 2016: 5):

> JAYNE: "Jan and I have been working together on the Big Lunch events, which we got micro-funding to run. Jan is the person who is named on the bank account, but we have tried not to get bogged down in policies and procedures. We only have one policy and it comes down to one sentence: 'Be nice to everybody'."
>
> DANNY: "We do deliberately minimise all the bureaucracy in order to enable individuals to act. But over the past two years, it has got to the point where we had to make some fundamental decisions. We did decide to constitute Ceramic City Stories as a Community Interest Company [CIC], this means we can apply for funding and so we do need to consider public indemnity insurance, health and safety, etc. But I also try and make sure that those of you who just don't want to deal with all that don't have to. I deal with it and it frees you up

to get on with what you want to do but that does/has created some micro-culture change, for example, I get some pay for my role in relation to the Fun Palaces Ambassadors project (albeit very limited and minimal hours and pay). This hasn't rocked the boat, but there is now someone with a 'professional' (paid) role and responsibility (and related status) working alongside the other voluntary activists, and that inevitably somewhat changes the dynamic.

But I know all of you want to ratchet up. The relationship I have with you individually might just continue at a small scale and that might be the level that it always operates at. Or, there might be an ambition to take it to another level. My concern with a lot of development is it is based on the economic model of exponential growth. It's not predefined that anything has to get bigger and bigger; it can remain at turnover level. and the nature of it changes as something gets bigger. Our own low-level turnover approach has something very much in common with some of The Potteries artisans we are working with. One of our collaborators, who owns a workshop making 'biscuit' tiles (pre-glazed ceramics), doesn't want to be more than two or three people. He wants to work at a scale where he knows they can control the quality. That said, none of this has to be set in stone; there can be individual micro-initiatives, working at that level, and you can chop and change and go up and down again depending on what you are trying to do. There also needs to be an adequate base-level resource (people and finance) to sustain the key individuals involved and core activities."

It is noticeable that as Ceramic City Stories has developed, it has required people to play different roles. Danny clearly plays the role of interfacing with a wide variety of agencies and funders but other people can both draw benefits from these wider and more formal connections without it then stopping them having small-scale ideas and running with them. The Fun Palaces Ambassadors programme has offered opportunities for team members to get actively involved in the UK-wide partner relationships and strategic shared learning process.

Funding

Karen, with her HLF hat on, is always interested in the facilitating role that funding can play. One idea that came out of the 'How should heritage decisions be made?' project through Danny's contributions and the contributions of Rachel Turner of Madlab in Manchester is that of micro-funding and funding individuals rather than only constituted community groups (Callaghan and Turner, in Bashforth et al, 2015: 52). How can funding also be tailored to fit purpose and scale flexibly, and to responsibly enable action and distributed leadership?

> JAYNE: "An important reference point for me is Incredible Edibles. Their approach is 'It is your idea, run with it, we'll support you but it is your idea'. That is the model that works best. Micro-funding is essential as part of that approach."
>
> JAN: "Micro-funding has been crucial to us and the Big Lunches. We've been facilitated to do a little bit of something, and from that, it spreads and spreads and spreads."
>
> KAREN: "To link back to Danny's point about not assuming exponential growth, we know we want to move away from the idea that there is a ladder – that you start with a small grant and then apply for a larger one. What we want to do now is start small and build the relationship. We want to say that you don't have to see it as a ladder, but if you do want to, then we can support you."

The challenge here is for very small amounts of money to just be there at the right time to make a difference and to nourish the networks that are growing, rather than – which is the danger with holding public money – transforming, formalising and coming to structure what it is. In other words, the challenge is for money to enable action and distributed processes rather than co-opting, taming and directing them.

The HLF has started to pilot this in Barrow-in-Furness through a new initiative, picking up Danny and Rachel's idea that a small amount of money can have a big impact in catalysing heritage activity, and that HLF's current threshold for grants of £3,000 is too high for those getting involved for the first time with local heritage. Danny and Rachel Turner from Madlab – as well as Lianne Brigham and Richard Brigham from York Past and Present – also made the case that the requirement to be an organisation to be eligible for funding, with a constitution and a bank account, was a barrier. Karen reflected at the end of the project:

> Funders, policy-makers and development agencies all influence how people participate in making decisions about heritage, but do we really know what's needed? You have to make time to get out, see how the system is working, talk to people on the ground and ask what they would change. Through doing just that in this project I've learnt that elements of the heritage ecology are more important than money: breaking down barriers; helping people to value their own heritage and act to give it a future; building a community of interest and creating a sense of ownership in good times as well as when there is the threat of loss. Clearly funding isn't irrelevant, but as little as £50 may be all that is needed to kick-start activity and make change happen. (Bashforth et al, 2015: 8)

When Esme Ward – Head of Learning and Engagement at the Whitworth Art Gallery and Manchester Museum, University of Manchester – approached HLF with a request to host her placement for her Core Leadership programme in December 2016, it gave Karen the perfect way to explore this issue further. Esme undertook an investigation *as* an 'insider-outsider, practitioner-researcher' (Ward, 2018: 6) into the question: 'How might HLF change its funding approach to support communities to catalyse new heritage activity?' (Ward, 2018: 7). Three distinct themes emerged from discussions with a range of people, including community change-makers and leaders, practitioners, researchers, and funders: HLF should be more relational; it should focus on the local; and it should find and support powerhouse people. One of three propositions for change made by Esme is that HLF should offer smaller grants, as little as £500:

> Critically, these microgrants would be targeted at individuals (though organisations could apply) and would be place-based (hyper-local). It's people that lead change, whether as activists, gardeners, community leaders, residents.

This proposition responds to the power of people and acknowledges that sometimes, when you care, it's personal. (Ward, 2018: 55)

In the summer of 2017, as part of work on HLF's next Strategic Funding Framework, Karen was able to feed this thinking – from the Heritage Decisions project, from Esme's work and from her own reflections – into a proposal to explore the practicalities and benefits of giving grants of under £3,000 and giving grants to individuals as well as organisations. HLF decided to work in Barrow-in-Furness, part of one of its existing Priority Development Areas (places that have received considerably less funding than the UK average and experience multiple social disadvantages) and the location of some of Esme's research.

On 9 November 2017, the initiative was launched to a wide range of community groups, organisations and local people, and HLF made the first grant within an hour. Karen sees the Barrow pilot as an experimental initiative to inform future strategy:

> "HLF is regarding this work as action research. We are taking more risks than we have so far, we are prepared for unexpected outcomes and we are prepared to fail in the interests of learning. We have external evaluators and we will feed the findings directly into shaping our funding from 2019 onwards." (Karen)

Political structures and long-term change

All the people involved in Ceramic City Stories want change in the sense that they want to see good things happen. One question that is often posed to people and groups that work in small-scale and DIY ways is whether their approaches really challenge underlying political inequalities:

> DANNY: "We have to wean ourselves off the idea that bigger is best. I think that one person doing something for one hour is intrinsically valuable. It is important to value the individual and their contribution. However, there is a basic level of relatively consistent resources needed to truly sustain grass-roots-led activity. The most precious funding is that which enables, in effect, 'micro-revenue income' for individual activists and groups, for example,

this is what the Fun Palaces Ambassadors programme has offered: low-level, consistent income against some paid time and base overheads over three years (as well as a UK-wide peer-to-peer network for structured support and to actively promote ongoing shared learning opportunities)."

HELEN: "A criticism sometimes made of the horizontal approaches you take – a distributed leadership model – is that it cannot be transformative on a large scale or that it does not intersect very well with formal political structures, like local authority planning, for example. But it feels like the argument Danny makes about economics applies to politics, too: that small things are significant in themselves and that even thinking in this way creates a mental shift, a way of thinking about political change differently."

DANNY: "Stoke is a frontier town; there is always a level of 'prospecting'. The history of this place lies fundamentally in commercial competition. There was always a spirit of innovation, of creative research and development (R&D), of copying and of improving, from the level of ongoing cottage industry to those Potteries companies that are still global brands today. Some become more established and long term but the activity – the action – is all complementary. I think it is not about saying we all have to be joined up (or agree with or even all know each other), it is about finding the Pings, the meaningful moments and connections across these different types of groups, organisations and activity. It is about encouraging the local authority, education providers, cultural organisations and many other influential bodies to see the value in the activity itself and seek to foster the conditions for it. A culture that seeks to encourage experimentation and innovation (especially in relation to wide public engagement) is ultimately based on trust and relative risk. Funders need to be prepared to take a leap of faith in relation to new investments (albeit with relatively very small/ring-fenced amounts of R&D funding) in individual activists and small activist groupings, rather than simply pour more money into the more established cultural organisations who are increasingly focused on/

adept at navigating the partnership politics and existing grant application forms."

JAN: "There's nothing revolutionary about it – what we're doing is not unusual, using networks and passing information and people round. Yet, maybe, what is different is we really value this as our way of working together and see change happening in lots of small ways that we notice and value."

These DIY approaches also challenge ideas of political change by shifting the scale from local authority and formal decision-making to the kind of change that happens through connections and conversations. Framed in this way, change is 'small change' (Hamdi, 2010), and making a difference is not about scaling up and top-down policy shifts, but about fostering the conditions for 'meaningful moments'.

Yet, clearly – as in the HLF example earlier – policy change can be prompted by 'Pings', and policy and funding can be geared to foster distributed, action-led 'small change' approaches:

"There is much discussion in academia of how to influence policymakers. To an outsider, 'policymaker' seems to be equated with Whitehall as if only Whitehall makes policy, invests money to bring about change and can use research to do this. HLF is a leader for heritage, investing £300 million per annum. The 'How should heritage decisions be made?' project, and particularly the conjunction of community partners with researchers, has had a direct impact on policy in the largest dedicated funder of heritage in the UK and could contribute to a significant shift in the dynamics of heritage in the future." (Karen)

Conclusion: to say research is a process and heritage is a process is just a starting point for designing collaborative community action

In this chapter, we have used the anatomy of a specific event to open up the DIY, action and distributed approaches developed by Ceramic City Stories. The Ceramic City Stories approaches are a challenge to conventional ways of thinking. Ceramic City Stories suggests: that knowledge does not necessarily need to be recorded or captured, but can simply be shared and passed on; that formal structures need to be very carefully used to enable and not constrain DIY action; that funding to support, rather than shape, activity needs to be micro and hyper-local; that action is valuable in itself and change comes through valuing and noticing lots of small DIY-type activity; and that conservation comes through building a community of care that allows things and significance to be sustained.

Crucially, all of these challenges rely on a way of thinking that values process itself. This point is often made and has perhaps become a bit of a cliché. Yet, what we have been able to show in this chapter is that the kinds of processes designed, used and enacted really matter. As our discussion about the Do-It-Yourself Heritage Day at Minton Library suggests, the group both created an event to reflect their emerging ethos and have come to articulate their ways of working together through reflecting on the events that they have run together. Ceramic City Stories has found that processes that enable people 'to run with ideas' tend to start with very porous boundaries. The group has found that DIY approaches to heritage are best enabled through events that have a strong theme but where people have space to find their own connections – where there is no pressure and where you can stay for 10 minutes or for two hours, but where any contribution you make is noticed and valued. Together, these approaches foster the conditions within which a Ping may well happen, and then more activity will, to quote Jan, 'spread and spread and spread'.

References

Bashforth, M., Benson, M., Boon, T., Brigham, L., Brigham, R., Brookfield, K., Brown P., Callaghan, D., Calvin, J., Courtney, R., Cremin, K., Furness, P., Graham, H., Hale, A., Hodgkiss, P., Lawson, J., Madgin, R., Manners, P., Robinson, D., Stanley, J., Swan, M., Timothy, J. and Turner, R. (2015) 'How should heritage decisions be made? Increasing participation from where you are?'. Available at: http://heritagedecisions.leeds.ac.uk/publications/

Bashforth, M., Benson, M., Boon, T., Brigham, L., Brigham, R., Brookfield, K., Brown, P., Callaghan, D., Calvin, J., Courtney, R., Cremin, K., Furness, P., Graham, H., Hale, A., Hodgkiss, P., Lawson, J., Madgin, R., Manners, P., Robinson, D., Stanley, J., Swan, M., Timothy, J. and Turner, R. (2017) 'Socialising heritage/socialising legacy', in K. Facer and K. Pahl (eds) *Valuing the impact of collaborative research: Theory, methods and tools*, Bristol: Policy Press.

Burns, B. (2007) *Systemic action research: A strategy for whole system change*, Bristol: The Policy Press.

Facer, K. and Enright, B. (2016) *Creating living knowledge: The Connected Communities programme, community–university partnerships and the participatory turn in the production of knowledge*, Bristol: Arts and Humanities Research Council.

Gilchrist, A. (2016) *Blending, braiding and balancing: Strategies for managing the interplay between formal and informal ways of working with communities*, The William Plowden Fellowship report, Birmingham: University of Birmingham, Third Sector Research Centre.

Graham, H. (2017) 'Horizontality: tactical politics for participation and museums', in B. Onciul, M.L. Stefano and S. Hawke (eds) *Engaging heritage: Engaging communities*, Heritage Matters, Suffolk: Boydell and Brewer.

Hamdi, N. (2010) *Small change: About the art of practice and the limits of planning in cities*, London: Earthscan.

Harvey, D.C. (2001) 'Heritage pasts and heritage presents: temporality, meaning and the scope of heritage studies', *International Journal of Heritage Studies* 7(4): 319–38.

Honeywell, C. (2011) *A British anarchist tradition: Herbert Read, Alex Comfort and Colin Ward*, London: Continuum.

Kirshenblatt Gimblett, B. (1995) 'Theorizing heritage', *Ethnomusicology* 39(3): 367–80.

Lowenthal, D. (1998) *The heritage crusade and the curse of history*, Cambridge: Cambridge University Press.

Massey, D. (1991) 'A global sense of place', *Marxism Today* 38: 24–9.

McKay, G. (ed) (1998) *DiY culture: Party and protest in nineties' Britain*, London: Verso.

Smith, L. (2006) *The uses of heritage*, London: Routledge.

Tunbridge, G. and Ashworth, J. (1996) *Dissonant heritage: The management of the past as a resource in conflict*, Chichester: Wiley.

Ward, C. (1973) *Anarchy in action*, London: Freedom Press.

Ward, E. (2018) 'The story of us: heritage and communities', HLF. Available at: www.hlf.org.uk/story-us-heritage-and-communities

EIGHT

From researching heritage to action heritage

Kimberley Marwood, Esme Cleall, Vicky Crewe,
David Forrest, Toby Pillatt, Gemma Thorpe
and Robert Johnston

Introduction

During 2012 and 2013, Researching Community Heritage (RCH) brought together community researchers in South Yorkshire and Derbyshire with a team of staff and students from the University of Sheffield to find out more about our local and regional heritage. Community and university researchers shared their expertise as both specialists in academic subjects and specialists in the places and communities where they live.[1]

A programme of workshops during the first year led to over 30 applications to the Heritage Lottery Fund's (HLF's) All Our Stories grant scheme. In many cases, the university researchers acted as advisors for these applications and the community researchers brought the ideas, inspiration and leadership. In other projects, the community and university researchers jointly devised the proposal, offering a shared intellectual and personal vision for the research.

We were delighted when 14 of the projects were offered funding by the HLF, and we devoted the second year of RCH to making these projects a success. Working together, we learned about our region and its history looking at both the fine grain of everyday lives (for instance, the pastimes and social lives of people in the Sheffield suburb of Heeley during the last hundred years) and the broader processes that were shaped by and that, in turn, shaped our communities (such as military training on Langsett Moor during the Second World War).

In this chapter, we present a few of the RCH projects in more depth, and introduce the activities of narrative, creative practice and engaged learning that were shared ways of working during the research. We reflect on how these activities engaged the participants with heritage as a creative and social process, rather than heritage as a body of immutable facts about the past. Through this attentiveness to process during RCH, we became conscious of how researching was a means of enfranchising participants, and of revealing and contesting inequalities within and beyond the projects. Inspired by Nancy Fraser's (2000) thinking on social justice and the application of her ideas in heritage studies (Waterton and Smith, 2010), we propose an 'action heritage' framework for undertaking co-produced heritage research. We began RCH with the seemingly straightforward aim of helping local community organisations find out more about their heritage. By the conclusion of RCH, we were all aware of the radical repositioning of roles engendered by co-production, and we were seeking ways to make this process fairer, more socially active and sustainable.

RCH

RCH benefited from an innovative partnership between the UK's HLF and the Arts and Humanities Research Council (AHRC). HLF supported year-long small-scale community heritage projects through its All Our Stories programme, which aimed to widen access to HLF funding and activities. Organisations were invited to apply for funding to undertake visits to historic sites, landscapes and museums, use collections such as archives and libraries, collect memories and record heritage (eg through archaeological excavations), and hold events where people could learn about, share and celebrate their heritage.

Through its Connected Communities programme, the AHRC funded higher education institutions to support the organisations applying for and delivering All Our Stories projects. At the University of Sheffield, we achieved this through a project somewhat uncreatively titled 'Researching Community Heritage'. Our primary aim with RCH was to link academic researchers with community organisations that had not previously engaged in heritage research, either due to a lack of capacity or because they thought that heritage was 'not for them'. This aim led us to work alongside communities who were underrepresented in our university and in the community heritage discourse in our region, for example, refugee groups, Hindu and Muslim women's charities, and a homeless hostel for young people. RCH involved academic researchers and students from a wide range of disciplines and at all stages in their careers, comprising archaeologists, ethnographers, historians, linguists and literature specialists, musicians, and musicologists. The All Our Stories projects also benefited from contributions by creative practitioners in film-making, photography, visual arts and music.

Figure 8.1: Images from RCH projects projected onto St Mary's Church

Note: The celebratory jamboree at the conclusion of RCH where the community and academic researchers shared the results of their projects with the wider public in Sheffield and beyond. The event was held in St Mary's Church and Community Centre, where Steve Pool projected films and images from the projects onto the exterior wall of the building.

Source: Photo © Gemma Thorpe.

A rewarding diversity of projects emerged from this eclectic mix of community organisations, creative practitioners and academics. For example, the Bengali Women's Support Group explored the rich musical heritage of South Yorkshire's Bangladeshi and Indian communities by collecting songs and associated reminiscences of immigrants from these communities. All Saints Catholic High School's 'Home of Football' project involved pupils investigating Sheffield's sporting history using archives, under the guidance of teachers and football historians, and recreating a traditional game of football using the Sheffield Rules from 1857. In 'Midhope at War', the Woodhead Mountain Rescue Team assembled a community archive of oral histories and documents about military training on the Langsett and Midhope moors during the Second World War. The Roundabout youth housing charity researched St Barnabas Road, which is a row of large Georgian houses that had recently been converted to provide accommodation for homeless and vulnerable young people.

In 'British Raj in the Peak District', we worked with Hindu Samaj, a Sheffield-based community group promoting Hindu faith, culture, arts and languages. The project aimed to uncover some of the shared heritage that has historically bound India and Derbyshire. We took two routes into doing this. First, we explored the use of Indian cotton in the mills that dot the Peak District and the surrounding area. Calver Mill, for example, spun Indian cotton throughout the 19th century, as well as cotton from the US, Egypt and elsewhere. Presenting the history of the East India Company, and its aggressive creation of an exploitative monopoly over Indian textile production, provides a useful supplement to the more traditional narratives of the Industrial Revolution told at Cromford, Arkwright's famous mill. Second, we looked at Edward Carpenter, the socialist writer and advocate of sexual freedoms who made his home in Millthorpe in Derbyshire. Carpenter was deeply influenced by Hindu teachings, particularly the Bhagavad-Gita, and studied Indian teachings and Eastern spirituality. He visited India and Ceylon, wrote *Adam's Peak to Elephanta* based on his travels and corresponded with key Indian thinkers, including Rabindranath Tagore and Mahatma Gandhi.

Stories matter

All Our Stories, the title of the HLF's funding programme that supported our projects, reminds us that all stories matter – not just the ones that we pore over, elevate and valorise. The stories of everyday life are essential to a deeper understanding of how we live, and they are part of our heritage.

Harrison (2015: 35) writes that stories emerge 'in dialogue among individuals, communities, practices, places, and things … assembled in the present, in a state of looking toward, and an act of taking responsibility for, the future'. How we hope and dream, how we remember, and how we forget are all enacted through narrative. Imagination and memory are formed of the stories we tell about ourselves and that we tell about others, the stories that we use to make sense of the world, to both bind knowledge and to share and communicate it.

Thinking about stories in this way suggests a commonality and a possibility for shared understanding that is, potentially, quite radical. The idea that 'everyone has a story to tell' might be re-imagined and imbued with substantial resonance if we modify it to suggest that 'everyone has a story to tell and everyone is a researcher'. 'Expertise' begins with our own stories; indeed, we are all experts in our own lives. RCH led participants to recognise that knowledge does not simply exist within the academy; everyday stories about how we live now and how we used to live are not always told in universities.

During the project at the St Barnabas Road homeless hostel, the residents used a scrapbook to record their discoveries and activities while researching the building's heritage. The outcomes of the archival researches were thin and the standard research activities (eg library visits) struggled, at times, to attract interest from the young people. The tone and engagement with the project shifted when we held a session linking the young people's personal stories with the scrapbook. This session provoked considerably greater participation and engagement from residents compared with the other activities. This could be framed as a failure since the project did not focus solely on the established heritage of the building. However, we interpret the changes in the use of the scrapbook as a productive process that represented a shift in the recognition of the residents and their stake in the project. Including personal histories in the scrapbook alongside the building's story broadened the research, gave it more obvious relevance to the participants and made their contributions more direct and accessible. This was itself dependent upon a recognition of the residents' stories as valid research within the project.

Recognising the value of stories in this way, and how the act of telling and sharing narratives might change the ways in which we produce and share knowledge, suggests an immediately more inclusive approach to research. This inclusivity should never be construed as in some way diluting academic integrity; rather, it suggests that the emotive nature of narrative as a way of knowing, a form of capital that we can all access, is ripe for exploration.

To identify with the emotional charge of narrative is to begin to utilise empathy and reflection as a form of knowledge: to read or hear a story is to imagine the story through our own lens, to think about where our stories differ or where they are united. As such, exploring the heritage of our communities through narrative anticipates a response not of passive consumption, but of active reading: meaning is formed by placing other people's stories in the context of our own life histories. As this happens, another set of stories might emerge that connects to or diverts from the original stimulus. This continues as an open-ended process of telling, reflecting and connecting that anthropologist Tim Ingold (2011: 162) likens to wayfaring through a landscape, and he regards this activity as fundamental to how knowledge is reproduced and carried on. In this sense, stories aid mutual understanding and shared recognition; they suggest a kind of fine-grained, intangible authenticity that might be harder to locate in a library book or archived record.

Creating, reflecting

What can creative practices such as visual art and music bring to heritage research? Heritage research and creative practices are often linked through the shared goal of telling stories and, on one level, they offer alternative ways of communicating heritage research to audiences who might not engage with more traditional forms of dissemination. More than that, creative practices can make us think deeper about the stories that we tell about the past. The experiences of taking part as artists, performers or audience can transform heritage into a living continuity between past and present. Creative practices can also tell 'unofficial' or painful stories about the past by conveying through images, music and drama what we cannot get across in words, and they can fill in the blanks in incomplete stories to allow us to imagine more fully what people and places were like in the past. Through all these means, we can connect with past communities in more direct and emotive ways.

During RCH, the projects harnessed the opportunities offered by creative practices to find out more about places, traditions, communities, identities, values and personal ancestries. As an example, film-maker Gemma Thorpe and university researcher Toby Pillatt produced a film in collaboration with the rural community of Mosser in Cumbria (Thorpe and Pillatt, 2013; Pillatt et al, forthcoming). Co-producing their film with local people, they used insights from Toby's PhD research into two 18th-century diaries that document the weather and its impact on people's daily lives in and around Mosser. Meanwhile, the residents of St Barnabas Road used video to document their processes of researching the hostel's Georgian building. The 'Transmitting Musical Heritage' project brought together community groups to explore cultural heritage through music, while Rotherham Youth Service's 'Portals to the Past' project invited children and young people in Rawmarsh to use their creativity and imaginations to 'enter' the past through magical portals. Even the football match played to original Sheffield Rules of 1857 by All Saints Catholic High School as part of their 'Home of Football' project was also a performance – a physical manifestation of sporting heritage, with actors and an audience.

A strength of creative practice is that it can be participatory and inclusive. It allows people of different ages and backgrounds to express their reactions to the past. Multiple voices can be heard, and these outputs can transcend cultural, economic and language barriers. For example, Shèffield Babel Songs, the film-maker Gemma Thorpe and a group of young people from Slovakia, now living in Page Hall in Sheffield, produced a film supported by RCH exploring the cultural and musical traditions within the Roma community in Sheffield (Pacan et al, 2014). Page Hall has been the subject of national debates regarding community integration and tensions between residents. By incorporating stories and oral histories (as used in RCH) and ethno-musicological methods of collecting music and lyrics (inspired by 'Transmitting Musical Heritage'; see Ball et al, Chapter Two in this volume), the film presented a quite different, uplifting and poignant representation of the Roma and Page Hall.

Through the creative work in RCH, we also explored ways in which film, photography and writing formed part of the research process. In some projects, artists' work was central to the process of discovery, contributing to the research itself and providing the opportunity to reflect on findings and pose new questions. An artwork can be much more than simply a record of 'what we did' at the end of a project. In 'Portals to the Past', primary-age children (10–11 years old) in Rawmarsh, Rotherham, began their exploration of the past by literally stepping through a portal built from timber by the project's artist, Steve Pool (Pool, 2013). By doing so, the children were transported back in time to when and where they wanted to research. The central premise of the project, designed in collaboration with Rotherham Youth Service, was to introduce children to the imaginative possibilities of history. As Steve Pool put it: 'the portal grew from the idea that the past wasn't fixed. The idea of history was kind of under question because we weren't looking for reality, we were looking for the idea of time travelling' (Johnston and Marwood, 2017: 822).

In 'Social Life in Heeley and Thereabouts', the Heeley History Workshop used their All Our Stories project to research the recreational life of residents in Heeley, a district in Sheffield, from the 1920s to the present. They used images, memories and stories to chart the way people socialised, formed relationships in the community and shared their time with others. They recovered memories of church life, Boys' and Girls' Brigades, and street parties using photographs, documents and oral histories. Much of the project's expertise lay with the Heeley History Workshop, while the university brought academic researchers, students to help with digital recording and a film-maker. Rather than documenting the outcomes of the group's research, the film-maker, Gemma Thorpe, collected images and audio recordings of the group talking about the process of researching. The film stimulated a reflection on the character of the 'social fellowship' that emerges through participation in the research (Heeley History Workshop and Thorpe, 2013). For instance, the group's Chair, Lilian Haywood, explained that participants return to the group for two reasons: 'because they enjoy the social contact'; and 'because they are interested in what we are finding and that they might have a link with more of the research that somebody might be doing' (Johnston and Marwood, 2017: 824). This sentiment was echoed in the film by another of the group, Sid. In addition to sharing his memories of Heeley, Sid said that he also comes for the 'company'. Through their research into Heeley's past, the group found connections with one another and, through these connections, made and reproduced their community in the present. The film was key in bringing this social fellowship to the surface.

Engaged learning

The community of researchers participating in 'Social Life in Heeley and Thereabouts' extended from the residents of Heeley to include undergraduate and postgraduate students from the university's archaeology, history and English departments. These students had diverse skills and participated both as volunteers and within accredited courses. Their experiences of community heritage research are also important to understand.

'Engaged learning' (a term used at the University of Sheffield for education that involves engaging with external communities and organisations) (Stone and Woof, 2015) offers opportunities for

Figure 8.2: Members of Heeley History Group discussing their project

Note: In Gemma Thorpe's film about Heeley History Workshop, members of the group described how their 'social fellowship' was born out of the connections they discovered with one another and with Heeley during their research.

Source: Photo © Gemma Thorpe.

students to share their academic knowledge, learn useful skills through 'real-world' experience and make an impact in the places where they live. This form of education is not the easy option. However, the hard work, risks and challenges bring rewards. Students presented overwhelmingly positive reflections on their experiences of working on All Our Stories projects. They highlighted the value of working with diverse groups of people 'outside the bubble' of the university, feeling like research can make a difference, seeing heritage from a different perspective and learning from the places and people where they live. The students' stories show that researching and learning together takes us on surprising journeys.

There is a link between the students' experiences on RCH and the pedagogy of place-based education, which 'engages learners experientially "in", "about" and "for" the places where they live' (Harrison, S., 2010: 1). It celebrates the complex layers of places and the connections between self, community and place, and it seeks to counteract education that is instrumental (designed to achieve a specific skill or knowledge), concerned with abstract concepts and processes, and that perpetuates a capitalist agenda of 'learn to earn' (McInerney et al, 2011). As three of the undergraduate students on placements with Heeley History Workshop observed: "they have taught me a lot about the area in a way that is far more personal and engaging than a textbook" (undergraduate, archaeology); "as an international student, it has been a very eye-opening and invaluable experience learning about community heritage in a different country" (undergraduate, Study Abroad Programme); and "I have learned so much about Heeley, but also about the city as a whole, which has made me feel more at home in Sheffield" (undergraduate, English literature).

Engaged learning also seeks to connect local experiences with broader social, cultural and political structures: '"place" is a lens through which young people begin to make sense of themselves and their surroundings' (McInerney et al, 2011: 5). Two of the students supporting 'British Raj in the Peak District' reflected on this connection between the local and global: "working on this project allowed me to both develop my skills as a historian whilst also seeing how people relate to history in the wider world" (undergraduate, history); and "as a researcher interested in the history of empire and of working people and their everyday lives, I was keen to get involved with a global history project that was grounded in local experiences" (PhD researcher, history).

The genealogy of engaged learning can be traced to key proponents of experiential learning, notably, philosopher John Dewey. It enables students to recognise and challenge the conditions that act upon the world, the places they inhabit and themselves. In this formulation, it explicitly and substantially draws from the critical pedagogies of Paulo Freire, Henry Giroux and others, where education reveals social, political and economic contradictions and empowers learners to act and transform their worlds (Freire, 1995: 17). This perspective was voiced by one of the PhD researchers participating in the 'Portals to the Past' project:

> "Using these texts [of local author Arthur Eaglestone] with young people in Rotherham schools … I have appreciated having my notions of knowledge and expertise challenged and found of great benefit discussing what is of relevance or can empower young people who are, and have been historically, put in a socio-economic and culturally deficit position." (PhD researcher, English language)

Engaged learning acknowledges that the boundaries between universities and the wider world are fragile, illusory or contrived. It creates open and unpredictable spaces for learning, which can be difficult and uncomfortable to inhabit but offer fundamentally different experiences to most other forms of learning. Students and staff involved in RCH appreciated the diversity of the ways of learning that they found among the communities that they worked with.

Action heritage

In this chapter, we have reviewed three themes that connect the activities within RCH: the value of stories and storying; the contributions of creative practice; and the setting that community heritage research provides for engaged learning. To conclude, reflecting on our experiences working on the RCH projects, we observed that heritage research, as a practice, forms and transforms people and communities. By this, we mean that aside from the formal results of research – the outputs of writing, exhibitions, artworks and so on – the practices and processes of researching are transformative in themselves. They have social and cultural impact around themes of cohesion, participation, social justice, community voice and identity. This is evidenced in the ways that telling stories, notably, the personal stories of the residents at St Barnabas Road hostel, proved critical in empowering and engaging the young people in the project. It was through researching that members of the Heeley History Workshop developed their 'social fellowship' and shaped the future of their community. Learning in places and communities gave students and university staff fresh and unpredictable perspectives on their local and wider worlds.

In a recent article, we proposed a theoretical framework for co-produced heritage research, which we termed 'action heritage' (Johnston and Marwood, 2017). If researching is active in shaping communities, then we should focus on the process and implications of this action as much as, if not more than, the outcomes. We identified four vectors to the action heritage framework: undisciplinary research; active rather than activist; with parity of participation; and that is sustainable and sustained.

A key strength of RCH was its undisciplinary character. The academic researchers were a multidisciplinary team representing subjects in the humanities and social sciences: anthropology, archaeology, history, language, literature and musicology. The projects brought us to interdisciplinary spaces and profitable collaborations with one another: an art historian working alongside a linguist; an ethnographer researching with musicians. By comparison, the community-based researchers approached questions and evidence with much weaker, if any, disciplinary claims. The community researchers and their projects were undisciplinary (*indisciplinaire*) – a category within the taxonomy proposed by Ayuko Sedooka and colleagues (2015: 375–6). While Sedooka et al place an undisciplined identity (a researcher who does not affiliate strongly with any established academic field) as a rarity at the margins of academic practice, we recognise this positioning as both commonplace and positive in the context of community-based heritage research. The community-based researchers we worked alongside did not ordinarily place sources in different figurative boxes – personal memories, oral history, architecture, industrial archaeology – nor did they compartmentalise and rank methods of inquiry according to their disciplinary origins or their perceived objectivity. We would suggest that the broad scope of the term 'heritage' and its roots in everyday life (the inheritance an 'ordinary' person may receive, not just that of the elite) has a powerful role in recognising the validity of this undisciplinary position and enabling the variety of activity that constitutes research within community heritage projects.

The second vector of the action heritage framework is the privileging of process over outcomes in heritage research. Recognising the transformative experiences of researching brings a responsibility to reflect upon the inequalities inherent in the process, and to self-consciously work in more socially just ways. If heritage can be both a condition of social action and a form of social action (Harrison, R., 2010: 245), then it is a small step from recognising heritage as social action to specifically directing that action towards social justice (eg Newman and Mclean, 1998; Byrne, 2008; Sandell and Nightingale, 2013). Indeed, it has been argued that there is a moral imperative to address issues of economic and social inequality through heritage activities. For example, retrieving and celebrating working-class heritage is 'intrinsically linked to projects of protest and social justice' because of the historical suppression and erasure of these histories (Smith et al, 2011: 13). Such political activism is intrinsic to the application of various strands of participatory research in archaeology, museums and heritage more widely (eg Atalay, 2012; McGhee, 2012). These research models foreground the research process as a means of 'generating knowledge that is both valid and vital to the well-being of individuals, communities, and for the promotion of larger-scale democratic social change' (Brydon-Miller et al, 2003: 11). While these are important inspirations, we experienced more diverse interests and priorities within the RCH All Our Stories projects. In our case, research was active rather than activist. The projects did not work towards achieving wider, large-scale social change – in other words, activist. However, they did attempt to undertake research about heritage in ways that recognised and sought to redress inequalities within the research process.

The third vector of our framework provides a theoretical basis for working in more socially just ways: a dispersed and redistributive model of research practice. This model aspires to parity of participation in research using Nancy Fraser's theories about recognition, redistribution and social justice (eg Fraser, 2000; Waterton and Smith, 2010). Fraser argues that social justice is achieved by enabling full participation through equality of both status and access to resources. This involves recognising the expertise that lies within communities and ensuring that the resources for research are fairly distributed to enable more equal opportunities to participate. The St Barnabas Road project, discussed earlier, provides an example of what parity in recognition and redistribution can mean in practice. When the emphasis in the scrapbook changed from recording the history of the hostel building to recording the residents' personal histories, the research became directly relevant to the participants and made their contributions more direct and accessible. This was dependent upon recognising the residents' stories as valid research within the project. The changing status of the scrapbook also enabled the redistribution of a resource – the hostel's archive – from the Roundabout charity to the residents. Reflecting on this change, one of the youth workers at the hostel commented on the way in which the scrapbook differed from the residents' digital files held at the hostel by being 'tangible' and something that the residents produced themselves (Johnston and Marwood, 2017). The scrapbook led to a shift in the project's objectives (away from the building and towards the personal histories of the residents), increased parity in the roles and status of the participants within the project, and changed the character of engagement.

The fourth and foundational vector of action heritage is being sustainable and sustained. The durations of the RCH projects we reviewed in this chapter were limited to 12 months by funding and the consequent availability of staff in the partner organisations and the university. This made it difficult for us to achieve or to trace long-term legacies from the research. Ours is not an isolated experience (eg Atalay, 2012: 128–66). In their review of the AHRC Connected Communities programme, Keri Facer and Bryony Enright (2016: 158) proposed that time is considered as 'critical infrastructure' for collaborative research: 'time is to collaborative research what a supercomputer is to big data'. This time can be 'bought' through grants and the redistribution of universities' and other institutions' funding. However, time can also be created through a loosening of the regulatory frameworks that monitor and influence researchers' practices. Such freedoms bring responsibilities for researchers, within and outside the academy, which, in turn, foster greater independence and potential for activism. These may be the conditions in which action heritage has more potential to flourish.

RCH began in 2012 with the relatively straightforward aim of linking community and university-based researchers so that they could collaborate on All Our Stories projects. The subsequent melange of activities, from archaeological surveys on Sheffield's moorlands to newly commissioned Creole music, led to some radical repositioning of the community participants as researchers and the academic researchers as participants. Action heritage is our attempt to distil this repositioning into a framework that can be applied widely and purposefully to achieve social justice through sustained participation in research.

Note

[1]   RCH comprised a wide network of researchers in both academic and community settings. They all contributed in various ways to the ideas and experiences we discuss in this chapter. The university-based researchers on our project were funded by the Arts and Humanities Research Council's Connected Communities programme (grants AH/J013498/1 and AH/K007769/1). The community-based researchers were supported by the Heritage Lottery Fund. We are also grateful for additional support from the University of Sheffield's Arts Enterprise initiative.

References

Atalay, S. (2012) *Community-based archeology: Research with, by and for indigenous and local communities*, Berkeley, CA: University of California Press.

Brydon-Miller, M., Greenwood, D. and Maguire, P. (2003) 'Why action research?', *Action Research* 1(1): 9–28.

Byrne, D. (2008) 'Heritage as social action', in G. Fairclough, R. Harrison, J. Schofield and J.H. Jameson Jr (eds) *The heritage reader*, London: Routledge, pp 209–18.

Facer, K. and Enright, B. (2016) *Creating living knowledge: The Connected Communities programme, community–university relationships and the participatory turn in the production of knowledge*, Bristol: University of Bristol/AHRC Connected Communities.

Fraser, N. (2000) 'Rethinking recognition', *New Left Review* 3(May–June): 107–20.

Freire, P. (1995) *Pedagogy of the oppressed*, New York, NY: Continuum.

Harrison, R. (2010) 'Heritage as social action', in S. West (ed) *Understanding heritage in practice*, Manchester: Manchester University Press, pp 240–76.

Harrison, R. (2015) 'Beyond "natural" and "cultural" heritage: toward an ontological politics of heritage in the age of Anthropocene', *Heritage and Society* 8(1): 24–42.

Harrison, S. (2010) 'Place-based education and a participative pedagogy', UHI Centre for Remote and Rural Studies.

Heeley History Workshop and Thorpe, G. (2013) 'Heeley history'. Available at: https://youtu.be/Frwi-orjkEg

Ingold, T. (2011) *Being alive*, London: Routledge.

Johnston, R. and Marwood, K. (2017) 'Action heritage: research, communities, social justice', *International Journal of Heritage Studies* 23(9): 816–31.

McGhee, F.L. (2012) 'Participatory action research and archaeology', in R. Skeates, C. McDavid and J. Carman (eds) *The Oxford handbook of public archaeology*, Oxford: Oxford University Press, pp 213–29.

McInerney, P., Smyth, J. and Down, B. (2011) '"Coming to a place near you?" The politics and possibilities of a critical pedagogy of place-based education', *Asia-Pacific Journal of Teacher Education* 39(1): 3–16.

Newman, A. and McLean, F. (1998) 'Heritage builds communities: the application of heritage resources to the problems of social exclusion', *International Journal of Heritage Studies* 4(3/4): 143–53.

Pacan, M., Sandor, M., Thorpe, G., Sheffield Babelsongs and Marwood, K. (2014) 'Roma stories'. Available at: https://youtu.be/_tY4VuERQZI

Pillatt, T., Thorpe, G., Johnston, R. and Marwood, K. (forthcoming) 'A break in the clouds: connecting community experiences in Mosser, Cumbria', *Journal of Contemporary Archaeology*.

Pool, S. (2013) 'Portals to the past'. Available at: https://youtu.be/IWC41_D_w9o

Sandell, R. and Nightingale, E. (eds) (2013) *Museums, equality and social justice*, London: Routledge.

Sedooka, A., Steffen, G., Paulsen, T. and Darbellay, F. (2015) 'Paradoxe identitaire et interdisciplinarité: un regard sur les identités disciplinaires des chercheurs', *Natures Sciences Sociétés* 23: 367–77.

Smith, L., Shackel, P. and Campbell, G. (2011) 'Introduction: class still matters', in L. Smith, P. Shackel and G. Campbell (eds) *Heritage, labour and the working classes*, Abingdon: Routledge, pp 1–16.

Stone, B. and Woof, I. (eds) (2015) *Engaged learning Sheffield: co-production and community in education at the University of Sheffield*, Sheffield: University of Sheffield. Available at: www.sheffield.ac.uk/staff/learning-teaching/our-approach/current/engaged

Thorpe, G. and Pillatt, T. (2013) 'A break in the clouds'. Available at: https://vimeo.com/gemmathorpe/abreakintheclouds

Waterton, E. and Smith, L. (2010) 'The recognition and misrecognition of community heritage', *International Journal of Heritage Studies* 16(1/2): 4–15.

NINE

Co-productive research in a primary school environment: unearthing the past of Keig

Elizabeth Curtis, Jane Murison and Colin Shepherd

Introduction

In the Introduction to this book, Vergunst and Graham argue that heritage is 'about relationships created through inquiry, between past, present and future, between people, and between people and things'. Here, we explore how this definition of heritage challenges attitudes and beliefs in relation to what school is for and the nature of curricula. Archaeology in the school-based community opens up possibilities for learning beyond the limitations of a content-driven model of learning. This chapter also considers the impact of the historical investigations carried out by children as heritage interpretation in the wider community.

We present a contextualised case study of work carried out in a small rural primary school in North-East Scotland. This work saw a community-based landscape researcher's commitment to the full engagement of non-experts in the planning, investigation and dissemination of landscape research being taken up by a head teacher, her staff and pupils. Participants recognised and valued the strength of putting children in charge of shaping what and how they learn. The experiences of all concerned resonate with Margaret Carr's (2005: 42) argument that 'education is an ontological project' because it is not just knowledge and skills that are generated, but also 'shifts and developments in identity'.

Elsewhere in this book, discussion of community and co-produced heritage research have problematised issues of power in relation to knowledge, skills, decision-making and voice. In this chapter, ways of knowing through co-production and enskilment are explored through the narrative of a school investigating the history of their village with the support of landscape researcher Colin Shepherd, a head teacher, Jane Murison, along with her staff and pupils at Keig Primary School, and a lecturer from a School of Education, Liz Curtis. Using this material, we argue that the Scottish Curriculum for Excellence (CfE) (Scottish Executive, 2004) is brought into being as a dynamic lived experience for all participants.

The ongoing nature of the work discussed here is significant. It began in 2011 as an element of the 'Bennachie Landscapes Project' (see Vergunst et al, Chapter One, this volume) that grew to incorporate a series of Arts and Humanities Research Council (AHRC) Connected Communities projects. These explored the nature as well as practice of work co-produced by the Bailies of Bennachie community group and academics from the University of Aberdeen.

Social relations thus play a key role in understanding the way in which the work has unfolded. A previous paper on this project highlighted how learning in schools is both situated and socially produced, and that the context in which learning happens matters (Curtis, 2015). Ingold's idea of dwelling, further developed as 'meshwork' (Ingold, 2000, 2011), and Bourdieu's notion of habitus (Bourdieu, 1977) provide a particular perspective from which to reflect on the experience of participation and on the unfolding nature of learning. Learning, when viewed as dwelling, is part of the everyday process of living in the world, of being in places with people and doing things together. As archaeologist Chris Tilley (2004: 25) has argued: 'places gather together persons, memories, structures, histories, myths and symbols'. From this perspective, learning is not about the transmission and receipt of a preformed standardised knowledge content within the formalities of the classroom, but rather about a dynamic co-production of knowing and feeling through the immediacy and directness of encounters with people, objects, earth, weather and documents (Ingold, 2011). This kind of practical knowledge is very relevant to discussions of heritage. Laurajane Smith (2006) has questioned the understanding of heritage as a noun, which encourages the past to be taken at face value as presented by others. Instead, Smith argues that a heritage is best thought of as a verb, something that is enacted through sets of practices. From this point of view, the past is brought into being through the actions and thoughts of people in the present in relation to their engagement with places, artefacts, documents and stories of the past; it is not a given thing, but a temporal process.

From the perspective of the landscape researcher and head teacher, the Keig project was designed to evaluate the practicality of using the principles of co-productive archaeological research to support children in leading their own historical investigation, while relating to the design principles and learning outcomes and experiences in the CfE

(Scottish Executive, 2004). Specifically, the Keig project set out to explore whether:

- children aged between five and 12 years could generate new and original historical research;
- such research carried out within the school might leach out into the wider community and generate greater concern for local cultural heritage;
- such research could achieve genuine educational benefits for the children involved; and
- such research might engender greater social cohesion within a rural community.

Curriculum and pedagogy

Between 2004 and 2008, the Scottish Government launched the 'Curriculum for Excellence (3–18)' into all state primary and secondary schools in Scotland (Scottish Executive, 2004). During the time between its launch and introduction into schools, the Scottish Executive and later Scottish Government issued a series of underpinning guidance through five 'Building the curriculum' documents (2006–11), which set out and explained the new architecture for learning and teaching for all of the subject areas of the curriculum. In their characterisation of the CfE, Priestly and Humes (2010) have argued that a close reading of the underlying architecture of this curriculum highlights a tension between core elements of the curriculum that actively encourage and support the development of a process-based and child-centred approach to learning within a broad framework, and those elements of the curriculum that are more instrumental in nature and outcomes based. In either reading of the curriculum, there is scope for both teacher and pupil to create the contexts in which they learn, and specifically in relation to this chapter, there are specific aims for children that are closely met through the experience of working with an archaeologist and researching the past of the area in which the school is located. What is key to the richness of learning discussed in this chapter is that the head teacher of the school in this project is committed to the idea of 'Curriculum as process and education as development' (Priestly and Humes, 2010: 346).

In the first of the 'Building the curriculum' documents, the then Scottish Executive (2006: 38) stated that 'It is important for children and young people to understand the place where they live and the heritage of their family and community'. How school leaders understand and facilitate the ways in which children explore and interpret the 'heritage of their families and community' (Scottish Executive, 2006: 38) is highlighted by Jane's account of how she and her school came to be working with Colin:

> "Our gut feeling was this is something really exciting, a great opportunity to work with an expert on real-life research, and we thought the historical and practical archaeology would be the main learning outcomes of the project. We really had to have a bit of faith as it was a very open-ended learning experience and steep learning curve for us all. We all had to be prepared to 'suck it and see' as we couldn't predict the Curriculum for Excellence Experiences and Outcomes covered in this learning." (Jane)

This focus on children and young people's understanding of the places in which they live and the heritage and culture that shape their experiences of family and community emphasises the role of the curriculum as a means of providing a platform from which children can play an active part in shaping their identity. Writing in the context of the New Zealand national curriculum, Te Whariki, Carr points to the way in which identity is embedded within it, and, in particular, the nation's aspiration for early years children that they have the opportunity to 'grow up … secure in their sense of belonging and in the knowledge that they make a valued contribution to society' (NZ Ministry of Education, 1996: 9, cited by Carr, 2005: 42).

Similarly, in 'Building the curriculum 3', the Scottish Government (2008: 20) actively encouraged schools to work in partnership with people and organisations from the wider community and to have the 'freedom to think imaginatively about how the experiences and outcomes might be organised and planned for in creative ways which encourage deep, sustained learning and which meet the needs of their children and young people'. This invitation to think imaginatively and creatively in relation to how and what children learn is reflected in Jane's reaction to Colin's invitation to develop a child-led archaeological project next to her school:

> "Keig School became involved in this Bennachie Landscapes Project when a wee voice popped up and said 'Remember me from a former life?'. That was Colin – archaeologist and Dad of a former pupil at another school. Inspired by the thought of a trowel, memories of *Time Team* and potential

headlines in the *Aberdeen Press and Journal* of 'Keig School Roman vase fetches £1 million in auction', the whole Keig School team – P1–P7 pupils, teachers, PSAs [Pupil Support Assistants] and parents – climbed on board." (Jane)

Unearthing the past at Keig

In the following part of this chapter, we describe the process of supporting children to investigate the archaeology of a small area of woodland near to their school. Research carried out on *'place-responsive pedagogy'* (Mannion et al, 2013) is relevant here, which is also underpinned by Tim Ingold's (2000) notion of dwelling, where the natural and cultural are intermingled and co-emergent, and from the perspective of 'curriculum-making … as a lived experience' (Mannion et al, 2013: 794). Curriculum-making is a key part of understanding the process through which Jane, Colin and Liz worked alongside each other and pupils and staff to design frameworks through which children could take ownership of the archaeological and historical investigation. Mannion et al (2013: 795) identify that 'significant adults', including teachers and other community members, can 'play a vital role in longer-term effects on proenvironmental behaviour'. This is borne out by the experiences of children carrying out archaeological investigations in the same woodland area that they regularly went to for forest school activities.

Elsewhere, Curtis (2015), following Cooper (1995), has argued for the importance of embodied learning in relation to making sense of time. In this project, learning involves understanding the world from a different, archaeological perspective through working alongside Colin and learning the skills of trowelling back the soil and collecting, cleaning, identifying, sorting and interpreting finds. Outdoor learning plays a regular part in the lives of all of the children and staff at Jane's school. All children spend at least one morning a week learning out of doors at all times of year and in all weathers. As a small school in a rural location, the children are fortunate to have an extended area of woodland within easy walking distance of the school. This commitment to regular and sustained outdoor learning could be seen to fall into what by Beames and Ross (2010) have characterised as 'outdoor journey pedagogies'. Central to these pedagogies is a shared responsibility for the planning and carrying out of learning between teachers, pupils and other adults. They identify three phases of negotiation between children and teachers: questioning, researching and sharing (Beames and Ross, 2010). These three phases are also central to Jane's conceptualisation of curriculum-as-process and of Colin's commitment to participatory archaeology in the community. Additionally, Jane's autonomy as head teacher of a small school played a key role in the way in which she created the time and space needed within the children's school week to work directly with Colin.

Fieldwork

Initial scoping had recognised archaeological features within a short walk (approximately 200m) of the school. An initial 'grid' of 10m × 10m was laid out and the children, with teachers and parent helpers, proceeded to excavate the site, layer by layer. Any finds were bagged and XY coordinates noted with reference to the site grid. The children were responsible for plotting, labelling and bagging their own finds. These were later cleaned, analysed and recorded on a University of Aberdeen pro forma finds sheet by the children. They worked to recognised university archaeological research standards.

In tandem with this work, groups of three or four pupils were taken out in turn to survey other archaeological features within the wood. This involved laying out linear baselines using only ranging poles and tapes and setting out survey grids along the baselines. This was done using tapes and Pythagoras' 3–4–5 theorem. The pupils then plotted in the features on drafting film over a grid, recording the features using topographical symbols, such as hachures for slopes.

All age groups were able to engage in most of the work, though the more physical excavation did prove difficult for the primary ones and twos. However, they did not want to be left out, so special, shorter periods were factored in to introduce them to the practice. It was quite eye-opening (as well as eye-watering) to observe primary ones and twos analysing pottery fragments and deciding on vessel type (flatware, hollow-ware, cup, teapot, etc), fabric (redware, whiteware, stoneware, etc) and surface treatment (glazed, unglazed, creamware, pearlware, sponge-applied, hand-painted, transfer-printed, etc). This was done as a class discussion with a show of hands to vote on each aspect of each piece of pot. It was time-consuming but very rewarding to hear them, at a later date, telling their parents about the finds in such detail. The older ones worked in pairs to write the descriptions and fill in the finds record sheets.

It is interesting to note that at the end of the last school year, the pupils who were leaving had experienced weekly archaeology and landscape studies for their entire seven years of primary school and probably left with more practical experience than most university

Figure 9.1: Keig Primary School pupils at work

Source: Photo © Elizabeth Curtis.

graduates in archaeology. On a site visit to one of the excavations run as part of the Bennachie Landscapes Project, the older ones were able to consider the site in the light of their own hands-on experience and were able to discuss the stratigraphic relationships within the site, consider the fabrics of some of the finds with a discerning eye and comment upon the archaeological strategies employed.

Of particular interest was the line of a former lade (artificial watercourse) leading from the Keig Burn to a sudden drop overlooking a further minor watercourse. This suggested a third, previously unknown, mill site laying between the Upper and Lower Corn Mills of Keig. The aim of this part of the project was to discover more about the construction and date of this mill and to try to understand how it functioned within its modified riverine landscape. The project succeeded in demonstrating that this had been a short-lived sawmill dating to the first two decades of the 19th century and was possibly constructed to prepare timber from the estate for the reconstruction of Castle Forbes at that time. The lade fed the mill wheel, which drove the saw. The latter was housed in a timber building constructed on large stones straddling the secondary watercourse. This was used to clear away the sawdust from the mill into the Keig Burn.

Children leading the way into the past

At all stages of the children's historical enquiry with Colin, they were given the opportunity to work with primary source material, including historical documents and fieldwork. They had real opportunities to pose informed questions and to offer informed analysis of what they found. In the later stages of their work, the children worked with staff from the University Museum and Liz to curate their own exhibition of their findings for parents and members of the local community during the parents' evening. This also resonates with research carried out in Sweden of high-school teachers' perceptions of the potential of learning outdoors (Fägerstam, 2014). Fägerstam (2014: 57) contextualises her study within the concept of 'Uteskole'. Drawing from Jordet (2007), she points to the underlying principle that characterises learning outdoors within the context of Uteskole: that 'the school surroundings are [not only] used as a *learning arena* but also as a *source of knowledge*' (Jordet, 2007: 57; emphasis in original). Head teacher Jane summarised her and the children's experience of this:

> "The field visits and digs went very well, although in abysmal weather conditions, and we dug up an extraordinary amount of 'treasure'. 'Colin come and see this!' became the cry and Colin spent his time dashing from find to find sharing his enthusiasm and excitement. New skills in archaeological excavation, working as a team (without standing on anyone else's cleared patch of ground!) and careful examination of the tiniest find to check for significance were only some of the many skills learned." (Jane)

The experience of children and adults of direct encounters with the past through the physical process of surveying and subsequently excavating in the woodland resonates with Mannion et al's notion of the intermingling of culture and nature as part of place-responsive pedagogies. Jane reflects on the way in which the weekly experience of going to the dig site with Colin and working in abysmal weather points to the children's resilience. This was borne out by one of the six-year-old children who, on reflecting on a photograph of her and her classmates digging out 'treasures' from the ground, described to Liz how she:

liked drawing and copying the pottery. I enjoyed digging, cos we found lots of pottery but I didn't like the rain but the next time we did it, it was sunny. I learned how it was for people in the old days. (Curtis, 2015: 46)

The social also plays a key role in relation to Carr's idea of identity building. When the children were carrying out practical archaeological work, such as surveying or excavating and sorting finds, so were the other adults. When children were digging in all weathers, so were their head teacher, parent volunteers and Colin and Liz. This experience affords the possibility for children of seeing familiar people in unfamiliar learning roles and learning new skills from Colin, together with adults. Working with Colin as part of a team and learning to not stand on somebody else's cleared patch of ground and to carefully examine the tiniest find to check for significance were learned as archaeological practices and as part of the process of creating heritage. Jane recalls that "one of the most memorable moments was when one pupil who was determined to find something discovered a piece of what we now know as 13th-century pottery. I was not sure who was more thrilled – the child or Colin".

Jane reflected that the children were also able to put forward their own theories as to where the mill might have been based on the finding of large stones, the positioning of the lade and the finding of an extraordinary amount of old domestic finds in a large widened area of the lade – 'The Midden':

"The children were convinced this was the site of the old mill but Colin was more wary and preferred the theory of the mill being further up the bank. However, after further excavation, the pupils seem to have been proved right!" (Jane)

This reflects, as also noted in Beames and Ross (2010), the positive impact of valuing children as competent beings, as able as any of the adults to pose purposeful questions, to make informed decisions and to interpret evidence. It also clearly demonstrates why it is important that children, as shown in this chapter, are given opportunities to work with primary sources of historical evidence and to take an active role in planning and carrying out excavations, collecting and sorting evidence, and interpreting it to create their own historical narratives.

Valuing children's understanding from the field to the classroom

Jane, Colin and Liz all held a similar view with regard to respecting the findings from the archaeological work that the children carried out. This is reflected in Jane's emphasis on creating the conditions in which children can be the leaders of their own learning, Colin's emphasis on enabling the children to develop practical skills in archaeological investigations and to publish their results alongside adult archaeological reports, and Liz's use of the University of Aberdeen's Collector's Cabinet to house the pupils' exhibition (a facsimile of one made for King Gustavus Adolphus of Sweden in 1632). Through the creation of a temporary exhibition of the findings of their investigation on a school parents' evening and through the more permanent publication of their findings, the children have shared their work with their families, local community and a wider audience interested in local heritage.

As a teacher-educator specialising in history education and located at the university, Liz situated herself in the classroom as an additional teacher with the role of working alongside adults and children alike to create an exhibition of the children's investigations in the Collector's Cabinet. Later in this chapter, Colin refers to the different levels of production and presentation afforded to professionals and to schoolchildren when showing the results of their work. This is also an issue that Aberdeen University Museum needs to negotiate and the loan of the Collector's Cabinet to schools is one way of readdressing such imbalances, even if in a temporary and fleeting manner. With the loan of the Cabinet came the opportunity for the children and their teachers to visit the university and take part in a workshop on collecting for museums and creating exhibitions. Jane recalls that:

> "As part of the project, the children visited 'The Cabinet' at King's Museum in Old Aberdeen. They were clearly mesmerised by the secret compartments and hidden drawers. The cabinet, with its 75 drawers and cupboards, became a focal point and we decided to display our research, dig finds and learning in an Open Evening Exhibition for parents and the community using the Cabinet." (Jane)

As a result of their experience of being at King's Museum, the children were able to use their learning experience to create their own exhibition and put their learning into action in a real experience: real-life assessment. Jane set up the initial planning session for the

Figure 9.2: Adding materials to the Collector's Cabinet

Source: Photo © Elizabeth Curtis.

exhibition as a whole–school activity in which pupils from a mixture of year groups worked together to create a mind map of the aims and content of the Cabinet. The planning and creation of the Cabinet exhibition by the children in the school reflects the third stage of the outdoor journey pedagogy approach: 'sharing'.

Colin was aware that children's work, unlike that of professional archaeologists, is rarely illustrated by professional illustrators and that this could lead to the children's work not being valued as highly. To readdress this, Colin ensured that the results were portrayed using the same graphic software as would be used to publish a professional report. The findings of the children's research are alongside the work of adults in the publications of the Bennachie Landscapes Project, in the same format and to the same standard so that the children's work is indistinguishable to that produced by a professional archaeologist. Colin argues strongly that in its low-cost school environment, the results represent an equal research value, irrespective of the educational and social benefits.

As a result of this work, the school introduced an 'Archaeological Responsibility Group', where the pupils lead the learning for the school and report back. This group meets every second Friday and the group is made up of children who have a special interest in archaeology and have selected it as their responsibility group. Their achievements have included finishing washing, sorting and cataloguing the finds to date, and writing reports for publication (in Shepherd, 2013) and for school displays. On the non-Responsibility Group Fridays, research with the upper-stage class includes continued study of the landscape history of the surrounding area. One particularly useful primary source is the 'Barony Book of Forbes'. This court record was used to help imagine local life in the 17th century and to understand the social environment of the time. The children chose to produce a historical 'comic cartoon' based on the exploits of the people as recorded therein. Pupils considered their own family names and, although not all originate in the village, the discussions led to a better understanding of genealogy in general. Trips to the local churchyard led to the recording of gravestones and a recognition of the range of social history contained in that source. Various 'lumps and bumps' and dyke stonework were also discussed as evidence relating to the developmental change of the graveyard itself. The graveyard setting resulted in a useful discussion concerning what societies have done with their dead from Neanderthal times to the present.

The nature of inquiry that underpins the conception of heritage in this book allows for the past to become a catalyst for thinking about what will become the heritage of the future (Introduction, this volume: 3). This is reflected in what has subsequently grown out of the original archaeology project. More recently, the school has acquired a former trophy cabinet that enabled the Archaeology Responsibility Group and the new P4–P7 class to put together the first exhibits for the School Museum. Jane reflected that she had a distinct feeling of déjà vu as the current pupils replicated the intense discussions and enthusiasm of the 'Cabinet Exhibition', and was heartened that the ownership of the project was still very much the children's:

> "The discussions were very intense and the reasoning and explanations put forward highlighted to me the incredible journey we have made from the start of this project to date. The pupils were articulate, confident, creative and willing to risk putting forward their ideas. It is maybe also a reflection of our school's journey with CfE as well as archaeology." (Jane)

The trophy cabinet has now been transformed into a display case that stands in the school foyer, which doubles as the local community hall foyer. A selection of finds have been displayed in an innovative way: rather than simply utilising a 'museum-case' format, the children have treated the finds as 'art' and created small 'installations' of grouped objects while also noting their provenance.

Learning for the school

In this section, Jane reflects on the evaluations of her and her staff and pupils of what they have learned through the ongoing process of historical investigation (see Box 9.1).

Box 9.1: Jane's reflections

The archaeology project at our school has enriched the education of all the pupils far beyond learning the craft of archaeology, the local history and changes to the landscape. Pupils have used primary sources to research information, have located places on maps, have participated in archaeological digs and followed the process from surveying the site, to cataloguing and displaying their finds. The skills that they have used span the whole curriculum and have given them a real-life experience for developing their literacy and mathematical learning. All our pupils are very proud that they are unearthing the past of our village and have pride in the new discoveries that they have made about the local area.

However, they have also learned to be open-minded and creative. They have developed their natural curiosity by asking questions and leading their own learning. The impact of the project goes beyond the obvious formal learning as pupils have developed their skills in communication, cooperation and teamwork, and, of course, have been able to experience the outdoor, local environment.

It has also helped them to take responsibility for their learning and the area of the site. We see this project not as a one-off event, but as a sustainable and long-lasting enhancement to the education of the pupils at our school. This, in turn, they share with their families and the local community.

Yes, pupils, staff, parents and the community have learned more about the local area and landscape, and discovered more about the past – how people lived and the part objects played in their lives. They have discovered the fascination of finding a piece of pottery and researching the find to discover how old it is and where it came from. Yes, we learned more about museums, presenting information and putting on an exhibition. We learned more about archaeology itself, the techniques, how to know where to dig and how to research parish records.

We have all learned to be open-minded about learning, to be creative, go with the flow, allow pupils to lead the learning. However, maybe, more importantly, we have learned more about how our pupils learn, and more about how projects like these can inspire and motivate even the most reluctant learner, how learning can truly be across and through the curriculum, allowing learners to explore their learning in a safe and real situation – and also that a bit of mud and rain does no harm. So, what now? Where do we go from here?

Each year, we plan roughly where the project is heading and how we are going to achieve this. We negotiate time, groupings, ideas and plans. It is a learning experience for all of us. We have integrated archaeology into our curriculum and as part of the learning at our school. Our next steps are to include this in our school rationale and revisit the part it plays in our overall curriculum. We are hopeful for the continuation of our project for the next few years at least.

Next session, we have plans to continue surveying and excavating, continue establishing our museum, and, of course, continue finding out about the old mill at Puttachie. We might not have found a million pound Roman vase, but we have discovered the educational equivalent. What format the project takes, where our learning is going, how we learn about the past and how we continue with our excavations? Well, it is up to our pupils – it is their dig after all. What we do know is that we want it to continue as we still have a lot to learn.

Recalling the visit of one of the council's quality improvement officers (QIOs), Jane reflects on the surprise of the officer at the level of involvement and responsibility that the children between the ages of five and 12 achieved through their participation:

"We were determined to continue excavating the mill site and have planned digs every year for various groups of children. It has moved from whole–class digs to group digs as the site areas are more specific and smaller. As part of this work, pupils undertook extensive site surveying and astounded Colin Shepherd with the accuracy of the eyes of youth. One of Aberdeenshire Council's QIOs came to experience a dig for herself. Despite having to borrow wellies and socks (I did warn her it was muddy), she revelled in the experience and declared that this was what Curriculum for Excellence was all about." (Jane)

Colin writes from an archaeological perspective (see Box 9.2).

Box 9.2: Colin's perspective

As noted in the Introduction, the Keig project was designed to evaluate the practicality of using a framework based upon principles of co-productive research within a primary school setting and to help answer a range of questions. These are now briefly considered.

Can children aged between five and 12 years generate new and original historical research? The answer is clearly 'yes'. The children used the recording and analysis sheets generated by the University of Aberdeen for their archaeological research project. The site surveys have been carried out by the pupils to a remarkable degree of accuracy across a difficult woodland terrain. The results were portrayed using the same graphic software as would be used to publish a professional report. Herein lies an important caveat: children's work is often presented in a method of production accessible to themselves in their school environment. Few professional archaeologists produce their own graphics for publication. They usually rely upon third-party professionals to carry out that work. By using the same approach, the children's work is indistinguishable to that produced by a professional researcher. The main difference resides in the time required to produce the results rather than the end results themselves. In the world of paid/funded research, the timescales taken for the children's project would be untenable. In its low-cost school environment, the results represent an equal research value, irrespective of the educational and social benefits.

Does this research achieve genuine educational benefits for the children involved? The project has permitted a practical application for many, if not all, curricular subjects. Place-name analysis has resulted in assessments of Pictish, Gaelic,

Scots and Latin formative elements in the generation of local farm names. Linguistic skills have been handled. Discussion of the physics and chemistry behind radiocarbon dating was prompted by the discovery of 11th-century carbonised grain at Druminnor. Digging leads to the observation of the biological world of worms, beetles, larvae and other creepy-crawlies, and these, inevitably, engender discussion. The numerical number-crunching and mental gymnastics required to convert pounds, shillings and pence, and acres, roods and perches, to contemporary equivalents for statistical analysis clearly underlines numerical accommodation. The list could go on to cover geography, history, comparative religions (not only faith-based), politics and sociology to eventually finish up in the world of art history and graphic presentation. There are clear educational benefits.

Clearly, the situation at Keig has been helped by a community member turning up at the school on a weekly basis to help. That has provided a focus for the activities, which might otherwise have fallen victim to a wide range of other competing projects:

> "I feel a little bit like the school mascot – the school's 'resident archaeologist'! Joking aside, I advise a bit and relate a few stories but it is very much the school that makes the project decisions – and Jane makes sure that means the children, not herself and the other teachers." (Colin)

Reflecting on Jane's earlier comments in relation to her experience of the visit from her QIO and Colin's discussion of the children's capacity to significantly engage in the whole process of an archaeological investigation, including reporting on their findings, Liz writes on the wider educational significance of the Keig project (see Box 9.3).

Box 9.3: Liz's reflections

A current concern of the Scottish Government in relation to children's education is the growing attainment gap in educational outcomes, particularly in relation to literacy, numeracy, health and well-being, between the children from the most and least affluent homes in Scotland. At the time of writing, the Scottish Government (2018) has just launched the National Improvement Framework and Improvement Plan. In the words of John Swinney, MSP, Deputy First Minister and Cabinet Secretary for Education and Skills:

> Tackling inequity is at the heart of the Scottish Government's education reform agenda and there is a collective responsibility to ensure continuous improvement for children and young people.... Decisions that shape the education of children and young people will be made in classrooms, schools and establishments, by those working with learners, their parents and communities. (Scottish Government, 2018: 3)

> The drive of the National Improvement Framework to reduce educational inequalities and to 'poverty-proof' educational outcomes for children is important and vital. However, with the drive for 'continuous improvement' (Scottish Government, 2018) comes an imperative to measure children's progress against nationally agreed benchmarks, which recalls Priestly and Humes' (2010) article, discussed earlier, in relation to the tensions between the underlying principles of CfE, which encourages process-based learning, and a more metrics-based instrumental approach to learning, which sometimes accompanies the need to measure continued improvement. Through reflections on the evidence, Jane has demonstrated the children's confident development and use of a wide range of literacy and numeracy skills embedded in the archaeological work, including reading, report and label writing, talking and listening, measuring, and working with data. Likewise, the children's reflections on their experiences of learning through photo elicitation points to the ways in which they developed team-working skills and learned to negotiate, to listen to others and to exchange ideas in relation to developing their initial exhibition and latterly their school museum, all of which reflect outcomes for health and well-being.

However, the learning is not restricted to the pupils and staff in the school. Through the process of team teaching, Liz has drawn from her experiences of working alongside pupils, teachers and Colin in the creation of a new course for primary education students, 'Making History', which enables student–teachers to acquire the skills and dispositions necessary to develop similarly creative and child-led local history investigations themselves as teachers in the future.

Learning for the community

The overall aim of the Bennachie Landscapes Project is to attempt to lay down the foundations of an interdisciplinary community and university research collaboration that has the resilience to be intergenerational. There are no overarching research goals other than to explore any or all aspects of the natural and built heritage of Bennachie and its surroundings and to utilise those findings for the benefit of present and future inhabitants of the area. A number of nested projects are operating both on the hill and in the surrounding communities. The results are shared around the area in a variety of formats coordinated by the Bailies/University of Aberdeen partners. The Keig School project is important as it provides one such focus within one of the parishes abutting the ridge of Bennachie.

As noted earlier, the Keig project links to the wider one in a variety of ways. Help has been afforded by adult members of the Landscapes Fieldwork group in aiding manually difficult aspects of the digging. The wider project has enabled the school's results to be spread to a wider audience through its publications. The printing of posters has helped to present the findings within the school and in a local heritage museum. The school has, conversely, provided valuable new research results concerning its portion of Bennachie, which has helped to further the aims of the wider project. Perhaps more importantly, it has demonstrated that a school with vision can produce original research and that the pupils can become educators within the community. Education does not have to be a unidirectional, top-down process:

> "Time plays an important part in Keig's explorations. Most 'professional' research is carried out under time constraints imposed by funding limitations. At Keig, there are no time constraints, but also few cost constraints. Research can take as long or short a time as is required. Herein lies a potential strength that a 'community way of doing things' can bring to co-productive partnerships."[1] (Colin)

Another important factor has been the open-ended access to the woodlands of the Forbes Estate by the Forbes family. The estate is managed for its resources but is left open for public access. The small piece of woodland explored in the archaeological project is regularly used by almost all the children after school and at weekends. To many, it was already a well-known landscape and exploring it in more depth merely extended their own personal explorations. This is another interesting reversal. Many archaeological sites are already seen as 'special' or gain that significance as soon as something is found there. At Keig, the change has been gradual: an already well-used area simply developing further layers of meaning within the past, present and future communal landscapes.

Over the last few weeks (at the time of writing), a wooden structure has appeared in the woods. This takes the form of a timber-laced framework with woven wattlework. It has footings of stones and the whole measures barely 2m × 1m. On questioning the pupils about it, it appears that a former pupil of the school (now in secondary education) is in the process of making it. He has used the knowledge gained from his own excavations of an 18th-century structure to try his hand at his own bit of experimental archaeology. This has also been made possible because of the open-handed nature of land management on the Forbes Estate.

Is it possible to say whether the research carried out within the school might leach out into the wider community and generate greater concern for the local cultural heritage? In terms of the landscape management of the area, the Forbes family has shown great interest in the project from the start. They, along with everybody involved with the project, have been startled to find out about the complicated history lying just below the surface of a small piece of woodland on their estate. Conversations with Lord Forbes have indicated that he is now more aware of the heritage for which he feels responsible. As noted earlier, as a landowner who has time and again shown himself to be very socially responsive, it is hard to imagine that this will not impact on the way in which future landscape management decisions are made.

With respect to the wider local community, it is difficult to assess the long-term impact. Certainly, a much larger number of people within the community now know a lot more about their cultural landscape. Furthermore, for as long as the school project continues, it is hard to imagine that this continual drip of knowledge from the children will not permeate the wider social network. Were the project to finish, it is interesting to speculate how resilient any gains would be. Presumably, the historic record would remain in its updated form but it is unlikely that any experiential or methodological gains would survive. This is a situation facing all community engagements: if the social fabric of a community cannot be altered to accommodate a new way of 'doing' prior to the cessation of an enterprise, all experiential lessons are likely to be lost. Long-term, low-input, sustainable engagements, such as the Bennachie Landscapes Project hopes to engender, may offer a better means of achieving such social change than short-term, high-input, non-sustainable approaches.

The question of whether such research might engender greater social cohesion within a rural community is clearly harder to determine. The Bennachie Landscapes Project hopes to achieve this through raising awareness and pride within local communities of their own unique sets of cultural heritage. It is hoped that when these are highlighted, through various projects, and shared between communities, the differences and similarities within and between these communities can be compared, contrasted and celebrated. It has already been noted that communities work at a slow pace due to circumstances of availability of time and other factors. So, even though the project has been running for five years and many exciting results have been seen (many being of much more than local significance), it is still too early to evaluate such a question. Only a small number of projects across a massive transect of landscape have been accommodated. It is hoped that the development of low-cost, though time-consumptive, methodologies will help the sustainability of the project for long enough for genuine social change within some of the communities to occur. This has to remain, however, a vision for the future.

Conclusion

In the Introduction to this book, Vergunst and Graham refer to heritage as a mode of action, and of the practice of 'heritage' as 'relationships created through inquiry' (p 2). In this chapter, we have demonstrated how these ideas are embedded in the ways in which the Keig archaeological project unfolded. From a theoretical perspective, Ingold's notion of dwelling and Bourdieu's idea of habitus are mirrored by approaches to outdoor learning taken by Mannion et al (2013) in relation to the intermingling of nature and culture that occurs through the actions embedded in place – responsive pedagogies and Beames and Ross's (2010) journey pedagogies. Experiencing this through the combined educational and archaeological practices and those of everyday life, we demonstrate Tilley's and Ingold's observations of the enmeshed way in which history and heritage is actively created through the gathering together of places, people, memory and history (Tilley, 2004; Ingold, 2011).

Through Colin's involvement in the project, the community came into the school, and through the children's investigations, the school became enmeshed in wider community practices of heritage. At the beginning of the chapter, we highlighted the role of social relations in creating meaningful and engaging contexts for learning. We can draw parallels with the way in which Jane has put into action the Scottish Government's emphasis on the importance to children of understanding the places in which they live in relation to family, community and heritage (Scottish Executive, 2006). From an international perspective, this echoes the New Zealand National Curriculum, which highlights the importance of providing the conditions for children to grow up with a strong sense of belonging, both socially and culturally (Carr,

2005). Community heritage projects such as this create rich and active contexts for developing children's core skills of literacy, numeracy, health and well-being, which are imperative to closing the attainment gap.

This project clearly demonstrates the value of a lived curriculum to the children in Keig Primary School but also to a wider community of people interested in the history and heritage of North-East Scotland. Through their involvement in the archaeological project, the children learned about the history of their local community, and through getting to know Colin, they came to know what archaeology is as a practice and its role in understanding their community in the past, present and possibly future. Perhaps, as Sonu and Snaza (2015: 261) put it, this project 'requires the reverse of what has always been familiar in education: for the adult to return to a child-like openness with the materiality around us'.

Note

[1]   The Bailies pay for Colin's mileage and this is a pattern followed for other volunteers acting for the Bennachie Landscapes Project.

References

Beames, S. and Ross, H. (2010) 'Journeys outside the classroom', *Journal of Adventure Education & Outdoor Learning* 10(2): 95–109.

Bourdieu, P. (1977) *Outline of a theory of practice* (trans by Richard Nice), Cambridge: Cambridge University Press.

Carr, M. (2005) 'The leading edge of learning: recognising children's self-making narratives', *European Early Childhood Education Research Journal* 13(2): 41–50.

Cooper, H. (1995) *History in the early years*, London and New York, NY: Routledge.

Curtis, E. (2015) 'The place of time in children's being', in J. Seymour, A. Hacket and L. Proctor (eds) *Children's spatiality: Embodiment, emotion and agency*, Basingstoke: Palgrave Macmillan, pp 39–53.

Fägerstam, E. (2014) 'High school teachers' experience of the educational potential of outdoor teaching and learning', *Journal of Adventure Education & Outdoor Learning* 14(1): 56–81.

Ingold, T. (2000) *The perception of the environment: Essays on livelihood, dwelling and skill*, London and New York, NY: Psychology Press.

Ingold, T. (2011) *Being alive: Essays on movement, knowledge and description*, Abingdon: Routledge.

Jordet, A. (2007) 'Naermiljoet som klasserom—en undersokelse om uteskolens didaktikk i et danningste-oretiskt og erfaringspedagogisk perspektiv' ['The local environment as a classroom—a study of the pedagogy of outdoor school from the perspective of education theory and experience-based learning'] (Doctoral dissertation). Oslo: Oslo University.

Mannion, G., Fenwick, A. and Lynch, J. (2013) 'Place-responsive pedagogy: learning from teachers' experiences of excursions in nature', *Environmental Education Research*, 19(6): 792–809.

NZ Ministry of Education (1996) Te whāriki: He whāriki mātauranga mō ngā mokopuna o Aotearoa, *Early Childhood Curriculum*. Wellington: Learning Media.

Priestly, M. and Humes, W. (2010) 'The development of Scotland's Curriculum for Excellence: amnesia and déjà vu', *Oxford Review of Education* 36(3): 345–61.

Scottish Executive (2004) 'A Curriculum for Excellence'. Available at: www.gov.scot/Publications/2004/11/20178/45862

Scottish Executive (2006) 'Curriculum for Excellence: building the curriculum 1. The contribution of curriculum areas'. Available at: https://education.gov.scot/Documents/btc1.pdf

Scottish Government (2008) 'Curriculum for Excellence: building the curriculum 3. A framework for learning and teaching'. Available at: https://education.gov.scot/Documents/btc3.pdf

Scottish Government (2017) *2018 national improvement framework and improvement plan: Achieving excellence and equity*. Available at: www.gov.scot/publications/2018-national-improvement-framework-improvement-plan/

Shepherd, C. (ed) (2013) 'Society and ecology in the history of North-East Scotland: Bennachie and the Garioch', Bennachie Landscapes Series 2, Bailies of Bennachie.

Smith, L. (2006) *The uses of heritage*, Abingdon: Routledge.

Sonu, D. and Snaza, N. (2015) 'The fragility of ecological pedagogy: elementary social studies standards and possibilities of new materialism', *Journal of Curriculum and Pedagogy* 12(3): 258–77.

Tilley, C. (2004) *The materiality of stone: Explorations in landscape phenomenology*, Oxford: Berg.

Conclusion: Co-producing futures – directions for community heritage as research

Helen Graham, Jo Vergunst and Elizabeth Curtis

Introduction

If, as we said in our Introduction to this book, the past is not what it used to be, then the future of the past – the future of heritage – is not either. Where we might once have envisaged more and more centralised control over heritage and the increasing professionalisation of what has, in many respects, become an industry, this no longer appears as the only, or even the most significant, way in which heritage will be in the future. Altogether different kinds of conversation are happening. These are shown by the approaches taken by the contributors to this book, which demonstrate the importance of shared inquiry and dialogue to what we have emphasised as the process of heritage. This is fundamentally what we mean by heritage as community research.

It is no coincidence that the projects explored here have come into being now in a way that can be viewed and are visible as they are in this volume. The new wave of participative research and participative heritage is coming at a time when institutions are renegotiating their relationships with wider society, prompted by the refiguring of the state since the late 20th century. Features of this change include declining deference to professionals, restructuring economies and flows of public money that require new business models for universities and heritage organisations, and increased cynicism towards government, including local government. At the same time, through the Internet and social media, notions of self-expression and the right to participate have become visceral, lived and expected, while recognising that the reliance of these forms on the exploitation of harvested personal data render this ambivalent to say the least.

In these contexts, radical traditions of the 1960s and 1970s have renewed relevance and resonance, and have come together with public funding initiatives, not least the Arts and Humanities Research Council's (AHRC's) Connected Communities programme and the Heritage Lottery Fund's (HLF's) commitment to community-led heritage as part of a reorientation of universities, museums, other cultural institutions and local government. It is easy to be sceptical of this confluence and it is by no means 'pure', but then no political situation ever is. However, what there have been are opportunities – opportunities, as our chapters here describe, for using this moment for something deeply social and sociable, collaborative and hopeful.

One reading that clearly emerges from this volume is that the future is open to ways of knowing and ways of acting that might just be beginning, and that have not yet been fully considered. To bring about the kind of future of heritage that our contributors would imagine, it is helpful to think about what we mean by the future itself. First, we should say 'futures' of heritage, in the plural, to emphasise the possibilities of diversity and multiple voices. Second, what we have in mind is not the future as a set of goals or outcomes to be achieved by a certain point, like a blueprint. Rather, it is based on a sense of emergence and becoming – without excluding the possibility of transformational or revolutionary change, but recognising that futures, like the past, are born of process as much as they are of the execution of a plan. Although such epochal thinking (ie considering the future itself as an entity) is probably an artefact of modernity, we might follow Peter Pels (2015) in contrasting the 'open future' of progress and radical difference promised by modernity with the 'empty future' of industrial capitalism in which time itself is controlled by the technology of time-keeping and reduced to money and exchange value. If we were to imagine open futures for heritage, what might they look like?

In the following, we briefly draw out some directions indicated by the preceding chapters of the book.[1] There is perhaps some utopian thinking here, but our suggestions are grounded in the work that ourselves and our contributors continue to be involved in, in ways that carry on into the future. Our task is to generalise a little from this work so that we might hope to join with others interested in pursuing similar paths. These directions are indicated through reflections on, and for, some of those who will bring the futures of heritage into being: funders, universities, schools, and activists and communities. The ideas have been made possible by the ways in which many of the projects described here have been prefigurative, in that they have sought to bring a desired future into the present by developing alternatives for working together *now*.

For funders

In our open future for funders of heritage projects and programmes, funding agencies would have built on the many successful experiments for developing co-produced and collaborative research. In the UK, funding by the AHRC, the HLF and others would, in many cases, be 'joined up' in the sense of being complementary and mutually supportive where appropriate. Rather than assuming that heritage professionals and/or academics should form the core project team, activists, amateurs and other community members would be embedded in research projects in a range of heritage disciplines, for example, in the role of community co-investigator that the AHRC has begun to enable. Further mechanisms for funding community involvement, including appropriate organisational overheads, expenses and honoraria for volunteers, would be diversified into a suite of possibilities to suit different forms of collaboration. Funders would frequently work together to create new initiatives – often with an emphasis on working from the bottom up – and cross-refer proposals to each other for assessment. Funders and other partners would successfully make the case to governments that heritage research creates multiple benefits for social inclusion and sustainability. At the same time, as the HLF has recently been piloting and as explored by Brookfield et al in Chapter Seven, funders would recognise that 'micro-grants' of very small amounts can enable community heritage research to happen at the grass roots in ways that large grants to established organisations can easily miss.

For universities

Research on heritage would be recognised as being at the vanguard of universities' roles in their communities, both local and global, as reflected in work such as that by Sherylyn Briller and Andrea Sankar (2013). Where the 'internationalisation' agenda has come to dominate the thinking of many in the university community, heritage research would instead begin to demonstrate the significance of connecting between local and global, and, in particular, to create stronger links with their local communities. Projects focused on contemporary place and community would be expected to include heritage research, while heritage projects would routinely create legacies for current and future generations. Universities would shift from valuing collaborative work with communities not just as public engagement or impact, but as primary research that is distinctive in its methods and outcomes. Universities' values, as described in their mission statements, would convey democracy and participation, rather than a narrow conception of specialist expertise that is simply passed on to others (for examples, see Rodin, 2007; Cantor, 2014). Historians, archaeologists and others would stand not solely on their academic records, but on how they involve others in their work, and how they make heritage resources such as archives and museum collections available for others. Expertise on the past would not in any sense be devalued, but rather be increasingly spread and decentralised, including by digital means. Universities would provide training themselves, and bring in training providers, for staff and community activists on how to work collaboratively, based on extensive experience and long-standing relationships.

For schools and teacher education

Schools that can find the curriculum in heritage, rather than in learning facts about the past, would create space for pupils and teachers to play an active role in researching the past in partnership with community and other heritage groups. They would support initiatives to close the attainment gap in literacy and numeracy through investigating local heritage in the form of historical records and the landscape, including enabling children to physically carry out fieldwork and interpret and share findings. Schoolchildren would be supported as capable investigators in their own right in a co-production of knowledge of, and with, the past between schools and community heritage groups. Teaching education would also be rethought from a community heritage perspective. The understanding of what it is to know about the past, and the skills and knowledge that teachers need to nurture dynamic and rich heritage-based learning, would all be well developed. 'Finding' rather than 'delivering' the curriculum would challenge all educators to have the confidence to work with the unfolding of knowledge. This would come from taking a place-based pedagogical approach to learning about the past.

For heritage activists and communities

Activists and communities would be enabled to have a much greater role in researching and telling their own heritage stories. This would include being involved in decisions made about heritage on a variety of scales but with a particular valuing of the small and local forms of heritage that are easily overlooked. Many groups would have built on their successes during initial programmes such as those run by the AHRC and HLF to develop long-term and broad-based research practices, including training for new recruits and in new specialisms. Some communities would take the initiative in connecting with universities and other community organisations, including internationally, in order to access and share heritage resources and plan projects together. Local heritage activists would be recognised and well connected into relevant networks. Members of community heritage organisations would be able to publish and disseminate their work to a wide audience in a variety of written, material and digital forms, while community heritage conferences and networks would continue to grow. Communities would have found a stronger voice in what happens to archaeological finds by partnering with museums and universities at the very opening stages of designing a heritage research project. Community-based organisations have become accredited holders of certain classes of finds, not just those unclaimed by museums, and they have the capacity to regularly be loaned items of national significance for research and display.

For places, planning and decision-making

Activists and communities – and community heritage – would also be involved in place-making and local democracy. Planning and long-term engagement processes would involve collaborative heritage, drawing on a commitment to plural ways of knowing and a participatory ontology that includes people, things and landscapes. Any local authority decision would begin early by working openly and with the ethos of inquiry to creatively identify the significance of place – what matters to people about the place – in order to guide future development (eg My Future York, 2018). Ongoing inquiries into place would be seen as fundamental to local authorities' long-term engagement strategies and would mean that any new development took place within pre-existing lively and inclusive conversation. Local knowledge would be valued in dialogue with other professional and technical knowledge in developing planning applications, and regeneration would always start from what is already there, the assets and energies of the place and its people, rather than seeing a place as a blank page. Formal decision-making process would sit alongside action-led, do-it-yourself (DIY) approaches as change would be viewed in a complex and interconnected way requiring different scales of governance. From these approaches, a renewed faith in local democracy would be cultivated, with the future being seen as a co-produced endeavour unfolding from collective sense-making.

The future is happening now

Of course, many of our ideas here for the future are already under way; innovation is happening, often not driven by large institutions themselves, but promoted by the loose collectives of people, some with institutional roles and many without, that our chapters represent. The projects described in this book are just a small collection of a wider movement – a movement that can trace its legacies to radical history, archaeological and pedagogic practices of the late 1960s and 1970s but have flourished in our current moment as museums, universities and governments seek different relationships with the people once described as visitors, students and citizens. The call on which we want to end is not for us all to become one coordinated body with a single and well-articulated focus, but rather to celebrate the parallel actions, the sparks between people and the small, powerful moments in any collaborative inquiry where the past and the future open up differently.

Note
[1]   We also draw here on the report for our AHRC project 'Heritage Legacies' (Vergunst et al, 2016).

References

Briller, S. and Sankar, A. (2013) 'Engaging opportunities in urban revitalization: practicing Detroit anthropology', *Annals of Anthropological Practice* 37(1): 156–78.

Cantor, N. (2014) 'Not taking democracy for granted: higher education, inclusion and community trust'. Available at: https://community-wealth.org/content/not-taking-democracy-granted-higher-education-inclusion-and-community-trust

My Future York (no date) 'My future York: ways of working'. Available at: myfutureyork.org

Pels, P. (2015) 'Modern times. Seven steps to an anthropology of the future', *Current Anthropology* 56(6): 779–96.

Rodin, J. (2007) *The university and urban revival: Out of the ivory tower and into the street*, Pennsylvania, PA: University of Pennsylvania Press.

Vergunst, J., Curtis, E., Curtis, N., Davis, O., Graham, H., Johnston, R. and Shepherd, C. (2016) *Researching the past together: Legacies of community-led and co-produced heritage research*, Aberdeen: University of Aberdeen Museums.

Index

Note: page numbers in italic type refer to Figures; those in bold refer to Tables.

.